فَادْعُوهُمْ فَلْيَسْتَجِيبُوا لَكُمْ إِنْ كُنْتُمْ صَادِقِينَ ۞ أَلَهُمْ

أَرْجُلٌ يَمْشُونَ بِهَا أَمْ لَهُمْ أَيْدٍ يَبْطِشُونَ بِهَا أَمْ

لَهُمْ أَعْيُنٌ يُبْصِرُونَ بِهَا أَمْ لَهُمْ آذَانٌ يَسْمَعُونَ

بِهَا قُلِ ادْعُوا شُرَكَاءَكُمْ ثُمَّ كِيدُونِ فَلَا تُنْظِرُونِ ۞

إِنَّ وَلِيِّيَ اللَّهُ الَّذِي نَزَّلَ الْكِتَابَ وَهُوَ يَتَوَلَّى الصَّالِحِينَ

وَالَّذِينَ تَدْعُونَ مِنْ دُونِهِ لَا يَسْتَطِيعُونَ نَصْرَكُمْ

وَلَا أَنْفُسَهُمْ يَنْصُرُونَ ۞ وَإِنْ تَدْعُوهُمْ إِلَى

الْهُدَى لَا يَسْمَعُوا وَتَرَاهُمْ يَنْظُرُونَ إِلَيْكَ وَ

هُمْ لَا يُبْصِرُونَ ۞ خُذِ الْعَفْوَ وَأْمُرْ بِالْعُرْفِ وَأَعْرِضْ

عَنِ الْجَاهِلِينَ ۞ وَإِمَّا يَنْزَغَنَّكَ مِنَ الشَّيْطَانِ

نَزْغٌ فَاسْتَعِذْ بِاللَّهِ إِنَّهُ سَمِيعٌ عَلِيمٌ ۞ إِنَّ الَّذِينَ

اتَّقَوْا إِذَا مَسَّهُمْ طَائِفٌ مِنَ الشَّيْطَانِ تَذَكَّ

The

PROPHET
Muhammad

The

PROPHET
Muhammad

A BIOGRAPHY

BARNABY ROGERSON

HiddenSpring

Published in Great Britain by Little, Brown

Library of Congress Cataloging-in-Publication Data

Rogerson, Barnaby.
The Prophet Muhammad : a biography / Barnaby Rogerson.
p. cm.
Includes bibliographical references and index.
ISBN 1-58768-029-7 (alk. paper)
1. Muhammad, Prophet, d. 632. 2. Muslims—
Saudi Arabia—Biography. I. Title.
BP75.R63 2003
297.6'3—dc21
2003013061

Published by
HiddenSpring
An imprint of Paulist Press
997 Macarthur Boulevard
Mahwah, New Jersey 07430

www.hiddenspringbooks.com

Printed and bound in the United States of America

To my father

'No father hath given his child anything better than good manners'

THE PROPHET MUHAMMAD

CONTENTS

TIMELINE OF HISTORY: 400–641 C.E.

ARABIA	CENTRAL ASIA, ABYSSINIA AND PERSIA

400–449 C.E.

| | 400 | Aksum destroys kingdom of Meroe (Egyptian Kush) in Sudan |

450–499 C.E.

| | 451 | Death of Attila |

500–549 C.E.

523–4	Dhu Nuwas massacres Christian Arabs at Najran	500	Probable completion of Babylonian Talmud, composed of the Mishnah (teachings) and Gemara (dialogues)
525	Abyssinian invasion of Yemen		
537–70	Abyssinian general Abreha and sons rule southern Arabia	520	Perfection of mathematics in India and invention of decimal system
		531–79	Chosroes (I) Anushirwan rules over Persian Empire
		540	Persians sack Antioch

550–599 C.E.

570	Birth of Muhammad	552	Destruction of great Mongolian
	Invasion of Mecca by Abyssinian-commanded army from Yemen		Empire by revolt of its Turkish vassals. The remnants, the Avars, join White Huns to create khanate over southern Russia and eastern Europe
583	Deposition of Ghassanid kings of Syrian desert by Byzantine Emperor		
595	Muhammad marries Khadijah		
		590–628	Reign of Chosroes (II) Parwiz

EASTERN ROMAN EMPIRE		BRITISH ISLES AND WESTERN ROMAN EMPIRE	
404	Translation of Greek scriptures into Latin by St Jerome in Palestine	406	Legions march out of Britain
		410	Emperor Honorius endorses British independence
			Visigoths sack Rome, invade Italy and overrun part of Spain
		426	Augustine of Hippo completes *City of God*
431	Second Church Council held at Ephesus; bishop Nestorius condemned	432–61	St Patrick converts Ireland to Christianity
451	Fourth Church Council held at Chalcedon; Monophysite doctrines of the ancient Churches of Armenia, Syria and Egypt condemned	c. 450	Jutes, Angles and Saxons invade Britain; St Germanus of Auxerre and Ambrosius Aurelianus rally British resistance
		475	Collapse of western half of the Roman Empire; deposition of last emperor, Romulus Augustulus
		475–537	Life of King Arthur
527–65	Rule of Justinian	525	Irish begin to colonise Western Scotland
542	Bubonic plague		
582	Accession of Emperor Maurikios	563	St Columba establishes monastery of Iona: the beginning of the conversion of Scotland
		590–640	Gregory the Great creates a distinctive Western Christianity (Roman Catholicism) from a simplified version of the teaching of St Augustine
		596	Gregory the Great sends Augustine to convert Ethelbert, Anglo-Saxon king of Kent

ARABIA		CENTRAL ASIA, ABYSSINIA AND PERSIA

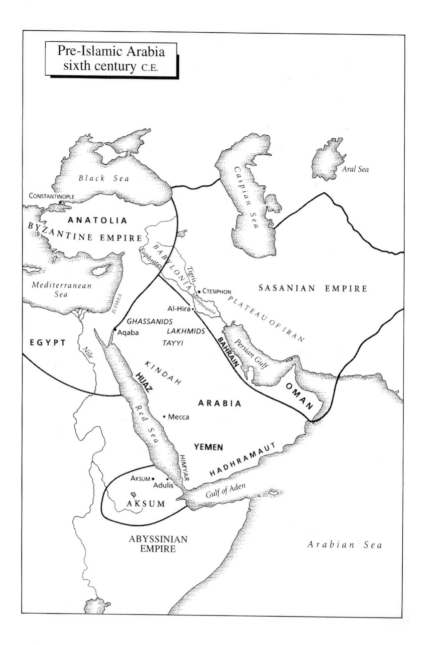

Pre-Islamic Arabia
sixth century C.E.

Black Sea

CONSTANTINOPLE

ANATOLIA

BYZANTINE EMPIRE

Caspian Sea

Aral Sea

Mediterranean Sea

BABYLONIA

Euphrates

Tigris

Mesopotamia

CTESIPHON

SASANIAN EMPIRE

PLATEAU OF IRAN

Al-Hira

GHASSANIDS

Aqaba

LAKHMIDS

TAYYI

BAHRAIN

Persian Gulf

IDUMEA

EGYPT

Nile

KINDAH

HIJAZ

OMAN

ARABIA

Red Sea

Mecca

YEMEN

HADHRAMAUT

HIMYAR

AKSUM

Adulis

Gulf of Aden

AKSUM

ABYSSINIAN EMPIRE

Arabian Sea

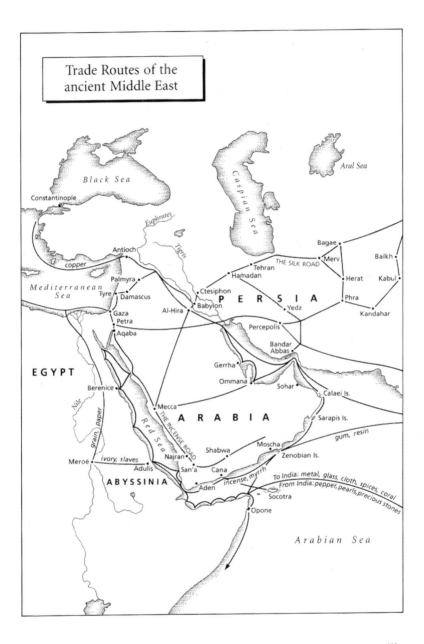

Trade Routes of the
ancient Middle East

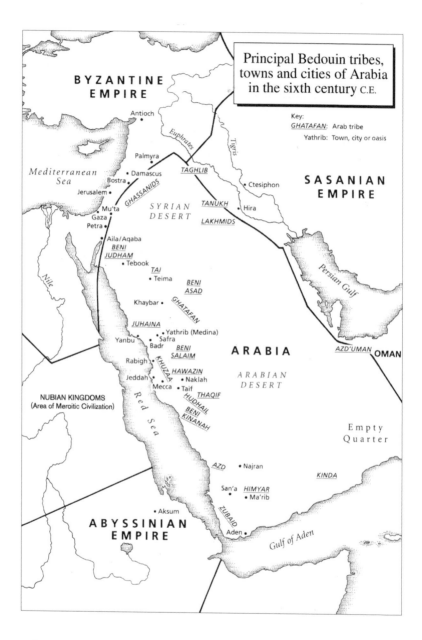

Principal Bedouin tribes, towns and cities of Arabia in the sixth century C.E.

Key:
GHATAFAN: Arab tribe
Yathrib: Town, city or oasis

BYZANTINE EMPIRE

SASANIAN EMPIRE

NUBIAN KINGDOMS
(Area of Meroitic Civilization)

ABYSSINIAN EMPIRE

Mediterranean Sea

SYRIAN DESERT

ARABIA

ARABIAN DESERT

Empty Quarter

Red Sea

Persian Gulf

Gulf of Aden

Antioch

Palmyra

Euphrates

Tigris

Damascus
Bostra
Jerusalem
Mu'ta
Gaza
Petra
GHASSANIDS

Ctesiphon

TAGHLIB

TANUKH
LAKHMIDS
Hira

Aila/Aqaba
BENI JUDHAM
Tebook
TAI
Teima
BENI ASAD
Khaybar
GHATAFAN
JUHAINA
Yathrib (Medina)
Yanbu
Safra
Badr
BENI SALAIM
Rabigh
KHUZAA
HAWAZIN
Jeddah
Mecca
Naklah
Taif
THAQIF
HUDHAIL
BENI KINANAH

AZD'UMAN OMAN

AZD
Najran
KINDA
San'a
HIMYAR
Ma'rib
ZUBAID
Aksum
Aden

Nile

xiv

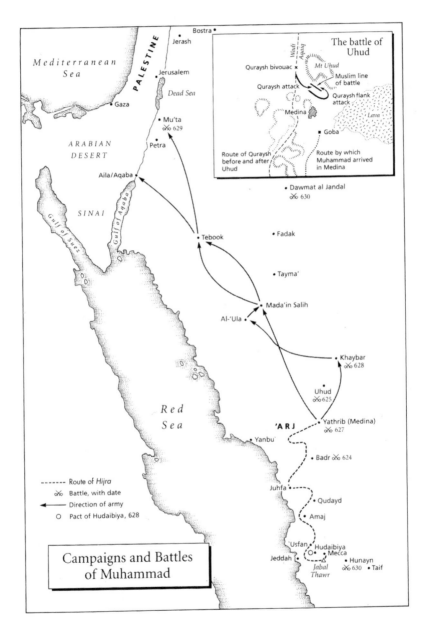

The battle of Uhud

Mediterranean Sea

PALESTINE

Bostra
Jerash
Jerusalem
Dead Sea
Gaza

Wadi Aqiq
Mt Uhud
Quraysh bivouac
Muslim line of battle
Quraysh attack
Quraysh flank attack
Medina
Lava
Goba
Route of Quraysh before and after Uhud
Route by which Muhammad arrived in Medina

ARABIAN DESERT

Mu'ta ⚔ 629
Petra

Aila/Aqaba

SINAI

Gulf of Aqaba

Gulf of Suez

Tebook

Dawmat al Jandal ⚔ 630

Fadak

Tayma'

Mada'in Salih

Al-'Ula

Khaybar ⚔ 628

Red Sea

Uhud ⚔ 625

Yathrib (Medina) ⚔ 627

'ARJ

Yanbu'

Badr ⚔ 624

Juhfa

Qudayd

Amaj

------ Route of *Hijra*
⚔ Battle, with date
◄─ Direction of army
O Pact of Hudaibiya, 628

Usfan
Jeddah
Hudaibiya
Mecca
Hunayn ⚔ 630 Taif
Jabal Thawr

Campaigns and Battles of Muhammad

PREFACE
Dreaming of
the Prophet

Late one afternoon some years ago I had returned from taking a group of well-educated Western travellers around the ruins of a great Roman city in a Muslim country. To a man and woman they were elated and were either swapping stories about emperors, olive oil and the gorgeous dusk-lit temples they had just photographed or sitting quietly scribbling notes. I noticed the bus driver and a huddle of local professional guides sitting outside a café. I was beckoned over to their table and given a glass of tea while an elderly postcard vendor continued his eloquent exposition. His Muslim audience was bright-eyed and attentive, alternately groaning, chuckling and tut-tutting at the familiar litany of events. From its reception I thought it must be political gossip spiced with burlesque sexual revelations. The story was halted for a moment to allow a translation for my benefit. It was the tale of how Mu'awiya had tricked the Prophet's son-in-law out of his inheritance. It was rhetorical, relevant and passionate, especially when told by an old man at the height of his powers. It was about thirteen-hundred-year-old events told with all the immediacy of yesterday. The storyteller's audience was pleased by my interest and questions. I was encouraged by smiling faces, who told me that this was the real thing, this was 'real history'. It was not to be compared with the tired old tales about fallen stones with their dates of dedication and architectural orders, which they knew so well. They all confessed to being profoundly bored by the classical ruins from the pre-Islamic 'time of ignorance'.

I was both shocked and excited. I had seen the same things, eaten the same meals, slept in the same hotels as the local guide, the coach driver and the sleepy-looking security man. We had all got on so well over the last ten days. But our memories of this time would include only the jokes and shared cigarettes. Although we had passed through exactly the same landscape, we would come out of it with completely different memories. Even under the ideal circumstances of an easy-going vacation, the gulf between the Christian West and the Muslim East yawned as deep as ever.

That night I wondered how I might try to emulate the success the old postcard-seller had had with his audience. I scribbled notes on the back of an outdated series of cards of Roman mosaics he had given me. Later that week I lit candles on a table after dinner, gathered the group around in a circle and told the story as best I could. The story I told was the life of the Prophet Muhammad. Although it was dark, I knew I had everyone's attention. Soon we were joined by the hotel waiters. They knew little English but could follow the progress of the story from the sound of the Arab names alone. Their enthusiasm added greatly to the intensity of the tale. I repeated it later, on other occasions, in other countries. I got used to knowing in advance that the first question from my fellow Western travellers would be, 'Are you a Muslim?', followed by, 'Do you intend to become a Muslim?' The same thing would happen later in London's Regent's Park mosque. Everyone wanted to know which side I was on.

I was on the side of a good story. The life of the Prophet Muhammad is a story of overpowering pathos and beauty. It is history, tragedy and enlightenment compressed into one tale. It is also a story virtually unknown to the West. Compare this ignorance with our enthusiasm for Father Christmas or the Three Kings: love them or loathe them, they stand only on the very outer fringes as spiritual teachers or historical characters, yet they are surrounded by a mythology of contrary ideas, perpetuated by recurrent images and historical novels. Set against even such peripheral mythical figures of Western belief as these, the Prophet Muhammad simply does not feature.

Within Islam, however, he represents almost everything of human value. Muhammad, Prophet of God, the last and greatest of that long line of men, from Adam through to Abraham, Moses and Jesus, who have struggled to bring the word of God to humankind. Even when viewed in an entirely secular perspective he remains a superhero. He was founder of the Caliphate, one of the greatest empires of the world; creator of classical Arabic, a new literature and world language; founder of a new national identity, the Arab; and creator of Islam, a worldwide culture that is now 1,200-million strong and growing more rapidly than you can count. Only by marrying the best qualities of certain characters from European civilisation – a combination, say, of Alexander the Great, Diogenes and Aristotle, or the Emperor Constantine, St Paul and St Francis – can you begin to understand the measure of the man.

Of course, his historical achievements were mere accidental spin-offs. His only purpose was to forge a new relationship between God and humankind. To those billions of believers who follow in his spiritual path he is omnipresent within the individual world of imagination, prayer and petition. He is perceived in many ways. He is the ultimate stern patriarch, that man of men who stands at the forefront of all the saints, heroes and good rulers from centuries of proud Muslim history. He is the implacable law-giver, the guide who has clearly pointed out the roads of destiny: this way leads to heaven, this way to hell. He is the loving grand-father, leading the prayers in the mosque while his infant grandson clambers upon his shoulders. He is the sacrificial hero who goes into the testing fire of the spiritual world for the benefit of humankind, shaken to the core of his very being by the terror of being addressed by God through the angels – and all the while per-secuted and reviled by his own people. He is the great lover of women – he required no other luxuries, no possessions, so com-plete was his joy and satisfaction in the company of his wives. He is the wise sage who despised the luxurious trappings of royalty, the halls, guards, courtiers, silks and gold that hitherto had always been associated with power. He is also the savant of the mystics, the guide who has led generations of dervishes, sufis, poets and lovers of God on their quests. He is the only man to have jour-neyed to heaven and back. He is the Hero of Heroes.

On a different journey I took a group of travellers around the courtyard of an ancient mosque, pointing out the architectural details and explaining Islam. As I approached the prayer hall – barred to non-believers by a low wooden screen – the old watchman in skull-cap and blue overalls stood up and ushered me beyond the screen. He had heard my talk and presumed that I was a Muslim and was now coming in for prayer. The vast, cool, dark hall, its countless marble columns polished by the touch of thousands of worshippers, beckoned. I blushed with pleasure and confusion. I had watched for years as the empty prayer halls of great mosques had filled up with the faithful – watched with the cold eyes of a professional observer – and for the first time I felt like a beggar looking on at a feast.

There are other barriers to conversion, besides low wooden screens. Could you go straight from being a ritualistically inclined Anglican to being a Muslim, without becoming an earnest convert in between? I realised that all my male Muslim friends would, within their own societies, probably qualify as bad Muslims. These were the ones I liked, who could laugh at and understand the attraction of the Western world yet stay true to their own inheritance. Who knew the newest, trashiest Hollywood films but also kept in touch with a wise old sheikh. Who would leave you watching their jacket in a portside café 'just for a moment' so that they could unobtrusively nip out and stand side by side with dock porters for the noonday prayer. Who could drink you under the table but follow the Ramadan fast to the last letter. Who could match the poetry of Keats with romantic Arabic ballads, fall constantly – and unsuitably – in love yet remain devoted to their families and, in their own minds at least, good husbands.

One Turkish friend confessed to me that overly devout converts could be a bore. He had adored his German girlfriend but now that she had become a Muslim mother, he said, 'it is like living with the Imam. And it's not just me,' he continued: 'her precise knowledge of the law alarms the whole street. I fear for our children.' He went on, as he poured more glasses of raki, 'instead of letting them play soccer she is now keeping them at home to study classical Arabic so that they can better understand the Qur'an. Turks do not need archaic Arabic to believe,' he finished, not without a note of scorn in his voice.

☾

The greatest travel writer from the old Turkish Ottoman Empire was Evliya Chelebi. He was descended from the very soundest Turkish martial stock: his father was a standard-bearer to Suleyman the Magnificent, his grandfather standard-bearer to Mehmet the Conqueror. He was a delightful and engaging character, an intellectual Puck, a literary Peter Pan, the Samuel Pepys of seventeenth-century Istanbul, fluent in Arabic, Persian and

Turkish, who flirted his way around the Empire with a keen eye for male beauty and a brilliant ear for language. Indeed, in one brilliant bound he exchanged the aridity of the theological classroom for a close friendship with Sultan Murat IV. To the rest of the Empire, Murat was both hero and monster, the last of his line to lead the army in person, whose military abilities were matched by a terrifying, homicidal temper.

In the inner garden of Istanbul's Topkapi Palace there is a pavilion that overlooks the waters of the Golden Horn. It was built by Sultan Murat to celebrate a military victory (the conquest of Baghdad) and as a private chamber from which to escape the cares of state. It is still possessed by an unearthly charm, grand but intimate, warm but austere. Here Evliya and his master would spend many a carefree hour in the company of the other boon companions of the sultan. Evliya seems to have acted like a balm to Murat's otherwise troubled mind.

On some counts Evliya might qualify as a bad Muslim. However, even with this dissolute character there is not a smidgen of doubt about the absolute orthodoxy of his faith. Indeed, within his writings there is a dream encounter with the Prophet Muhammad. It is a classic of its kind: 'then flashes of lightning burst from the doors of the mosque and the room filled with a crowd of saints and martyrs. "It was the Prophet!" overshadowed by his green banner, covered by his green veil, carrying his staff in his right hand, his sword girt on his thigh, with the Imam Hassan on his right hand and the Imam Husayn on his left. As he placed his right foot on the threshold he cried out, "Bismallah!" and throwing off his veil, said, "Health unto thee, O my people!" The whole assembly answered: "Unto thee be health, O Prophet of God, Lord of the Nations!"'

Evliya trembled in every limb of his body but was able to provide an exact description: 'The veil on his face was a white shawl and his turban was formed of a white sash with twelve folds; his mantle was of camel's hair inclined to yellow; on his neck he wore a yellow woollen shawl. His boots were yellow and in his turban was stuck a toothpick.' Sa'd Vakkas (one of the twelve evangelists and the patron saint of archers) took Evliya by the hand and escorted him into the Prophet's presence. Evliya remembers weeping in his excitement and confusion, kissing the Prophet's hands and receiving his blessing (and that of other saints). He describes the assembled company: 'Their hands were perfumed with musk, ambergris, spikenard, sweet basil, violets and carnations: but that of the Prophet himself smelt of nothing but saffron and roses, felt when touched as if it had no bones, and was as soft as cotton. The hands of other prophets had the odour of quinces, that of Abu Bakr had the fragrance of lemons, 'Umar's smelt like ambergris, 'Uthman's like violets, Ali's like jasmine, Hassan's like carnations, and Husayn's like white roses . . . Then the Prophet himself pronounced the parting salutation from the mihrab.'

The same ecstatic visions are recorded by every age and condition of Muslims. The aspiration of being blessed by the Prophet in Paradise cuts across race, class and time within the Muslim world. This pious hope is part of the essence of Islam. It is reinforced by the Prophet's account of his own mystical journey to heaven where he is greeted by the prophets who have gone before him. It is also imprinted on Muslim minds as a shared childhood memory. On the day of the great annual festival of Aid el Kebir (commemorating Abraham's sacrifice) a young boy will accompany his father to a great gathering of the faithful in an open-air mosque. On this day the entire congregation will be beautifully attired, bathed, scented and resplendent in the full robes of tradition. Here the young Muslim boy will briefly be treated with the formal manners of adulthood. The respect of one's peers is a powerful aspiration, which in Islam comes only to those who walk the sure path of tradition.

When a Turkish Cypriot diplomat talks about forty thousand martyrs he is not referring to the murderous division of his island in 1974, but rather to a successful sixteenth-century Ottoman siege. When Colonel Gadafy regrets the fall of Granada he is not talking about a province of the Libyan Sahara lost to the colonial powers but about a Spanish city that fell in the fifteenth century. When every year some Shiite Muslims whip themselves into an emotional and bloody frenzy during a ten-day festival, they are not weeping for their nation but commemorating the death of Husayn in seventh-century Iraq. History is the very warp and weft of life, into which Muslims are themselves woven. This is not to say that every man in a Middle Eastern street can recite a list of rulers and dynasties going back to the Sumerians. Indeed THEY (meaning current rulers, those charlatans behind the smoked-glass windows of their limousines and the well-guarded walls of their palaces) are often waved away dismissively – as you might brush away a fly from your cup of coffee – while in moments of extreme passion an old man will scream out to a crowd, 'Why are our rulers all thieves?'

The real 'living history' of the Muslim world is compacted into the hundred years around the life of the Prophet. It is this story that remains vital to modern life. It is a story that can be discussed, analysed and argued over. It provides all the parallels one might ever need for the goodness, the wickedness, the comedy, majesty and tragedy of humankind. It is the Shakespeare, the Aeschylus, the Euripides, the Milton, the Pinter, the complete works of humankind combined in one coherent tale. It has all the ingredients that a Muslim might ever require for reflection on the ways of the world: how the precious message of God survived against the wiles of Satan during the life of the Prophet Muhammad; of the heroic bravery of the Companions of the Prophet; of the first mesmerising Arabic conquests which extinguished – as if they were a pair of candles – the two thousand-year-old empires that dominated the old world; and of the time of the first Caliphs, the four 'rightly guided' successors of the Prophet. But even during this period of glory, when the achievements of the Arabs were writ in the heavens, there begins the slow fall from that high estate. Within a hundred years of the death of the Prophet it is the Umayyads – descendants of the Prophet's most bitter opponents during his lifetime – who rule as hereditary emperors over the vast Muslim Empire, while the Prophet's own grandson was left to ride alone to his death. The path trodden by the Prophet Muhammad, so soon neglected by his followers, has ever after been sought by the righteous.

There are no new facts about the life of the Prophet Muhammad though there are and always will be a demand for new versions of his life. Each generation, each decade, each passing year breathes its own new needs and knowledge on this endless project. The corpus of relevant material was however first assembled in Baghdad under the Abbasid Caliphate in the eight century. There are three great primary sources: the Qu'ran (believed by Muslims to be the word of God through the mouth of the Prophet), the Hadith (the various collections of the oral sayings and actions of the Prophet) and the first histories, biographies and collections of legends written under the sponsorship of the Abbasid court. Even to pick a narrative from these great central sources, the well-ploughed field of more than a thousand years of scholarship, requires a degree of personal choice. To give an example, there are two distinct narratives available for the Prophet's death, one giving a central role to the Prophet's daughter, the second to the Prophet's favourite wife. In this and a thousand other instances I have read the histories, absorbed the traditions and listened to the sacred legends and then told my version of the Life of the Prophet Muhammad.

Knowledge of the details of Muhammad's life is vital if one is to enter the imagination of the Muslim world. On a trip I undertook some years ago, I was once again admiring some classical ruins set against a desert landscape. The place was one of great beauty and considerable remoteness, though there had been some damage to it since my previous visit. By chance my arrival coincided with that of a film crew and a journalist from the state-controlled media. In front of the assembled village elders from this part of the pre-desert, arranged in a semicircle in their sparkling white, Friday best, I was interviewed. Part of me wanted to explode with an impassioned diatribe about litter, about the destruction of archaeological sites by casual treasure hunters and about the desecration caused by allowing builders to dump their waste here. I also wanted to talk about conservation, about the role of the World Monument Fund and how one could learn from both the good and the bad work done in Great Britain by the National Trust and English Heritage.

Instead I found myself talking about the Prophet. I suggested that this place must have been built during the childhood of the Prophet; that it must have looked much as Mecca did when the Prophet was a young man; that the first Muslim missionaries must have arrived here just as the last of the great pagan mausoleums was being finished. As the interview ended I thought, what a fool I have been not to talk about litter, illegal digging, illicit dumping and art theft. It was then that I overheard one old man talking to another. Who is he? *Ingliz*, (English) the other replied. Who are they? The *M'rabet Rumi* (the holy men of Europe) whispered his neighbour. Litter could wait.

1

Dawn over Mecca

Mecca, the sacred city of Arabia, is spread below us, home to twenty thousand souls. No walls guard its perimeter. It is a Monday morning. The twelfth day of the month of Rabaa in the year 570 C.E. Dawn first lights up the summits, for the city is defined by a surrounding wall of mountains, polished clean by the desert winds and baked black by the unrelenting sun. Once it has risen, the sun climbs quickly to show plumes of smoke drifting up from the tightly packed warren of houses. Now the light pours on to the rooftop terraces. Deep shadows exaggerate the different heights and idiosyncratic features of the walls. From the hidden yards and alleys rises gently, but with increasing tempo, the cacophony of life. Indistinct brown bundles laid out on biers beside the doorways shift slightly. Then, with a swift movement, a blanket is transformed into a cloak and a figure rises to greet the dawn. It is the habit on hot nights for the men of Mecca to sleep outside their doors to catch the cooling breeze. Cocks crow, children scamper, goats bleat; older girls can be seen moving swiftly through the alleys, fetching water, firing small clay ovens while

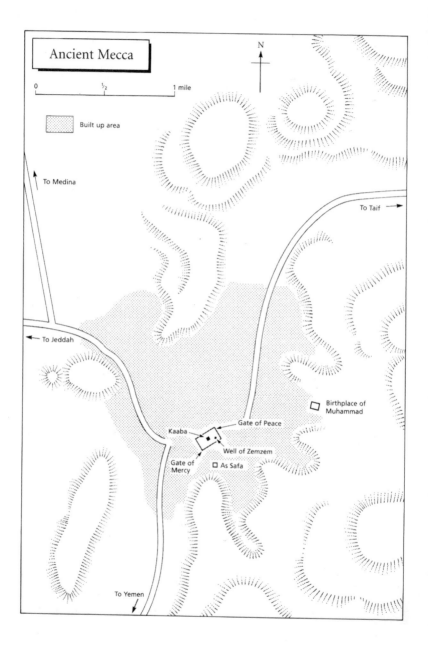

Ancient Mecca

N

0   ½   1 mile

Built up area

To Medina

To Taif

To Jeddah

Birthplace of
Muhammad

Gate of Peace

Kaaba

Well of Zemzem

Gate of
Mercy   □ As Safa

To Yemen

cloth-shrouded bundles of dough are hurried from door to door. Slowly the dense cluster breaks down into individual houses. There are some fine imposing manor houses, whose proud dry-stone walls rise vertically, inset with narrow windows and protected by massive wooden doors. They stand side by side with humble mud-wall compounds whose perimeters contain nothing more substantial than a brushwood hut or a tent.

Unlike other cities of our experience, no teams of oxen can be seen pulling wagons noisily along the rutted stone pavements. The sand and gravel streets of Mecca catch and muffle traffic, whether it be the soft thud of camels' hooves, the slightly quicker trotting of a mule or the exuberant gallop of a mare. But nothing can dam the deep, disgruntled, throaty roar of the camels as they are marshalled into caravans, saddled, burdened with packs and led out, in single file, along the roads. Mecca has grown like a star, its houses reaching out along the available level ground of the valley floor, following the sand roads that lead out to the four corners of the world.

The western road leads directly to the ports of the Red Sea, a doorway to Egypt, Abyssinia and the India and China trade concentrated in Ceylon. It is but forty miles away, a distance a determined messenger could cover in a day with a change of horses. This way, the road south takes you out of the city on the road to the Yemen, to *Arabia Felix* (Arabia the Blessed) and the priceless source of incense. That road which heads north-east cuts through the bleak centre of Arabia, across an arid plateau that shelves down towards the rich agricultural land of Iraq, the many cities of Mesopotamia and the way east, up into Persia. This way north leads across the awesome sands of the Syrian desert towards the ancient oasis cities, the bustling trading markets of Damascus and Bostra, gateways into the empire of the Byzantine Caesars.

As your eyes follow these roads your gaze passes beyond the tattered edges of the spreading city, through the city of the dead, vast fields of nameless cairns of stone. It passes through a suburb of huts, thorn-bush corrals and odd, cleared patches surrounded by rings of stones. These are the camel stables of the great merchants, pens for herds of goats and sheep and the seasonal camping grounds of the Bedouin. There is no bright green forest, no fertile orchard of date palms, though viewed from afar some of the dry river beds support a haze of thorn trees. Thin elegant trunks rise up, their under-foliage neatly clipped, as in some ornamental parkland, by the feeding goats. They are also harvested by man, for the sap, when dried, is the source of the medicinal balm of Mecca.

Mecca stood at the centre of the Arabian caravan trade and was one of the great spiritual capitals of the peninsula. Like a desert gourd, it grew and retracted extravagantly with the season. The trading seasons – when the two great annual caravans set out and returned – were frantically busy. By contrast, when the caravans had left town, Mecca felt like an empty husk. Nothing, however, could match the time of the annual pilgrimage when all Arabia packed itself around the city and the camps of the Bedouin stretched out for mile upon mile.

Let us look back again into the heart of the city. The sun has risen high over the mountains and the great open space at the centre of Mecca glows with light and life. Thin shadows are cast by the three hundred and sixty stone idols that circle the solid, box-like temple, the Kaaba, which commands the centre of this ritual space. A small knot has formed around the sacred wellhead of the *zemzem* spring and a handful of newly arrived visitors are circling the central temple of the Kaaba at the curious jog trot of the pilgrim.

The usual form of worship is for pilgrims to circle the Kaaba seven times at a trot and then to drink from the holy spring. This rite seems to have a straightforward interpretation, with the square Kaaba symbolising the four corners of the earth which is circled seven times, just like the seven planets (or spheres of heaven) which were believed to circle the earth. We still live today in a yearly calendar ordered by these ancient beliefs, from the names and numbers of our days of the week, to the four weeks that form our lunar months and the stellar signs of the zodiac.

Aside from this accustomed act of prayer there are other small knots of pilgrims pursuing their own ritual actions. For the inviolate sanctuary, situated right at the heart of Mecca, encompasses the worship of a disparate pantheon of gods. Many gods, many beliefs and many stories coexist in this sacred temenos. One Meccan might tell you that each of the three hundred and sixty idols is sacred to a different Arabian tribe; another would add that they also represent the days of the year and have been designed to mark out the divine passage of the solar year. One might tell you that the Kaaba is the altar of Adam; another that it was built by Abraham; yet another that it was once open to the sky. It is now enclosed, with roof and a raised doorway, to form a sacred cube. Inside this holy of holies are stored all manner of sacred objects and images. These are said to include an icon of the Virgin Mary with the Christ Child and a portrait of the Prophet Abraham. But the shrine is dominated by a representation of the war god Baal Hubal, who watches over the city's political destiny. At times of trouble the city elders can seek his advice by casting a quiver of divinatory arrows before the idol and reading the future from the answers they give.

Despite the evidence of Christian and Jewish cult objects within the Kaaba, the vast majority of the Arabs of Mecca adhered to their traditional pagan beliefs. It was a loose and eclectic paganism yet it contained a reasonably sophisticated body of belief which operated on a number of levels. There was no expectation of any life after death beyond the honour and continued prosperity of your clan. This was deeply related to a fundamental belief that you should meet your fate, your preordained destiny, with dignity and without indulging in an indecent and useless struggle to extend your allotted term. Beside these stoic virtues there was a widespread acceptance of an all-encompassing but basically malign spirit world which included powerful ancestors and jinn-spirits (who assumed the form of desert winds or rainstorms, or inhabited certain characteristic rocks, mountain peaks, caverns, springs and forests) which had to be propitiated, or at least treated with respect, if you were to reduce their malevolence. To assist in these actions there were the *kahins*, wandering seers and soothsayers, who dabbled in magic, in love potions or in reading a future for their paying clients from the shapes formed by throwing sacred bunches of twigs, scattering divinatory arrows, watching the flights of birds or reading the wind-blown patterns in the sand. Some of the *kahins* could be encouraged to go into shamanistic trances and though they were often consulted, and not a little feared, they remained on the edges of society. They never formed a priesthood and the Arabs of Mecca, just like the ancient Romans, simply entrusted the care of their shrines to the most respected and capable men of the community.

There was also an Arabic version of the worldwide fertility cult, the worship of the mother goddess, known variously as Isis in Egypt, Cybele in Anatolia, Aphrodite in Greece, Astarte in Syria and Ashteroth in Mesopotamia. The mother goddess was often worshipped as a trinity, to include her characteristics of creator, nurturer and destroyer, and so could be portrayed as nubile nymph, curvaceous mother and vengeful crone. The goddess was always worshipped in association with a virile male god who shared in the triple aspect, and could be lover, brother and child. This heroic young fertility god was doomed to a sacrificial death but was recreated each year by a redemptive rebirth, often assisted by a beneficent all-powerful father god normally associated with the sky. This cycle, as in all Middle Eastern societies, was linked with a whole mythical literature, the four agricultural seasons, the movements of the stars and the cycles of the sun and moon. The fertility goddess was addressed in Arabia as al-Lat, literally 'the Goddess', or as Banat al-dahr, 'the daughters of fate'. Just a few days' ride from Mecca there were three famous shrines to the goddess. At the oasis of Taif she was addressed as al-Rabba, 'the sovereign', at Nakhlah she was al-Uzzah, 'the mighty one', while at the port of Qayd she was simply Manat, 'doom'. The youthful, male rain-giver and thunder god was addressed as Thuraiza or Muzdalifa. The supreme all-powerful father god was simply but emphatically addressed in Arabic as al-Lah, or Allah, which is not a distinct identity but simply means 'the God'.

The Yemen boasted great bronze cult statues in such open-air sanctuaries as the one dedicated to al-Maqah at Marib, while the temples of Palmyra were filled with stone carvings of the deities. In central Arabia there was little representational stone carving. As in ancient Palestine the deities were represented by unshaped god-stones. Some of these, like that of the Kaaba, were unearthly meteorites; others were natural formations that followed the old requirements in Exodus (20: 25): 'make me a stone altar, do not build it of dressed stone; for if you use a chisel on it, you will profane it'.

During the annual month-long pilgrimage held in the autumn, the radius of the sacred sanctuary of Mecca was extended to twenty miles. All the tribes of Arabia were welcome and all forms of warfare, even blood feuds, were forbidden. It therefore became customary to leave all arms and clothing outside the sanctuary and to perform the pilgrimage naked. Among the ritual actions to be undertaken by pilgrims was a running ascent of the two hills of Mecca, to be repeated seven times, an all-night vigil of prayer beside Mount Arafat, offerings addressed to three stone pillars at al-Mina and a blood sacrifice. Interpretations of these actions must remain speculative but it seems likely that at the holy time of the autumnal equinox the sacred rites of the Middle Eastern fertility cult were performed to insure that the cycle of life continued. Most, if not all, of the specific original details may have been lost on the worshippers by the sixth century, but the pilgrimage to Mecca clearly held a place of unique importance within Arabian society. We know that even Arabs who had converted to Christianity continued to perform the pilgrimage.

Mecca also held a unique place in the development of the Arabic language. For the annual market at Ukaz, which was held outside the precincts of the city during the month of Dhu l-Qa'da, was as much about poetry as about trade. This attracted all the great wandering poets of Arabia who would compete with each other in recitals and boasting competitions. Not only would all the old epics be recited (many of which had been composed for the courts of the rival Ghassanid and Lakhmid kings) but new verses would be revealed or spontaneously composed, praising some great patriarchal chief for his generosity and wisdom, some young warrior for his heroic daring or lauding the beauty of the loved one, be it a camel, a horse, a youth or an unattainable girl. Side by side with martial interests and the stoic virtues of the desert, the Arab poets loved to dwell upon the endless trials, inspirations and pitfalls of love as well as describing the beauty of the random patterns that were formed by the shadows of passing clouds upon the desert. Ukaz brought all this together, along with a political agenda that thrashed out the settlement of blood feuds, a truce or a new alliance through marriage. Ukaz was uniquely important but it was not alone, for there was a recognised schedule for the ten annual markets of Arabia. Each had its role: Sohar, on the Persian Gulf, was paramount for the Indian Ocean trade, the fair at Aden was necessary for the trade with Somalia and Abyssinia, while the market at Mahra that sprawled beneath the mountain where the prophet Hud had been buried was an important gathering point for the tribes of southern Arabia.

Illiteracy in central Arabia was the norm, even among poets. One of the most striking facts about Arabian society was that the spoken language was kept in its purest form by the nomadic tribes. It is almost as if the lack of material objects and the lack of written forms kept the joy and exuberance of language at its most acute. It alone maintained a breathless virility and inventiveness, though all the written forms evolved in the more settled areas in the far south or in the north. We know from archaeology that there were at least four distinct lettered languages in existence in ancient southern Arabia and at least four in the north. Among the more famous of these northern languages are Aramaic (the language spoken by Jesus) and the Hebrew of the Jews. Both of these influential tongues seem to have been formed at about the same time, around 1200 B.C.E., by nomadic tribes migrating out of the Arabian desert into the fertile crescent. In the Hellenistic period Aramaic had emerged as the language of the street throughout the Middle East, in preference to either Greek, Latin or Persian. It was further widened, evolved and disseminated as the native tongue of the great trading cities of Petra and Palmyra and in the Syriac dialect used by the Church. However, all of these northern and southern tongues, despite centuries of official and literary use, would ultimately be eclipsed by the unwritten speech of the desert. The poets may have played a critical role in this transformation, and by the fourth century C.E. Arabic can be said to have evolved. It was understood across the length and breadth of Arabia.

☾

Mecca is many things to many different people. The centre of the world to its citizens, a sacred centre for all of pagan Arabia, a central entrepôt of the caravans that crisscross Arabia with the beneficial profits of trade as well as a marketplace bustling with local traders.

The markets are on the edge of the sacred enclosure of Mecca and feed the city. For although Mecca has holiness and water aplenty, practically everything else has to be imported. Bedouin bring in the pick of their herds of sheep and goats to be bought by butchers and slaughtered in the market. Beneath palm-frond shades piles of grapes, melons, watermelons and cucumbers are sold in season, mostly the produce of the oasis gardens of Taif, a two-day ride away. Less perishable goods such as dates, pressed dates, barley and wheat come from a wider field of suppliers including the oasis of Yathrib, a ten-day ride to the north.

That Monday, a messenger arrives at the house of one of the dominant merchant sheikhs of the town. He is 'Abd al-Muttalib, the acknowledged leader of the Beni Hashim clan, one of the many kinship groups that make up Mecca's ruling Quraysh tribe. He is a paramount figure in Mecca's clan-based society, a man worthy of the greatest respect, a rich and powerful merchant whose every word is listened to in the councils of his clan, tribe and city. The messenger is from Aminah, his daughter-in-law: 'An infant is born to you; come and see him.' 'Abd al-Muttalib rises and hastens on his way, for since the death of his youngest son, Abdullah, he has become the responsible male. The old man stoops beside Aminah's bed and listens carefully to what she has seen, dreamed and heard during her pregnancy. He approves her choice of name. The boy will be called Muhammad, which means 'the Praised One'. 'Abd al-Muttalib then takes his brand new grandson in his arms, carries the child into the dark, gloomy interior of the Kaaba shrine and gives thanks to the High God Allah for this gift of life.

How happy they had been just nine months earlier. Everyone in his family knew that Abdullah had been the old man's favourite. Not that 'Abd al-Muttalib had been short of choices: he had ten sons and six daughters. They were a good-looking family, every inch the proud hawk-featured Arabs. Indeed, it was said of his sons that 'there were no more prominent and stately men, none of more noble profile. Their noses were so large that the nose drank before the lips.' And not that the life had gone out of their father either. To prove that he was still full of natural spirit, 'Abd al-Muttalib had decided to take a new wife to coincide with Abdullah's first marriage. For Abdullah he had chosen carefully – Aminah, daughter of Wahb, who was related to one of his business colleagues and was one of the leading merchants from the Zuhrah clan. After a shared celebration, father and son had both 'entered' into their new wives on the same night. Muhammad had been conceived on that first night. Now Abdullah was dead and buried, already two months cold in his grave. Thank God for this gift of life.

Abdullah had died before he could make anything on his own account from trade. The newborn Muhammad and his widowed mother had but five camels and a little slave girl, Barakah, to their name. But at least the child had a lineage to be proud of. Muhammad, son of Abdullah, son of 'Abd al-Muttalib, son of Hashim (founder of the Beni Hashim clan), son of 'Abdu Manaf, son of Qusayy (the founder of Mecca's ruling Quraysh tribe). He would never lack for cousins, he would never be alone and he would never starve or lack protection, for he was of the Beni Hashim of the Quraysh. To be born of the Quraysh of Mecca was as good a start in life as was possible in central Arabia. For four generations the profits made from guarding Mecca and organising the caravan trade had been in the capable hands of the Quraysh. However, the Quraysh had only achieved that dominance by expelling a previous tribe, the Khuza'ah, as guardians of Mecca a hundred years before. They had also thrown off the suzerainty of the al-Kinda kingdom which had once dominated central Arabia. The Kinda had been based in Qarayat Dhat Kahl, a way station on the caravan route between southern Arabia and Iraq. As the paid allies of both the Byzantine Empire and the powerful Himyar kingdom of the Yemen, the Kinda had been able to summon a great tribal army in time of war. In the middle of the fifth century Qusayy, the eponymous heroic ancestor of the Quraysh, seized control of Mecca. Qusayy had vanquished but had not destroyed his rivals. The tents of the Khuza'ah Bedouin could still be found scattered over the marginal grazing lands of central Arabia, while the al-Kinda (or Kinta) dynasty survived in magnificent retirement, and ruled over a small group of oasis villages to the east of Palestine.

So the Quraysh had always to be on their guard. On top of this, there was considerable friction within the tribal confederation. From the earliest days there was a division between the Quraysh 'of the hollow' (in control of the vital central market and shrine of Mecca) and the Quraysh 'of the outskirts'. It is likely that those 'of the hollow' were descended from Qusayy's immediate kin, while those 'of the outskirts' were allies co-opted into the confederation. Even within the tight network of Qusayy's immediate descendants there were further rivalries and schisms. In particular the clans descended from Qusayy's two sons, 'Abd ad-Adr and 'Abdu Manaf, perpetuated this sibling rivalry. And whichever clan was the most successful – making the most money from the caravan trade, owners of the most camels, producing the largest number of warlike young men – could be sure it would face the others' overt rivalry.

At the time of the birth of Muhammad these rivalries had coalesced into two antagonistic groups: 'the Confederates' and 'the Scented Ones'. Although this could paralyse decision-making it was also a natural process within any Arabian tribe, a system of checks and balances designed to frustrate tyranny and ensure a rough equilibrium. The only danger was that the infighting might grow so violent that it threatened tribal unity. This was especially dangerous if, in its desperation, a defeated faction called upon an outside tribe for help. All around Mecca, in the highlands of the Hijaz, there were tribes of desert Bedouin such as the Hawazin or the Ghatafan, which looked enviously at Mecca. They would gladly use any excuse to intervene in the politics of Mecca and in the process topple the Quraysh from their perch.

Nor was the city of Mecca absolutely secure in its position. Certainly its role as a centre of pilgrimage was permanently fixed in the Arabian constellation, but not so its dominance of the caravan trade. Even the nearby oases of Yathrib or Taif (the latter's town protected by fine walls) would gladly have taken over the lucrative trade from 'sister Mecca'. If you look back into Arabian history, or keep your eyes on the old trade routes, you will stumble across the ghastly ruins of once great trading cities. Spirit-haunted graveyards; ruined fields overrun by thistles and attended only by the wind; cities such as Petra and Palmyra that had dominated the life and the trade routes of central Arabia in their time just as effectively (and rather more magnificently) than Mecca did in the sixth century.

Mecca had so far survived the turning wheel of fortune quite well. Its isolation and its inhospitable hinterland were its chief bulwarks. But these defences would be tested in 570 C.E., the very year of Muhammad's birth, by the Christian Empire of Abyssinia.

2

Arabia and Her Neighbours

To fully understand the times, and therefore the life of Muhammad, it is important to see his land, Arabia, in relation to its three imperial neighbours. Let us stand on the bleak hills that overlook Mecca and gaze out over this far, far horizon, peering like inspired savants towards those three distant thrones in Abyssinia, Persia and Byzantium, whose arbitrary and autocratic decrees had the power to give this sacred city decades of peace, or wreak on it the horrors of war.

In 525 the Christian Abyssinians became the rulers of the Yemeni kingdoms of southern Arabia. The Yemen is different from the rest of Arabia, its terrain and geographical characteristics being created by the tail end of the Indian monsoons that wash the highlands with rain. Here alone, among all the countries of the Arabian peninsula, there has been enough water to support permanent agricultural settlements. The gardens of Arabia tend to be concentrated in oasis-like valleys whose verdant vegetation contrasts dramatically with the arid slopes of the surrounding mountains. Since at least 1000 B.C.E. (perhaps much earlier) this region has been home to a continuous succession of kingdoms whose art, temples, class structure, written language and architecture bear instant and worthy comparison with those of Egypt and Babylon. Marib, the largest city, was protected by a 4,500-metre-long curtain wall while the twenty-storey palace of Ghumdan at San'a, which stood during the lifetime of Muhammad, was one of the wonders of the world. On each of the corners there were hollow copper lions which funnelled the passing wind into a roar. On the summit of the palace was a pavilion made of marble with a ceiling of alabaster through which the birds could be seen. From the thousands of inscriptions deciphered we hear only of the deeds of kings and priests and catch the echo of a distant poetic nomenclature, of such monarchs as Queen Shamsi and of the Yemeni kingdoms: the Minaeans, Sabeans, Qatabanis, Attramatei, Hadhramautis and Himyarites.

There has always been a tradition that this region, closely connected to Abyssinia, is the true cradle of the Arab people and the Arab language and there is some archaeological evidence to support this. It is known that the central desert was not occupied until around 1300 B.C.E., when the indigenous Arabian camel was first successfully domesticated. It was only with the aid of the camel that the Arabs were capable of successfully exploiting the sparse grazing and identifying the scattered water holes, oases and wells within the central desert. The bulk of the population always remained firmly based in the southern kingdoms.

The southern kingdoms were doubly blessed for, besides the fertile valleys, the arid slopes of the goat-grazed highlands abounded with a variety of shrub-like thorn trees whose bark or sap were collected to produce frankincense, myrrh and balsam. Such spices and incenses were prerequisites for any religious rituals or honourable burials, quite apart from their luxurious use in scents, in cooking and in domestic fumigation. They were among the most valuable trading commodities in the ancient world and remained unique resources of these kingdoms.

The jostling for power of the rival kingdoms within the Yemen suited everyone, not least the famously independent-minded tribesmen of southern Arabia. It also meant that no single power could control the production of incense. In the 520s the capable young King of Himyar threatened to upset all this. He had converted to Judaism and under the popular title Dhu Nuwas ('He of the Hanging Locks') threatened to unite all southern Arabia under his charismatic authority. He seems to have acquired backing from Persia, which was always keen to extend its zone of influence further along the Arabian coast. Dhu Nuwas identified the Christian Arabs of the Yemen as enemies to his ambitions. He sacked the famous monastery church at Najran and began to purge the region of Christians in 523. All those who continued to profess their faith were herded in the direction of a furnace which had been lit in a moat. There, to the jeers of the crowd, they faced the ultimate test of faith. Tales of their martyrdom – and the steadfastness of their faith – spread throughout Arabia. Muhammad was obviously deeply affected by their example, as a later Qur'anic passage would testify:

> Cursed the masters of the trench
> of the fuel-fed fire
> when they sat around it
> witnesses of what they inflicted on the believers.
> (Surah Al-Buruj, no. 85, verses 4–7)

The persecuted Christians appealed for help from the Negus Kaleb, the Emperor of Abyssinia, who was the nearest Christian monarch. The Negus had also been in correspondence with the

Byzantine Emperor Justin I, who had asked his 'brother emperor' to save the Christians of southern Arabia.

It was this appeal that in 525 led to an Abyssinian army crossing the Red Sea. Dhu Nuwas was defeated but rather than be taken captive he rode his horse into the sea. A Christian chieftain, Sumyafa Ashwa, was set up in his place. When this puppet monarch was deposed a few years later in a local revolt, the Abyssinians decided to step in and rule directly. In a methodical campaign the Abyssinian army commander Abreha subdued all the independent kingdoms of the Yemen. A blind Yemeni poet, Alqamah ibn Dhi Jadan, mourned the passing of the old order:

> Himyar and its kings are dead, destroyed by Time;
> Duran by the Great Leveller laid waste.
> Around its courts the wolves and foxes howl,
> And owls dwell there as though it never was.

In 547 one of Abreha's expeditionary forces pushed north right into the Hijaz mountains around Mecca but it was forced to return without establishing a permanent foothold in the region. In due course, Abreha's two sons, Yaksum and Masru, succeeded to his authority. From the proud inscriptions that Abreha had carved we also know that churches destroyed by Dhu Nuwas were rebuilt, new buildings such as the celebrated cathedral at San'a (fragments of which can be seen rebuilt into the city's mosque) were constructed and the irrigation works, damaged by the bursting of the Marib dam, were repaired. The Coptic mother Church at Alexandria in Egypt responded to Abyssinian requests and despatched a bishop and a number of priests to rebuild the Christian faith in the Yemen.

The Abyssinians were sincere in their beliefs. The Negus, the Emperor Kaleb, voluntarily relinquished his throne in order to become a monk in one of the mountain-top monasteries outside his capital at Aksum. He sent his crown as an offering to the great pilgrimage centre of Jerusalem where it was placed in the church of the Holy Sepulchre. However, under the rule of his equally pious son, the Negus Gebre Maskal ('Slave of the Cross'), it was clear that the Abyssinians, having come to southern Arabia as liberators, planned to stay on indefinitely as rulers.

☾

In 570 the Abyssinian viceroy of southern Arabia decided to 'inspect' Mecca, backed up by an army complete with a war elephant – the tank of its day. So struck were the Meccans by this Abyssinian weapon that they thereafter labelled 570 the 'Year of the Elephant' in their mnemonic chronology. It was never very clear what the Abyssinian viceroy was planning. It was widely feared that he intended to establish a permanent garrison in Mecca, and where there were foreign soldiers (however well behaved they might be) there was invariably trouble. Food had to be 'found' locally, an annual tribute topped up by tariffs and customs duties imposed by foreign officials. It all made good sense from the Abyssinian point of view as Mecca was the halfway point of the Yemen to Syria caravan route. It was therefore the logical extension of their rule over southern Arabia whose frontier had never been clearly established. Fortunately the elemental logistics of central Arabia intervened. The population abandoned the city and took refuge in the barren mountains. The Abyssinian army was hit by a form of plague or an outbreak of cholera and forced to evacuate their camp at Mecca within a matter of weeks. The Quraysh of Mecca breathed a sigh of relief and the population flooded back into the city. The High God of the Kaaba was thanked for sending the plague, believed to have been spread by poisonous stones dropped by a flight of birds.

Muhammad would grow up to the story of the political relationship between Arabia and Abyssinia; to that of Mecca's
miraculous deliverance from the Abyssinian army in the year of his
birth. It was a dramatic event that shook the city to its core, but
Muhammad never felt any residual hostility to Abyssinia. Indeed,
quite the reverse is true. Although there is no evidence that he travelled there as a young man, there seems to have been an intimate
relationship between Abyssinia and Muhammad that is not evi-
dent with any of the other imperial powers close to Arabia.

This intimacy was partly a result of family background.
Muhammad's own grandfather 'Abd al-Muttalib (and his great
grandfather) were heavily involved in the trade between Mecca and
Abyssinia. They would have enjoyed frequent access to the households of the various Abyssinian Christians, traders, craftsmen and
slaves who were resident in Mecca. Indeed, this relationship was
sufficiently well recognised for 'Abd al-Muttalib to be chosen to act
as the spokesman for Mecca to the encroaching Abyssinians in
570. 'Abd al-Muttalib's personal standing with the invading general was certainly good enough to ensure that his own herd of a
hundred camels, captured during the campaign, was returned to
him. There is also an old tradition that at some time in his boyhood Muhammad was cared for by an Abyssinian nurse. If this is
true, Muhammad might have developed a natural affinity with
and sympathy for Abyssinian patterns of speech and ways. It is an
historical fact that he would later send a substantial number of the
first Muslim believers (including his own daughter) to take refuge
with the Negus so that they could escape persecution. An even
greater influence has been detected by a linguist. In the 1930s A.
Jeffery identified some two hundred classical Arabic words that
may be derived from Ge'ez, the ancient liturgical language of the
Abyssinian Church. As an example, the Abyssinian word *hawari*,
helpers, was borrowed to describe Jesus' disciples in Arabic. This

should be no great surprise as the cultural exchange between Semitic Abyssinia and Semitic southern Arabia has ricocheted historically over thousands of years. The great barrier of the Red Sea narrows to a mere twenty miles at the Bab al Mandeb between Abyssinia and southern Arabia.

☾

The Abyssinian military expedition that had reached Mecca in the year of Muhammad's birth was justifiably considered to be a very serious threat. The wise old sheikhs of the Quraysh could stand on the hilltops above Mecca and look at the roads to the south. Who could know if the Abyssinian army might return the next year and destroy the freedom of their city and their faith? Subsequent events, however, were unexpectedly to reverse this gloomy prognosis. In 572 a general revolt against the Abyssinians among the tribes of the Yemen summarily destroyed their military rule over southern Arabia. That particular threat to the freedom of tribal Arabia and to Mecca dissolved like mist on a summer morning.

However, it soon became clear to the sheikhs of Mecca that the destruction of Abyssinian rule in southern Arabia had not been quite as spontaneous as it had first appeared. There was talk of secret agents distributing Persian gold among the tribes, a Persian-backed force of eight hundred Arab exiles and a fleet of eight ships moving down the coast in support. This came as no great surprise to the Meccans, who were well aware of Persia's desire for revenge on the Abyssinians for the death of their ally Dhu Nuwas back in 525. The only wonder was that it had taken them so long.

☾

Any Meccan merchant who took the road east knew all about the power of Persia. The Sasanian Empire of Persia was the effective ruler of the whole eastern coast of Arabia. Whether you were taking goods in or fetching merchandise out, you came under the authority of a Persian governor and a Persian tax collector. There was a 25–50 per cent customs surcharge placed on Chinese silks brought into the Persian Gulf from Ceylon in ships borne by the trade winds. This was a hefty tax but the demand was constant, for the exoticism of silk meant that it always had its own, ready market. The Persians were also very protective of their profits. One of the stories often recounted in the bazaars told of the foreign fleet that tried to cut out Persian middlemen from the profits of their eastern trade. As they headed for one of the ports of Ceylon the ships' captains were exultant at having finally outsmarted the Persians. But as they drew closer to the port their smiles froze, for they saw that between them and their goal sat the Persian battle fleet: rather than lose his cut of the profits, the emperor had ordered his ships to cross the Indian Ocean to blockade the ports of Ceylon.

In Mecca, therefore, the merchants knew that they crossed the Persians at their peril. Smuggling brought enormous rewards, but had its own risks as there was no easy excuse to hand. On the frontier of the Persian Empire there could be no possible confusion between the desert and the town, between free tribal Arabia and the lands of the empire.

In 570 the name of Persia's emperor, Shapur II, still prompted a shiver of fear throughout Arabia. Shapur had invaded central Arabia, massacred the most troublesome Bedouin tribes and then proceeded to transplant whole communities of Bedouin, such as the Beni Hanzala, to new grazing grounds hundreds of miles within his empire. It was the same Shapur II who had ordered the construction of the Khadaq Sabur, a frontier dyke on the edge of what the Persians described as *badiya* – the desert. The Khadaq Sabur was guarded by frontier watchtowers manned by the Arab tribes of the frontier region. These frontier Arabs, who were excused payment of the Persian land tax, were under the authority of the Arab Lakhmid king. An hereditary monarch, he had absolute control of the frontier, though in the hierarchy of the Persian Empire he was no more than a provincial governor, the *marzban* (warden of the marshes) of the south. The Lakhmids had their own capital, the city of al-Hira, which was strategically placed on the junction of the desert, the farmlands of Mesopotamia and the extensive marshlands of southern Iraq. They were implacable rivals of the Arab Ghassanid kings who in turn were sworn allies of the Byzantine Empire. Absolute and inflexible though this shared animosity was, it was never allowed to interfere with trade but it did show itself in matters of religion. Although both the Ghassanids and the Lakhmids were Christian, their natural rivalry allowed one dynasty to support the Syrian-based Jacobite Church while the Lakhmids were intimately connected with the Iraq-based Nestorian Church.

In terms of magnificence the Lakhmids were acknowledged to have a definite edge over their rivals. For as well as the desert frontier of Iraq they governed the entire eastern coast of Arabia along the Persian Gulf, the coastline of Oman and, when the opportunity presented itself, they spread their influence and power into the Yemen. The only chink in the Lakhmid armour – and one that the Ghassanids exploited to the full – was that they were too much part of the Persian system. The Ghassanids liked to boast that they were allies of the Caesars while the Lakhmids were servants of the Persian emperor.

Most of the merchants of Mecca involved in the eastern trade routes attached absolute importance to their relationship with the Lakhmid kingdom. In the 570s everybody in Mecca agreed that the Persian Empire seemed to be in its prime. The state was not shy of pomp and circumstance; in fact it positively revelled in it. Scholars have yet to sort out the exact hierarchy and purpose of the many dazzling titles that were given to the officials of the court at the Persian capital of Ctesiphon. Since the foundation of the Sasanian Empire by Ardashir I (227–241 C.E.) they had gone to great lengths to set themselves up as the legitimate heirs to the ancient Achaemenid Empire of Cyrus, Darius and Xerxes. The Achaemenid Empire had ruled over the entire Middle East and the Sasanids aspired to restore this vast empire. There was an inbuilt political momentum to seize back the 'lost provinces' from the Byzantine Empire, no matter that they had originally been 'lost' to Alexander the Great some eight hundred years earlier. This political illusion would ultimately help to destroy the regime, though in 570 absolutely no one could have predicted such an outcome, and even less that within sixty years the Arabs of the desert would be the new masters of the empire.

☾

The Persia of King Chosroes I (531–579 C.E.) positively bristled with imperial authority. Chosroes (known also as Khosru or Kisra) presided over a perfectly ordered society, a state that embraced many languages and cultures but enforced universal laws. Although it had had its bad moments, compared with the Byzantine Empire it was essentially tolerant of different religions. Jews and Christians prospered beside the state-supported Zoroastrian fire-temples. As imperial authority had increased over the centuries so had the importance of the cities and towns. The authority of the great aristocratic lords had gradually been eclipsed and replaced by an urban bureaucracy directed by a centralised court. The capital city of Ctesiphon was a vast amalgam of seven towns, known as al-Mada-in, 'the Metropolis', to the Arabs. The four points of the compass corresponded to the four borders of Persia, each guarded by a *marzban*. Society was neatly divided, again like the compass, into four groups: priests, warriors, scribes and the labouring peasants and artisans.

This class hierarchy would be blown apart by the equality brought about by Islam, but other features of old Persia would survive. Although Islam would have no truck with a priesthood, the Persian priest, doubling as judge and protector of the poor, would be the role model for the cadi, the scholar-judge of Islam. Similarly, the Persian habit of setting up legal trusts to support religious institutions would be expanded into the *waqf*, the Muslim system of pious endowments that enriched all the medieval cities of Islam. The Arabs were great admirers of the Persian postal system and the respect given to sealed letters. They also delighted in the traditional Persian walled gardens – yet again divided into four quarters – that were fed by ornamental fountains and well-ordered irrigation trenches. Indeed, the very Arabic word chosen by Muhammad to describe heaven, *paradis*, was the Persian word to describe these walled gardens.

The Arabs shared the Persian respect for learning. The university city of Jundisabur/Gondeshapur is a true legend of the East. It was to this city, famed above all for its devotion to the healing art of medicine, that the philosophers of Athens fled when their university was closed down by Christian fundamentalists in 529. As well as courtyards for scribes, learning and debate, Jundisabur had one of the world's first teaching hospitals. Tariq Ali has described how the first Arab who earned the title of physician, Harith bin Kalada

was later admitted to the Court of the Persian ruler Chosroes Anushirwan and a conversation between the two men was recorded by scribes. According to this the physician advised the ruler to avoid over-eating and undiluted wine, to drink plenty of water every day, to avoid sex while drunk and to have baths after meals. He is reputed to have pioneered enemas to deal with constipation.

When the great library of Alexandria was burnt (by Christian fundamentalists in 391) Jundisabur kept knowledge alive. Here Greek
and Syriac texts were translated into Pahlavi, the written language
of Sasanian Persia, and from these were made the Arabic translations that would be spread across the known world. The great
Arab philosopher-physicians ibn Sina and al-Razi were always
happy to acknowledge that they were indebted to a small town in
Persia for their learning. The very word 'Arab' was coined in Persia,
for the Persians described the Syriac-speaking province within
their empire as 'Beth Arabaya'.

From the point of view of a merchant of Mecca looking towards
the east, the Persian Empire seemed to be one of life's certainties.
Persia's grip over the coast of eastern Arabia was tenacious, though
her influence in the Yemen would no doubt continue to wax and
wane just as the moon did.

☾

What about the north? In 570, did the merchant city fathers of
Mecca fear the great empire that lay to their north? The Byzantine
Empire brooded over all the lands of the Near East. The legions of
Byzantium occupied Egypt, Palestine and Syria and her governors
looked back on a heritage of absolute dominion that went back
five centuries to the Hellenistic kingdoms and further back to
Alexander's empire. Although the western half of the Roman
Empire had been swamped by barbarian invasions, the eastern
half had brilliantly renewed itself. During Justinian's long reign
(527–565) the emperor's armies had expelled the Ostrogoths from
Italy, the Vandals from North Africa and the Visigoths from southern Spain. Justinian had spat out vast fortunes in a hugely
ambitious building programme. Explore any part of the eastern
Mediterranean and you will stumble upon his creations: fortresses,
forts, city walls and vast underground cisterns abound. He also

adorned the holy places of Christianity with a reckless but innovative piety. At the very end of his long reign he was able to reinaugurate his great cathedral of Ayia Sophia at Constantinople. He solemnly entered that breathtaking sanctuary with its heaven-suspended golden dome in the clear light of Christmas morning. Bowed with age and clothed in the black cowl of a monk, Justinian was heard to whisper, 'Solomon, Solomon, I have surpassed thee.'

The Byzantine emperors were only ever interested in territory that paid its way. They were interested in prime farmland, mines, quarries and ports that controlled foreign trade. There was no profit in ruling Mecca and central Arabia for their own sakes. The roads that connected the domains of the emperor with the markets of Mecca crossed thousands of miles of desert that could neither be taxed nor garrisoned. For a man accustomed to undertaking this journey it still took forty days. It was much more cost-effective for the empire simply to hold on to the Syrian market towns on the edge of the desert: the desert herdsmen would be forced to drive their camels and their precious caravans of trade goods across the frontiers of the empire to sell at these provincial markets. At desert border posts throughout the empire, inscriptions have been found that neatly tabulate the customs duties payable on various goods as the merchants entered and then departed from the empire. Thus it was never simply a one-way flow of cultures of the powerful external empires rippling out from their imperial capitals to influence the desert periphery. Arabs passed through the customs posts on the desert frontiers: as merchants of the caravans; as Bedouin herdsmen seeking grazing for their flocks; as migrant workers helping out with the seasonal harvest; as dealers in livestock; as mercenary soldiers on ten-year contracts; as travellers in search of fortune and adventure; or as entire tribes leaving the desert in search of their version of the land of milk and honey.

From a Byzantinian perspective the 'other side' of the desert frontier was the land of the Sarakenoi, 'the people who dwell in tents'. From the word Sarakenoi, medieval Christian Europe would later coin the name 'Saracen', a catch-all term for its Muslim-Arab foe. The resources that any empire could extract from these people were never deemed worth the price of military occupation, especially since the inhabitants could at any time fold their tents and decamp, depopulating entire regions situated anywhere near a tax-gathering garrison. But although the Byzantine Empire might not care to rule the land of the Sarakenoi it liked to be able to police the edges of it. The empire had two basic strategies available to it: 'forward reconnaissance' and 'client kingship'.

'Forward reconnaissance' involved sending military patrols beyond the fixed frontier, mobile detachments of the army that could observe the seasonal tribal markets and gauge local feeling. This could be combined with the recruitment of Arab cavalrymen into the Byzantine army, from the free tribes of the borderlands. These recruits, the auxiliaries of the Byzantine army, were placed under the command of a Byzantine officer, deliberately kept in small units and usually sent far away from their homelands. Traces have been found of Arabs stationed in Germany, Romania and north Britain.

'Client kingship' meant that through his local governors the emperor could support a local tribal chief who showed loyalty and elevate him to become a king among his people. An annual cash stipend from the imperial treasury was usually sufficient to support a permanent bodyguard. This could be reinforced with grants of citizenship to other members of this client local dynasty, gifts of regalia (gilded and enamelled crowns, swords and silver dinner services, for example) and exquisite textiles from the work-shops of the palace at Constantinople. The result of all this was to raise a loyal subject or client swiftly to a vaunted position over his peers.

Both policies had their problems, however. Forward reconnaissance was more expensive, more assertive and more efficient but could, in the hands of the wrong officers, actually serve to irritate rather than calm a border area. Client kingship was cheaper but there was always the risk that the empire might create a subject who was altogether too powerful.

In the year of Muhammad's birth client kingship was the policy of the day, and the Byzantine Empire had chosen the chief of the Ghassanid tribe of Arabia as its client. It was a good choice, especially as the Ghassanids had a firm hold on that vital part of the Arabian desert that acted as a buffer zone between Byzantium and Persia. Not only did the Ghassanids control the tolls on the direct Syria to Iraq caravan route but they guarded the classic invasion route between the two empires.

In 570 the ruling chieftain of the Ghassanid tribe was al-Mundhir. The traveller can still wander through one of his royal audience halls, which stands just outside the rectangular city walls of Byzantine Sergiopolis, near Syria's frontier with Iraq. It is a classic example of Justinian's building programme; indeed, Justinian's favoured court historian Procopius gives a fulsome account of the transformation of the town in his *Buildings* book. The beautiful triple gateway of Sergiopolis was worthy of comparison with that of Diocletian's palace at Split. Cisterns and barracks for the army, three magnificent churches, civic courtyards and a caravanserai for the use of passing merchants were all enclosed in a circuit of walls overlooked by fifty towers, all of which glittered and sparkled with reflective light from the crystal mica in the building stone.

Al-Mundhir's hall was famous throughout Arabia. The king would sit on his throne in the raised eastern apse, his counsellors ranged around him, with honoured guests seated in the flanking aisles. The main aisle, once surmounted by a tower – where now the desert sun pours through – would be packed with his bodyguards and supplicant visitors. The flanking pair of royal beasts and the heraldic phoenix carved in stone on the walls of the apse were matched by figures in gilded wood and ivory that supported the Ghassanid throne. Around the walls you can still identify sections of carving that include the Greek inscription that translates as 'Long Live al-Moundaros'. It is a place steeped in atmosphere even if aesthetically it is inferior to the imposing buildings of the adjacent town. Compared to the great domed cathedral of the bishop, the long-naved basilica of the Holy Cross or the celebrated shrine of the martyr St Sergius, it is undeniably crude. However, in its heyday, surrounded by a sea of tents and lit by a constellation of innumerable campfires at night, it must have glowed with splendour. It was constructed to be used just once a year, at the feast day of St Sergius, which had grown into an empire-wide cult. Here one can imagine the Arab king and Byzantine governor jointly presiding over the week-long festival. St Sergius was then at the apogee of his popularity.

Only when the official audiences were finished could the Arab king return to his true culture. In his royal hall outside the walls the bards of ancient Arabia would chant their fierce poetry. They would not speak of columns, of mosaic floors or gilded domes but of love, passion, heroism, fame, beauty and regret. The writer Isfahani's eyewitness account glows with the splendour of these receptions:

> I have seen ten singing girls, five of them Byzantines, singing Greek songs to the music of lutes, and five from Hira . . . chanting Babylonian melodies. Arab singers used to come from Mecca and elsewhere for his delight. And when he

would drink wine he sat on a couch of myrtle and jasmine and all sorts of sweet-smelling flowers, surrounded by gold and silver vessels full of ambergris and musk. During winter aloes-wood was burned in his apartments while in summer he cooled himself with snow. Both he and his courtiers wore only light, single garments in the hot weather and fenek fur or the like in the cold season. And by God I was never in his company but he gave me the robe which he was wearing on the day . . .

In 584 there was a sudden reversal of policy when the Emperor Maurice (or rather Maurikios, for this was the time when Latin was finally dropped in favour of Greek) cut off the annual subsidy to the Ghassanids. This was not a malicious act, though it turned out to be a foolish one. Maurikios, an otherwise efficient ruler, was obsessed with balancing the budget. Costs were slashed here, there and everywhere. Four years after he cut off the Ghassanid subsidy he reduced military rations by a quarter. In 602 he took parsimony too far. He decided it would be cheaper to keep his field army under canvas over the winter months than to march them back to their barracks and the comfort of their women. He was dead within the month.

☾

It was Maurikios's usurpation by the centurion Phocas that provided the Persian king Chosroes II with the pretext of invading Byzantium in 603 to restore legitimate authority. For the tribes of central Arabia this offered a golden period of freedom. The all-powerful empires to the north, east and south were so consumed by their own rivalry that they gave no thought to the politics of Arabia. Mecca, safely sited in the geographical, commercial and religious centre of Arabia, was now left alone in the centre of the Arabian stage.

Over the lifetime of Muhammad the power of these three great imperial empires receded even further from Arabia. It was as if fate had conspired to create the most exceptionally positive environment in which the Arabs could work out a new destiny.

3

From Boy Shepherd
to the Caravans
of Old Arabia

It is market day in Mecca in 570. A party of Bedouin from the Beni Saad (literally, 'the sons of Saad') clan of the Hawazin tribe have come into the city from their customary grazing lands, a nine-day ride away. The women have left their husbands at the stock market and are enjoying themselves as they work their way around the streets of Mecca; they form a noisy, boisterous train, all mounted on donkeys, part heckling, part charming their way around the doorways of the noble households of the Quraysh. They are asking the women of the house if there are any newborn children who require a wet nurse, for fostering the children of the comparatively wealthy Quraysh is one of the ways in which these women can earn a little extra. No money changes hands, though it is acknowledged that they will receive a handsome gift when they deliver the child back to his Meccan home, which thereafter will also be obliged to provide hospitality to old foster mothers passing through Mecca for the market. One by one the Bedouin wives pick up an extra charge, until only one of them, Halimah, is left without a foster child. On the grapevine they have already heard that there is a young Quraysh wife who needs a wet nurse for her newborn son, Muhammad. But that same grapevine also warns the Bedouin that the father of the child is dead. They fear that the reward from a young widow may not be worth the extra work involved. Halimah hesitates. Should she approach the widow or should she not? She returns to the marketplace and asks her husband for advice. He is in a good mood and gives his approval, saying: 'Perhaps he will be a blessing to us.'

Thus was the young Muhammad passed from his mother to the care of a Bedouin woman. Halimah and her husband rejoin their kinsfolk in time to pick up with the long cavalcade of the Beni Saad as they trot out of Mecca on the north-eastern road.

☾

To the villagers and town dwellers, the tented Bedouin seemed an anarchic and rulerless people with neither priests, judges, governors nor kings. In fact they were bound tightly within their own social organisation. No Bedouin would contemplate a life outside the tent he shared with his immediate family, surrounded by the dwellings of his extended family of cousins, all of whom shared common descent from a heroic male ancestor. (Though property, interestingly enough, was often inherited through the female line.) A hundred or so families might constitute a clan, which held rights over wells and pasturage in common as well as fighting and migrating together as a unit.

A council of forty of the most respected men met to decide any issue and choose one of their number to act as a leader – a sheikh – in war, migration or negotiation. Loyalty to the clan, *asabiya*, was an absolute virtue. There were no courts of law in central Arabia, no written codes of conduct, while the only protection against murder was afforded by the blood feud or vendetta, when a clan would avenge the death of one of its members by killing an equivalent member of the murderer's clan. The rule was an eye for an eye, a tooth for a tooth, with clan feuds stretching back over generations. Theft, particularly of herds from a rival clan, was an admired rather than a despised act. Above the clan was the tribe, which was formed of coalitions of clans and tended to have little internal strength unless threatened by a common enemy or united by the prospect of trade or booty.

Muhammad's early childhood was spent in the desert with his Bedouin foster mother Halimah, who cared for him alongside her own children. Not only did such a system enable the Bedouin to supplement their income, it also gave a Quraysh child a healthy start in life, away from the infections of the town, an opportunity to grow up in the harsh, clean air of the desert on a diet of fresh milk and flesh. And it freed the aristocratic ladies of the Quraysh from the burden of child rearing – or at least it reduced some of the pressures on them in their continuous cycle of pregnancy. Such fostering also cut across class and clan divisions, binding the comparatively rich merchants of Mecca into close relationships with the Bedouin who were all around them.

Halimah and her own offspring thus comprised Muhammad's family in his first years. He shared the left-hand side of the tent with the women and children, while the men inhabited their own space beyond the flimsy hanging that symbolically as well as physically divided the tent in two. Possessions, other than clothing, were few and were stored in bags, either of skin, woven wool or matted grasses. These could be used as cushions or flung on the backs of camels when it was time to move on to new pastures within the sparse desert hills of the Hijaz. Their immediate cousins, the other kin of Halimah's father, Abu Dhuayb, would be grouped in a crescent of tents pitched at calling distance but seldom numbering more than a dozen. The boy Muhammad thus lived the life of a nomad in a world that gradually extended from the black tent to embrace the surrounding desert.

Long afterwards, memories of the childhood of Muhammad were lovingly collected by his biographers. Halimah fondly recalled that the years in which she cared for the boy had been a time of abundance for her. Before she had found him her breasts had been empty, but once she started wet nursing the infant Muhammad she remembered how they had become filled with an abundance of milk for her own son and his new foster brother. On their first night together they both drank their fill and slept through the night. At the same time their exhausted old she-donkey perked up so much that their neighbours could almost not recognise her. Even their she-camel was found to have plenty of milk. To crown it all, 'when we arrived at our habitation in the country of the Beni Saad – a more sterile land than which I do not know on the earth of Allah – our sheep met me in the evening filled with milk so that we had only to milk and drink, whereas others could not milk a single drop'. Whatever the truth of these happy memories, Muhammad was weaned at two, passing from the milk of Halimah to that of her flock.

There was, however, a very disturbing incident, which caused Halimah immediately to return her charge to his home in Mecca when he was six years old. Her own son told her that two men dressed in shining white garments had taken hold of Muhammad and cut open his chest. They had removed his heart, cleaned away a black clot and then washed the organ and his chest in purifying snow from a golden platter. This miraculous account of angelic sanctification is contradicted by the Prophet's own denial of any miraculous occurrence in his life. However, the imagination of the faithful delights in this tale.

So Muhammad was returned to Mecca and to the company of his widowed mother, Aminah. His foster mother was paid off and his childhood friendships came to an abrupt end, though throughout his life Muhammad was always delighted to entertain his Bedouin step-family and would invariably send them away loaded with gifts.

The cherished reunion between mother and child was fated to be all too brief, for Aminah was dying. The proud widow took her young son to visit his maternal uncles, joining one of the Yathrib-bound caravans. In Mecca she had succeeded in hiding her illness from everyone, but the rigours of a desert crossing exposed her fatal weakness. After a few days of slower than normal progress the caravan grew impatient. Ailing mother and her son were left behind at the little oasis halt of Abwa where it was hoped that Aminah might recover her strength. In the long days of painful idleness she taught her son how to make and fly a kite. Then, one day, as the young Muhammad was flying his kite, his mother slipped away from him for ever. He had known her for less than a year; now he was required to bury her in a desert grave, marked only by a pile of dark, sun-baked rocks.

The orphaned Muhammad waited until a passing caravan could return him to Mecca. There he found shelter in the large household of his paternal grandfather, 'Abd al-Muttalib. His grandfather was still a man to be reckoned with: he remained the acknowledged sheikh of the Beni Hashim clan of the Quraysh, though his days of travelling with the caravans were now over.

Muhammad clearly basked in the love and concern of this wise old man. It was his grandfather who would lead the hunt when young Muhammad (fresh from the desert) got himself lost in the labyrinth of Mecca's alleys. When he was at last tracked down, wandering in a street in the upper town, 'Abd al-Muttalib hoisted the youngster on his back and carried him around the Kaaba, calling upon God to protect and watch over his orphaned grandson. The rest of his large family maintained a distant respect for the grand old patriarch, but the lonely Muhammad seems to have cut straight through to his grandfather's heart. Muhammad was the only one of his grandchildren who was allowed to sit with the old man on the day bed that was placed outdoors, either outside his front door or in the shadow of the Kaaba. Here they would chat or doze away the afternoon heat; sometimes Muhammad would massage the aches and pains from the old man's shoulders.

This loving relationship would too soon come to an end. 'Abd al-Muttalib died in 578 when Muhammad was eight and the boy now passed into the care of his uncle Abu Talib. It is believed that this was done on the orders of 'Abd al-Muttalib on his deathbed, although, as the only surviving full brother of Muhammad's own father, Abdullah, Abu Talib was in any case the obvious guardian for the boy. All his many other uncles were the children of 'Abd al-Muttalib's other wives and concubines. Abu Talib inherited many responsibilities from his father but not his power. Leadership, or more exactly, the chairmanship of the clan council of the Quraysh, now passed to the children of one of 'Abd al-Muttalib's many cousins – the Beni Umayya clan.

Muhammad would always be cared for by Abu Talib but it was also clear that, despite his proud lineage, he was nonetheless still a poor orphan. He would have to work for his keep and work especially hard if he was ever to be able to amass enough wealth to possess his own herd of camels, to pay the necessary bride price for a wife and establish his own household. Tradition, in some quarters, has it that he immediately started work as a herdsman for his uncle.

The age of eight marked a powerful change in the life of a Bedouin boy. It was one of the major thresholds of manhood. The ancient Semitic ritual of circumcision marked the transition from boyhood to youth and was an excuse for feasting and public celebrations. Curiously, considering the essential part it plays in the life of a Muslim male, there are no stories about the Prophet's circumcision, while that of Jesus is marked by a festival in the Christian calendar. Some obscure little religious booklets might suggest that Muhammad's circumcision was performed by angels. But this is no more than a pious thought. Muhammad would probably have been circumcised at the same time as one of the sons of Abu Talib.

After circumcision boys could sleep on the male side of the tent, would no longer eat in an extended gynaeceum, that scented, bosomy, competitive network of aunts, mothers, step-mothers and grandmothers, but would proudly take their place around the communal platter of the men. No longer smothered with kisses and attention, they would take grave satisfaction in existing silently on the bottom rung of male society. At this stage in life it was their privilege to listen and to serve. This new status was also reflected in a change of animal husbandry. Gone were the days spent looking after the sheep and goats. If he was fortunate a youth would now devote himself to the lord of the desert, the king of beasts in the Arab world – the camel. For a boy this was true glory indeed.

The camel was everything to the Arabs of the desert. Without a camel, as a man you were nothing. You could neither be a war-rior, a merchant, a lover or a free-spirited wanderer. You had no status, no voice, no ambition, no sex appeal, no pride, no poetry and little future. Instead of boundless opportunity and an ever-expanding horizon, the desert closed in, like a crabby, malicious claw, upon a camel-less man. The camel was the knight's steed, the modern-day lorry of the hard-working trader, while in its slaugh-tering a man automatically ascended to the position of munificent host. It was the one unit of currency that could buy a man an hon-oured wife, pay off the blood guilt of a murder and offer irrefutable evidence of his status within society. In reading the seven surviving poems of pre-Islamic Arabia, it is frequently necessary to check if the poets are praising a lover or a camel. The amoral warrior-poets of pre-Islamic Arabia would not have been offended by the confusion. For in that famous pagan catalogue of the three male pleasures of life – to ride flesh, to eat flesh, to enter flesh – the camel scores well.

So Muhammad, entering the adult world of the merchants of Mecca had, first and foremost, to learn about the care and breeding of camels. Much of this would be instinctive, things that he had heard and seen all his life. How to hobble the wandering beasts at night, how gradually to wean the young from their mothers, how to tie a girth, how to arrange a saddle and how best to load a camel so that it suffered no debilitating sores. How to weave ropes from palm fibre, how to prepare goatskin water bags; what food it was possible to feed a camel in addition to its own grazing. Certain species of the palm tree family are poisonous and even dates – though useful in an emergency – overheat the blood. The camels also had to be trusted and given their head. In the words of Hassanein Bey, one of the greatest of the twentieth-century Arab explorers of the desert, 'Nothing is more important . . . than the condition of your camels. Not only must they be fat and well nourished from the start, but they must be allowed to drink their fill with deliberation and permitted to rest after the drinking.' This resting of camels was an essential part of desert lore. Even the greatest of the desert crossings needed to be broken down into periods of intense activity combined with prolonged rest.

Camel management was only the beginning of the apprenticeship of the young Muhammad. Knowledge of the desert was also vital. Maps now mark the trade routes across the Arabian desert. These are useful to the modern mind but cannot express the realities on the ground. At one point a trail might narrow to a thin pathway of red dust suitable only for single file as it snakes its way through a bleak landscape of jagged black rocks. At another the tracks across a wide wadi bed will divide into a thousand different paths and allow for some good grazing on the way; while the route through a stretch of sand dunes might be well known but the familiar pathway obscured every evening by the wind that blows up after dusk. Elsewhere it may lead through a gorge, the only way through in this direction, a well-trodden route indeed, dotted with traces of the campfires fuelled by camel dung.

Muhammad also needed to know about pasturages. Different tribes had their own habitual seasonal grazing grounds and these were connected by tracks that were deliberately designed to avoid encroaching upon the pasturages of a rival tribe. Others led off on a long detour that seemed to make no sense in terms of the direction they took except that they passed by a reliable well. In short, there were hundreds of different routes for different peoples, each picking their own way delicately across the landscape, avoiding foes and greeting allies. Each camel caravan would connect two centres together but the various tracks followed were innumerable.

The boy Muhammad would have learned that the size of the caravan also helped dictate the route. The larger the caravan the safer its passage through the desert. It could undertake the crossing of some notorious badland or bandit-infested gorge that a small group could only take at its peril. However, these large caravans brought on additional problems if they exceeded the available water sources and the grazing. Both of these themselves depended on the season, the desired speed of travel and on a highly erratic weather pattern, which might in one year bless a valley with rain sufficient to produce a 'land filled with milk and honey' but leave it a barren wasteland for the next nine. Muhammad would know that there was no such thing as idle gossip in the desert. Detailed local knowledge was vital: which clans were friendly, which wells were dry, which pasturages had been eaten out – all such knowledge was of vital concern. Wars without truce might close down one route just as a newly signed peace treaty opened up another. The caravan had to negotiate with each Bedouin tribe to be professionally guided across its grazing territory – a form of protection money not far removed from a tax. Equally important was the relationship with the trading cities at the caravan's final destination. Though stable enough compared to the Bedouin clans they were in other ways less reliable. Changes in government policy and staff come easy to autocratic states. Old trading connections sanctified by three generations of fair prices could be superseded overnight by the arrival of some new, more mercenary governor.

The young Muhammad had to learn all of this if he was to survive as a merchant in Mecca working on the caravans of old Arabia. His education came fast. Some sources say he first accompanied Abu Talib on the caravan from Mecca to Syria at the age of nine, while others claim he was twelve. Half his life, from the years 582 to 610, would be spent on the caravan trade. If he was to profit at all he had to understand each and every one of the strands of the trade. He had also to learn about the hierarchy of wealth. He would have watched and listened in on the endless rounds of consultations and discussions in which his uncle took part. An Arab caravan was a joint stock venture, not a military campaign. Much of the actual carrying was done not by the servants or slaves of the great merchants but by cameleers, free men who rented out the porterage of their camels and their own service as attendants. In their own words (as recorded by a coffee merchant), 'their backs are yours but the beasts remain ours'.

Knowledge of the goods with which to trade was the second half of the education of a young merchant of the Quraysh of Mecca. Trade was the lifeblood of the city, as the Qur'an confirms: 'For the protection of Quraysh: their protection is their summer and winter journeyings' (surah Quraysh, no. 106, verse 1). The Arab tribes of the central desert subsisted on their herds. In good years they could make a little extra by selling their surplus livestock to those who occupied the richer agricultural lands. Here they acquired grain, dried fruit and textiles. They also came to admire the cooking utensils, weapons, jewellery and armour, which they could rarely afford to purchase. Nature seldom blessed them with an abundance but she did at least ensure a reliable market. Neither horses nor camels (the one vital for war, the other useful for trade) could be successfully bred in the irrigated flatlands that supported all the earliest states in Egypt and Mesopotamia. Therefore there was a continuous demand for the livestock reared by the Arab nomads, who could easily include a certain amount of trading during their year-round migrations. In winter they would graze the remote reserves in the central desert known only to them, before moving out in the spring to catch the arid pastures briefly in bloom after the sporadic rains. By summer they had migrated towards oasis villages or farmlands, taking up any casual labour required during the harvest and using the opportunity to graze the fields after harvest. This was the season of the markets. The simple exchange of the products of nomadic society for those of a settled agricultural society was the first strand of the caravan trade.

The second strand of trade for the merchant of Arabia was leather. Skins could be picked up cheaply from the Bedouin throughout the year and then packed up for the long journey to the cities and towns of Syria and Iraq. Leather was in a sense the plastic of the pre-modern world and was in continuous demand. Apart from the high status items – the plush slippers, tooled saddles, leather jerkins and pages of parchment – there was an endless demand for leather bags, bottles, bed straps, red leather tents, chairs, bridles and halters. In terms of volume this was the biggest business by far. Hashim, the Prophet's great-grandfather, is known to have secured permission to export skins and textiles into Syria.

The third strand of trade was incense, the single most lucrative ingredient of the caravan trade. Yemen, as we have seen, was the source of frankincense and myrrh. Pliny describes the process by which both are acquired: 'the earliest gathering takes place at about the rising of the Dogstar, when the summer heat is most intense . . . from the incision a greasy foam bursts out, which coagulates and thickens, being received on a mat of palm leaves . . .' from where it was collected and packed into small wicker baskets. The locals were determined to make the most of this resource. Foreign merchants were encouraged to stay away from the regions of production, around which circulated strange tales about how they were protected. The outside world was encouraged to believe that frankincense and myrrh were gathered by priests from groves hidden away in mountains sacred to the sun that were guarded by flying serpents. These stories, which were faithfully recorded by many of the Greek geographers of the day, helped further to raise the profile and profit of incense.

Despite the mark-up the Yemenis applied and the lucrative royal monopolies over the selling of incense, the profits from the trade could still be staggering. Provided that they could get their caravan safely across the mountains and deserts and avoid the bellicose Bedouin tribes of Arabia, the merchants could expect to turn a handsome 500 per cent profit.

To be an effective merchant Muhammad would have to know his way instinctively around the incense markets. Aside from the grades of colour and the different potencies, affected by the age, the condition of the tree and the season of tapping, there are actually nine different species of frankincense tree. The mist-shrouded mountain slopes of Dhofar, the eastern province of the Yemeni kingdom of the

Hadhramaut, produced the best, though that shipped out of the island of Socotra was also highly valued. Myrrh was sold either as a pure oil or as a crystal. Of the latter, Erythraean myrrh is believed to have been extracted from trees in Arabia while Troglodytic myrrh (the most expensive) probably came from Abyssinia. There were ten different kinds of balsam traded in the Near East. It was known as *kataf* in the Yemen, though a wider geographical range made it a much less valuable commodity for the merchant. The balsam of Judea and of Mecca were, however, both useful trade items.

This was all big business. Demand was assured for the religions of the ancient Middle East had an almost addictive dependence on incense. Frankincense had to be burned at all major rituals, it was used to fumigate shrines and during funeral rites. From Hellenistic times it began to be used in royal courts and by Justinian's time, although it had been dropped from Christian funerary practices, the great basilicas of Christian Byzantium were once again filled with clouds of incense. It cut across all creeds, be they Jews, Christians, Zoroastrians or pagans: there was not a god among them that did not demand it. Myrrh was used for preparing the dead for burial and in Egypt for mummification. At the height of its profitability (around the second century C.E.) it has been estimated that six hundred tons of myrrh and three thousand tons of mixed incense were exported from southern Arabia every year. Over the centuries enterprising Arab merchants had also developed additional trades, journeying south and west to acquire rare woods, incense and spices from the remote highlands and steppes of Sudan and Somalia as well as from their agents established along the East African coast. Indeed, it seems likely that most of the oil of myrrh was produced on the Somali coast which boasts five indigenous species of the thorny shrub from which myrrh is obtained.

☾

The caravan travelling to the Yemen from Mecca generally set off in the winter. It is said that Muhammad made this journey at least once (with his uncle Zubair) though there is no precise evidence. His family connections with the Abyssinian trade would suggest that this caravan route was a regular part of his early life. The caravan's destination was one of the royal cities of the Yemeni kingdoms, such as the Hadhramaut capital of Shabwah. Certain verses from the Qur'an suggest that Muhammad had an intimate knowledge of the terrain. The once-fertile domain that existed in the shadow of the Marib dam may possibly have supported a population as large as fifty thousand. The collapse of the dam sometime in the sixth century reduced this thriving farmland to a desert within a few years. The Qur'an eloquently describes this catastrophe: 'We have given them, instead of their two gardens, a harvest of camel thorn, tamarisk and a few ilb trees.'

At the great market centres of the Yemen the camels would be rested while negotiations started. Incense, Yemeni textiles and whatever else could be found at a reasonable price that had been imported from India, Somalia or Abyssinia would be haggled over, bartered, bought and bound up in bundles. From there the trail – known as the Incense Road – stretched back north across a sea of sand. The caravans would stop off at the string of oasis communities that lie parallel to, but safely inland from, the pirate-infested Red Sea. The route from San'a to Mecca was known as 'the Way of the People of the Elephant', as it had been the route used by the Abyssinian army that had marched on Mecca in 570.

All being well, the caravan returned to Mecca where it then disbanded. The goods were broken up, divided among the various merchants, disposed of in the markets and the camel guides paid off.

The second great caravan of the year set off in the spring to take goods north. This is the route with which the Prophet is most strongly linked and we must consider the lessons he might have learned as he followed this familiar route. Bundles of stinking leather were strapped on to obstinate camels, while other beasts were loaded with bolts of cloth, or carefully wrapped packages of spice, tightly packed sacks of dates and parcels of incense. The caravan stayed a safe distance from the dangerous coastline but also had to skirt the sand sea of the Arabian desert. Each year a specific route would have to be selected from out of a cloud of variable concerns. All things being equal, a line of march that led through Yathrib (Medina), Khaybar, Mada'in Salih, Tebook, Mudawwara and Fassua to Ma'an would represent a typical route. Ma'an, east of the mountains that shield the famous rock-guarded city of Petra, was an important stopping off point, for here the caravan often split. The Palestine and Egypt-bound traders would then strike directly north-west to Gaza, the ancient citadel of the Philistines, and in the sixth century one of the great ports of the Mediterranean. The other half of the caravan would strike north up through Syria, stopping at the important administrative centre of Bostra before continuing on to Damascus. From Damascus it was possible to join the Iraq-bound caravan, which passed through the ruins of Palmyra on its way to the River Euphrates.

The journey to Syria from Mecca was also a journey through the history of Arabia. As the Qur'an says, 'Ways of life have passed away before you. Travel in the land and see what was the end of those who listened not to God's messengers' (surah Al-Imran, no. 3, verse 137). The caravan trail led directly past half a dozen places of great mystery and power. These places set the rise of Islamic Arabia in perspective – part of a continuous cycle of history that has seen Arabian culture blossom time and again from the heart of the desert. The great monumental ruins from these cultures, especially those of Petra and Palmyra, are testaments to the enduring resilience of Arab culture and the

brilliance that they could achieve. Both cities were destroyed by
Roman armies and Muhammad saw the ruins of the past as evidence of the judgement of God on the failings of humankind.
He placed them alongside those of Sodom and Gomorrah and
the other myriad citadels symbolic of humankind's vanity said in
the Hebrew Bible to have been destroyed. Their destruction was
an example of the terrifying force of divine punishment. The
imminence of divine wrath never left Muhammad. It was said
that he could never look at a thundercloud without thinking of
the punishment the prophet Hud had unleashed on a great city
in southern Arabia. In his eyes the ruins of Arabia were not a
spur to a national revival; they were an edifying moral example.
They spoke very powerfully to those who could listen; as the
Qur'an has it, 'Are the people of the cities then secure from the
coming of Our wrath upon them as a night-raid while they
sleep?' (surah Al-Araf, no. 7, verse 97).

Mada'in Salih was a place well known to Muhammad from his
days as a trader; its rock tombs are still one of the most impressive
sites along the old caravan route to Syria. The most celebrated
tomb façade stands like some lonely gateway to the Temple of
Solomon. Its bold shadow-casting cornices, proto-capitals and
towering crow-stepped acroteria proclaim the architectural heritage of Tyre, Assyria and Egypt rather than Athens and Rome.
Indeed, it gets a recognisable mention in the Qur'an: 'and hewed
out houses among its mountains' (surah Al-Araf, no. 7, verse 74).
Although only the tombs now remain, it was once the twin sister
of Petra. Mada'in Salih was the southern capital of the Nabateans,
Petra their northern capital. According to the Qur'an it was
destroyed by an earthquake after its citizens had rejected the ethical teachings of the prophet Salih. When he returned there towards
the end of his life Muhammad forbade his men from camping
anywhere near the accursed ruins.

Petra, that 'rose-red city half as old as time' was rediscovered for the Western world by the Swiss historian Jean Louis Burckhardt in 1812. At that time it seemed fantastically remote, a sanctuary of antiquity hidden in the mountains. There would have been no such mystery for an Arab merchant such as Muhammad working the trade routes in the late sixth century. Petra stands astride a geological fault, which made for the easiest east–west crossing of these highlands to the Mediterranean port of Gaza, the favoured destination of the Arabian caravans. Muhammad would have known Petra when it was no more than a village with a church, haunted by its magnificent past. Stories of Petra's years of glory must have been told around the campfires. From the first century B.C.E. to the first century C.E., when King Aretas IV of the Nabateans would give his daughter in marriage to Herod, the neighbouring King of the Jews, it dominated the caravan trade. Though a loyal ally, its alliance with Rome would ultimately be the undoing of Nabatea. First Augustus stole their trade, then Trajan stole their liberty. On the death of the old King Rabbel II in 106 C.E., Trajan ordered units of the Roman army to march in and quietly occupy the strongholds of Nabatea. Ten years later a brand new road named after the Emperor Trajan – the Via Nova Traiana – had been completed, connecting Bostra, the new capital of 'Roman Arabia', with the port of Aqaba some four hundred kilometres away on the Red Sea.

The caravans that Muhammad accompanied would have skirted to the east of the Byzantine military installations between Bostra and Aqaba. On such a passage they would have smelt and seen the ghastly state-run work camps at places such as Wadi Feinan. These vast, state-owned copper mines, worked by convict labour on the edge of the desert, were the death camps of the classical and Byzantine world. For centuries these pits spewed out slag, metal oxide vapours and caused frontier desiccation as the scant water resources of the desert fringe were channelled into running these hells on earth.

☾

Muhammad would probably have been less interested in the Nabatean dynasty than in stories about the old biblical kingdoms such as Moab, Edom and Ammon, for the history of the people of the Arabian desert was intimately linked with the proud testimony of the prophets of the Hebrew Bible. An ancient tradition ascribed the origin of the kingdoms of Moab and Ammon to the daughters of the prophet Lot. The origin of the militant Edomites had a different source. They were descended from Esau, the favoured son of Isaac, who was tricked out of his inheritance by Jacob. Instead Esau was given the empty-handed paternal blessing 'And by the sword shalt thou live . . .' The family of Herod the Great came from Edom and the ruling dynasty he established over the Jews was known (rather scornfully by his subjects) as Idumaean. The Arabs of the desert (known as the people of Midian in the Bible) could trace an even more exalted ancestry. They believed that they were descended from Ishmael, the son of Abraham. Bible texts seem to confirm this belief; for instance, during Gideon's war there is a passing reference to the men of Midian wearing gold earrings 'because they were Ishmaelites'. For a travelling Arab merchant with the slightest religious awareness, the caravan route to Syria passed through any number of sacred landscapes. The holiness of these sites could be confirmed by listening to biblical tales told by the light of the campfires: how the kings of Midian travelled into battle with sacred crescents hanging from the necks of their camels; how Balaam, the revered prophet of the five kings of Midian, spoke with God and so refused to do what was asked of him; and how Moses had to climb up to a Moabite sanctuary, Mount Nebo, in order to be vouchsafed a view over the promised land. Indeed, the central spring at Petra was widely considered to the one that Moses had miraculously opened. It still bears the name Ain Musa, the spring of Moses.

Rabbath Ammon was another way station on the caravan road. It had been the great city of the Ammonites so frequently described in the Bible, though more often as a theatre of war than a home of spirituality. This city of many different names – Philadelphia of the Decapolis to the Greeks and the capital city Amman to modern Jordanians among them – was also the site of King David's administrative murder. The Bible tells us it was here that David placed Uriah the Hittite in the first rank of battle so that he would be killed, thus leaving David free to possess Uriah's wife, Bathsheba. It is known that this story appalled Muhammad, who could not believe that God's anointed could have committed such a crime. It was just such a story that led him to believe that the Hebrew Bible, though filled with the words of God, had also been corrupted.

Muhammad was also fascinated by the prophet Shu'ayb whose tomb could be visited in a valley to the west of Ammon. Shu'ayb is mentioned in three different chapters of the Qur'an. He is better known to readers of the Bible as 'Jethro, the priest of Midian'. Jethro is that engaging, peripheral character from the Book of Exodus who provides the young refugee Moses not only with hospitality and a job but also gives him one of his seven daughters. Jethro would later reappear in the life story of Moses to give the prophet practical advice on how to administer the twelve tribes of Israel. Muslim tradition has it that Jethro, having been rejected by his own people, eventually journeyed south and settled in Mecca.

Of all the sites, camps, cities and shrines strung out along the Syrian caravan route Bostra is the only place to have been positively associated with Muhammad. The tale goes back to his very earliest years, when he was a boy learning the ropes; it tells of Muhammad's lowly status when he was acting as an apprentice camel driver under his uncle Abu Talib's supervision. At Bostra there was a monk's cell that had been inhabited by generations of Christian hermits. The cell was filled with gospels, commentaries and the inspired predictions of these holy men. In the Arab traditions the last of the monk occupiers of this hermitage was Bahira, Syriac for 'Reverend'. Bahira believed that the time of 'the comforter' prophesied in the Gospel of St John was nigh.

One day Bahira was meditating on the landscape, observing the dust raised by an approaching caravan. As it came closer he saw that an illuminated cloud seemed to follow the caravan. He thought nothing of it. Dust, heat and refracted light conspire to throw up many such spectres in the desert. Only when the caravan had halted and pitched camp a little distance away from him did he notice that this cloud of light was now still. It hovered above a thorn tree whose branches seemed to bend down to the seated figure below it. Bahira became interested.

The hermitage had great stores of food that were continually being topped up by the gifts of pilgrims. Bahira sent word that a feast would be prepared for the men of the caravan – 'every one of you, young and old, bondman and freeman'. In due course the Quraysh merchants from Mecca arrived and, as Bahira stood to welcome them with the traditional exchange of greetings, he also carefully scrutinised the face of each guest. Nothing was revealed. Bahira hid his disappointment from his guests but could not resist inquiring, 'if they hadn't mistakenly left someone behind'. 'There is no one left at the camp,' they answered, 'save only a boy, the youngest of us all.' As they spoke they felt guilty that young Muhammad had been excluded, so one of the men went back, embraced the lonely young boy and brought him over to join the rest of his people. At a glance Bahira recognised the enormous spiritual qualities in Muhammad. While they ate he gently questioned the boy about his faith, his life, his family and his ambitions. With each answer Bahira became ever more certain that this orphan boy was the one who had been so long awaited. When he caught a glimpse of a strange welt on Muhammad's back, which he identified as the seal of prophecy that had been borne by all the old prophets, he felt he should keep silent no longer. Later that evening he took Abu Talib aside and advised him, 'Take your nephew back to his country and guard him carefully for, by God, if certain people see him and find about him what I know, they will do him evil. A great future lies before this nephew of yours.' Abu Talib heard these things and kept them in his heart.

There are different versions of this tale even in the original sources; local variations are legion. In one account the young Muhammad is nine, in another he is twelve. The episode is also repeated fifteen years later, when Muhammad is again recognised as a prophet but this time by another hermit monk of Bostra known as Nestor. When I first came across the story I imagined that Bostra was a small isolated oasis deep in the desert. This is pure fancy. By the time Muhammad visited Bostra it had been the capital of eastern Syria for five hundred years. It bustled with officialdom; it was the seat of the Byzantine governor and the commander of a legion and the Archbishop of Bostra lorded over some thirty-three junior bishops. At the time Muhammad would have known it Bostra was a great walled city whose skyline was dominated by the newly completed domed cathedral. This might have served as a working model for the great Muslim shrine of the Dome of the Rock that would one day dominate Jerusalem. Bostra was surrounded by the Hauran, a productive hinterland of agricultural villages. Roads led across this busy landscape to Antioch, Damascus, Palmyra and the Red Sea. It was appropriate that the caravan from Mecca should stop there; indeed it may well have been an administrative necessity. The tradition of scholar hermits also ties in with the Christian sects known to be active in this period, such as the Jacobites and Nestorians. Even now Bostra is impressive, though the local black basalt can cast a melancholy shadow over the place. The mosque of Mabrak is traditionally considered to be the site where the young Muhammad dismounted from his camel, while an old Roman basilica has long been considered to be Bahira's church.

If Bostra was the administrative capital of Byzantine Syria, Damascus was the commercial heart. It was the final destination for most of the northbound caravans from Mecca, the place where cargoes were broken up and sold at auction, or by private treaty. It was also the one city, even more so than Jerusalem, that seemed able to move seamlessly from one culture to another. This is tangibly apparent at the city's spiritual centre, graced as it is by one of the world's most hallowed shrines, the Great Mosque of Damascus. Before the eighth-century Umayyad mosque it was the site of the great Byzantine cathedral of St John, which stood over the sanctuary of Jupiter Damascenus, which was itself raised upon the holy place of Baal Hadad. If any Syrian city could boast of a link with Muhammad, one would surely imagine this to be the place.

Muhammad did drive his train of caravans up to the walls of Damascus; he did load and unload goods outside courtyard inns but he never once passed beneath the shadow of its Roman arch or paced in front of the thousand shops that line the central thoroughfare, the Via Recta, or Souk al-Tawil. Rather, it is said that he was content to observe the city from the summit of Mount Kassion, that he would not allow himself to be tempted by the place he could see below. He already knew that there was but one paradise for man and he was resolved to meet the heavenly rather than the earthly paradise. This is recalled in Alexander Kinglake's early nineteenth-century travel book, *Eothen*. 'This "Holy" Damascus, this earthly paradise of the Prophet, so fair to the eyes, that he dared not trust himself to tarry in her blissful shades, she is a city of hidden palaces, of copses, and gardens, and fountains and bubbling streams.'

Palmyra was another landmark in the Syrian desert not to be missed. From the first to the third centuries C.E. it had been the commercial center of Arabia. It had risen in the wake of Petra, just as Mecca would rise after Palmyra's fall. It had many similarities with Mecca. It had first come to prominence through its control of the caravan trade; it sat on the midway point of an important desert crossroads; it had learned to police the trade route and to send out its sons to dominate both ends of the trade; and, like Mecca, it also had to strike a careful political balance, for it stood between the rival empires of Rome and Parthia. By the time the Emperor Hadrian visited the city in 129 C.E. Palmyra was well and truly on a roll. The city feted the emperor so magnificently and so inventively for three weeks that when he departed he gave them a gift their hearts must have yearned for – tribute-free status with the right to collect their own taxes. For the next three generations Palmyra ruled as the absolute queen of the desert, decorated with an imperial grandeur, ringed by the monumental tombs of its plu-tocrats and bursting with a population that may well have exceeded two hundred thousand.

In the late third century a violent confrontation between Persia and the Roman Empire shattered the old certainties and threat-ened the trade routes. The Persians captured an entire Roman army and the reigning emperor. It was left to Odainat, an Arab general in the service of Rome, to restore the honour of the empire and secure the eastern frontier. After Odainat's death, his widow, Zenobia, used the confusion of the times to establish an Arabian empire. She declared herself the successor of the Ptolemies, the Augusta of the East, and sent her armies into Egypt, Anatolia and Syria. For a dazzling couple of years Zenobia did indeed rule the whole of the Near East from her native city of Palmyra. Her empire is a curious precursor to the eventual rise of the Arabian Muslim Empire. Her armies were, however, eventually defeated and her desert capital stormed. Zenobia was captured and taken in chains of gold to Rome, the prize ornament in a triumphal possession. A second rebellion by Palymra was crushed even more brutally by the Roman legions, and the city was turned from a proud, thriving metropolis into a desolate ruin.

Palmyra had always managed to combine trade with a spectacular devotion to the old gods of Arabia. A monumental way, a 1,200-metre-long procession of stone columns, led straight from the outer gates to the city's central shrine. The avenue passed beneath triumphal arches to reach a great arcaded temple courtyard that was dominated by a vast central shrine dedicated to a trinity of gods: to Bel, master of the heavens, who was flanked by Yahribol, the sun, and Aglibol, the moon, assisted by the seven planetary deities.

The young Muhammad, who loved his home town of Mecca, may have considered carefully the fate of Palmyra. So much power, so much wealth, so much beauty had been squandered and lost. Surely no faith could be placed in worldly possessions? As the Muslim historian al-Tabari would later write, 'They reigned, they prospered, yet their glory passed, now deep entombed they be this many a year.'

We cannot know how much Muhammad learned of the world on the caravan trails of old Arabia, but we do know that it was the making of him as a man. By the age of twenty-one he had won the epithet al-Ameen, 'the trusty', for his skilful and honourable management of the camel caravans. He was of average height with a good bearing and a head of thick, curly hair. He was trained like all his clan in the use of the sword, the bow and in wrestling. His manners were exemplary: when in conversation with someone he never looked over his shoulder, allowed himself to be distracted or let his attention wander. When he met people he gave them his complete attention, turning his whole body to address them and clasping their hands affectionately, so that it is said he was never the first to withdraw from a handshake. His most striking feature, much commented upon by all his contemporaries, was the glow that lit up his face.

4

Muhammad:
Man, Husband,
Father, Seeker

Muhammad grew into manhood among the markets of Mecca, on the long desert crossings with the caravans and amidst the tribal culture of pagan Arabia, which was dominated by the cult of the warrior. Only the military power of the tribe, the fierce loyalties that existed within the clan, the sharing of blood guilt and the duty of revenge provided individual security. For those who had fallen outside the protection of clan and tribe there was no safety or justice to be found anywhere in the land. Yet, for all the inherent brutality, the callous killings, the cycles of murder and revenge within Arabia, it was also a society that could be lit up by extraordinary instances of bravery and generosity. Indeed, it was Arabs of the desert who virtually created the concept of chivalry, celebrated in some of the great epic poetry of the desert.

The two celebrated incidents of Hatim and Rabia from the period of Muhammad's manhood allow us to appreciate the extraordinary extremes found within pre-Islamic Arabian society. Like all the young men of his generation, Muhammad must have delighted in these tales of great chivalry.

Like Muhammad, Hatim Tai was an orphan who was brought up in the household of his grandfather, a sheikh of the Tai tribe. Unlike Muhammad, however, when Hatim came of age he inherited his father's great herds of camels and goats. Hatim was so prodigal with his entertainment, slaughtering animals for his guests and making gifts, that his vast inheritance was soon dissipated. On one occasion he slaughtered three camels just to feed three men who had ridden past his camp. They happened to be poets, and they immortalised the young man's generosity in verse. Hatim complained to them, 'My idea was to do a kindness to you but your poem has put me in your debt.' However, to his grandfather, who had complained bitterly about Hatim's prodigious hospitality, he was able to boast, 'If I had kept my camels, they would have all been dead in twenty years. But in exchange for them, I have won a poem in praise of our family, which will pass on from mouth to mouth until the end of time.'

Another of the great figures from sixth-century Arabia was Duraid ibn al Simma, equally famed as a poet and desert raider. On one such raid he was leading a war party into the mountains south of Mecca, the grazing land of the Beni Kinanah tribe. Coming over the brow of a hill Duraid and his men spied Rabia, a lone warrior leading a camel upon which a woman was mounted. Duraid called out to the warrior that if he left the woman and camel to them they would not harm him. The warrior did not for a moment consider such a dishonourable offer. Indeed, though greatly outnumbered, he turned his horse back three times to fight off his pursuers, each time returning to his duty as an escort. On the third encounter, although his lance was by now shattered, Rabia once again returned to the lady's side and, without altering their stately pace, sung out this verse:

> Ride on in peace, my lady fair,
> Secure and safe and calm.
> Be confident and debonair

And free from all alarm.
I cannot flee before a foe
Except he taste my arm,
The boldness of my charge he'll know
Who seeks to do thee harm.

Duraid was so impressed by this gallantry that he himself rode
after them and cried out, 'O horseman, such a man as you does
not deserve death. But my men hunger for revenge and are just
behind me, and you are now unarmed. Take my lance, my friend,
and I will see that my men do not pursue you.' In another skirmish Duraid himself was taken as a prisoner into the Beni
Kinanah camp but was rescued by Rabia's widow who threw her
cloak over him – a potent symbol – and declared, 'O warriors! This
man is under my protection – for he is the one who gave his lance
to Rabia, when he was unarmed in enemy country.'

Even at the end of his life Muhammad liked to remember the
time when, his young heart well charged with a questing nobility,
he had joined a band of like-minded men of Mecca who had
formed themselves into a chivalric association. This brotherhood
had been created in response to a particular injustice in which a
powerful Quraysh merchant had taken possession of the goods of
a Yemeni merchant but had then refused to pay for them. As a
notable within his own city of Mecca the Quraysh merchant felt
invulnerable whereas the Yemeni merchant was powerless. This
injustice disturbed many, although they were reluctant to take
action lest the whole case deteriorate into another round of clan
rivalry. Instead a number of them founded the non-clan-based
brotherhood 'the lovers of justice', which was sealed with a collective oath. They poured water over the black stone of the Kaaba,
collected it in a bowl and swore loyalty as they drank from the
loving cup. They ensured the man from Yemen was paid his due.

Its immediate effect on the politics of Mecca was short-lived but the seed it planted – of a brotherhood that could reach beyond clan loyalties to unite humankind – would come into fruition as Islam.

☾

These years when Muhammad was in his twenties were not all devoted to justice. He was also in love. He had long adored Fakhita, his beautiful cousin with whom he had grown up. She was the daughter of his guardian uncle Abu Talib, and they knew each other as only young cousins can. She had three brothers: Talib, who was the same age as Muhammad, Aqil, who was just a little older than her, and Ja'far, the four-year-old darling of the family. Both Muhammad and Fakhita delighted in joining in Ja'far's games and, as they played, Muhammad fell ever further under the spell of his young cousin.

The relationship was, however, to go no further. By the time Muhammad had steeled himself to ask his uncle for Fakhita's hand in marriage she had already been betrothed to Hubayrah, a well-connected young man of the Beni Makhzum clan. It was a wounding blow. In the process he was also reminded that, as a poor orphan, his marriage prospects did not look promising. If he wanted a good wife he would first have to acquire a substantial herd of camels with which to pay the bride price. He devoted himself anew to the caravan trade. The profits he was to wring from this would bring him a wife, but not in the way that he might have imagined.

Muhammad's reputation as a trustworthy young merchant preceded him. In 595, just as the Syria-bound caravan was preparing for the trip north, he was entrusted with some goods by a distant cousin, the widow Khadijah, who asked him to sell them on her behalf. Such a request was not unusual. Mecca was full of

Muhammad's cousins and this handsome, well-organised twenty-five-year-old who knew the ropes was an obvious choice for Khadijah. They agreed on a fee, the price he should try to get for her goods in Syria and the merchandise she wanted him to acquire for her. To help him cope with this additional responsibility she sent her manservant Maysara to accompany him on the journey.

Khadijah had interests in Muhammad other than trade. She had begun to take an interest in him personally. Khadijah sent Maysara to join the caravan so that he could find out if Muhammad was as trustworthy, good and true as she had heard. For, other than sharing a bed, there is no better way to learn about someone's character than to accompany them on a long journey. When Muhammad returned with a scrupulous balance of the accounts, Khadijah was even more intrigued to hear Maysara's story of the journey. He gave his mistress a glowing report of Muhammad but also hinted that there was something other-worldly about him. Muhammad had once again been recognised by a Christian hermit as a holy man, while Maysara was himself convinced that he had seen Muhammad being shaded from the sun by a pair of angels. Such stories might have put off many other women, but Khadijah was enthralled and hurriedly consulted her cousin Waraqa, who was also her wisest and most experienced friend.

Her mind made up, Khadijah needed an intermediary, for such things could not be done face to face. No one wanted to embarrass another person with a public refusal to an offer of marriage. Khadijah did not know if Muhammad had yet recovered from the heartbreak of losing Fakhita or if he would be prepared to accept a wife fifteen years older than himself. She therefore called upon the services of Nufaysah, the matchmaker, to ask Muhammad if he was interested in the idea of marriage. Such a question from such a person was not to be idly dismissed. Muhammad was open to the idea though he felt it was out of the question until he had acquired the necessary dowry. Nufaysah replied, what if you were given the means? And what if there was a woman who combined beauty with property, a noble bloodline with an abundant coffer? 'Who is she?' asked Muhammad. 'Khadijah!' she replied. 'For my part I am willing,' declared Muhammad.

It was an astonishing turn of events. Khadijah was a beautiful, intelligent, wealthy woman who, through the death of two previous husbands, now commanded a considerable fortune. In a clandestine meeting that she arranged at her house she explained herself to Muhammad. 'I love you for many reasons: you are well centred, not being a partisan amongst the people for this or for that; you are trustworthy and have a beauty of character and I love the truth of your speech.' The engagement was then entrusted to the hands of their closest male relatives. Muhammad's token offer of twenty camels for Khadijah was formally accepted. Muhammad celebrated his marriage by giving Barakah (the slave girl whom he had inherited from his father) her freedom. For her part Khadijah gave her new husband as a wedding gift a fifteen-year-old slave boy called Zayd.

It was a love match from the outset. Muhammad made no use of Khadijah's wealth (other than to give alms to the poor) and maintained his same simple existence and his life as a merchant. His wife was also his closest confidante and friend, and shared his spiritual yearnings. In times of trouble or anxiety Muhammad turned first to Khadijah for support. Muhammad was a passionate man but, unlike many of his contemporaries, he also found that he loved the company and society of women. It was he who first coined the expression, if you would know a man's character first look to the health of his wife. He never took another wife while Khadijah was alive, and during their marriage she bore him six children.

Their two boys – Qasim and Abdallah – both died young, but the four daughters – Zaynab, Ruqayyah, Umm Kulthum and Fatimah – survived into adulthood. Apart from the burial of the boys, the tragic separations that had punctuated his own childhood were not repeated and he delighted in the company and the games of his children. Nor did his foster mother Halimah lack for an honourable welcome or a departing gift whenever she passed through Mecca. On one such visit, during a time of drought and famine, Khadijah revealed her own innate generosity. Halimah was given a new camel and a herd of forty sheep.

The cheerful humanity of Muhammad and Khadijah's household also manifested itself in the treatment of their young slave boy. Zayd grew to love his master so much that when his own family eventually traced his whereabouts and offered to buy him back Zayd asked to be allowed to remain with Muhammad. Faced with such loyalty Muhammad refused the sum of money, gave Zayd his freedom and adopted him. Later, to ease the congestion and the growing poverty within his uncle Abu Talib's household, Muhammad invited his young cousin Ali into their house. The arrival of the young boy must also have helped to fill the gaping wound left by the death of their last child, Abdallah, when he was only a few months old. Ali became the son that fate had taken from Muhammad and Khadijah, and a brother to their four daughters.

These were not arbitrary acts of generosity but part of a determined pursuit of a responsible moral life that stood side by side with the prayers that Muhammad addressed to the High God of Mecca. He fasted, he questioned the wise and gave freely to the poor with his time and from the abundance in his kitchen. His standing within the community of Mecca was now sufficiently high for him to be called in to arbitrate in a squabble that threatened to break the unity of the Quraysh. The Quraysh had agreed to rebuild the old Kaaba shrine but fell out among themselves about who should have the honour of replacing the sacred god-stone to its honoured position. A white meteorite that had been stained black by centuries of blood offerings, it was believed to be a gift from heaven. Muhammad's solution – that the holy stone should be placed on a blanket and jointly lifted into place by all the sheikhs of the clans – was instantly accepted.

As Muhammad grew in wealth and wisdom he joined a select group of religious thinkers in Mecca known as the *hanif*, the seekers. The *hanif* searched for a coherent religious identity for the Arabs, a clear doctrine to replace the welter of deities and the shambles of blood sacrifices held around the temple at Mecca. They focused their attention on the all-encompassing father god Allah whom they freely equated with the Jewish Yahweh and the Christian God the Father. They revered the tradition that Mecca had originally been dedicated to this one God. They looked for references to the true religion of ancient Arabia, the religion established by the Patriarch Abraham. There was much to be sought out. Arabia nurtured a fascinating cross-section of foreign merchants, artisans and refugees, escaping not only from the endless destructive fighting between Persia and Rome, but also from vicious doctrinal purges within the empires. There were Jews, persecuted Manicheans, Persian Zoroastrians, Nestorian Christians, Jacobite Christians from Syria and Coptic Abyssinians. Aside from these mainstream beliefs there were also a score of lesser practices condemned by the ever more orthodox emperors in Constantinople. For the Arabs of the desert interested in religion there was a rich profusion of beliefs and practices on offer, some of which came with the backing of a wealthy foreign power.

Among the *hanif* in sixth-century Mecca we know of four remarkable individuals. 'Ubayd Allah ibn Jahsh was a cousin of Muhammad. He was a great seeker after the truth who would be one of the early converts to Islam, though during his period as a refugee in Abyssinia he ended up embracing the doctrines of the Coptic Church. Waraqa ibn Nawfal was another celebrated *hanif,* a cousin of Khadijah who had made a special study of Christianity. He may even have translated some passages of the Gospels into Arabic. 'Uthman al-Huwayrith followed the same Christian centric path as Waraqa, though his studies ultimately took him away from Mecca to Constantinople. At one point in his life he offered to become the official ambassador of Mecca to the Byzantine Empire. He guaranteed better trading relations with the Byzantine territories but his peers in Mecca feared that he was conspiring to set himself up as a king. Later he would formally embrace Christianity.

Perhaps most remarkable of all was Zayd ibn 'Amr, whose impious questioning of the traditional pagan beliefs scandalised the entire city of Mecca. Zayd refused to attend the blood sacrifices to the pagan gods, or to touch the dole of meat from these sacrifices and publicly denounced the practice of burying unwanted female babies. His strait-laced half-brother, Khattab, felt so ashamed of Zayd's behaviour that he took it upon himself to rid the city of this pest. He hired a band of toughs to deny Zayd access to the sanctuary and later their persecution drove him from the city. Zayd crossed the great desert and travelled through the cities of the Middle East, visiting a number of the great spiritual masters of the day, be they Jewish rabbis, Christian hermits, hidden heretics, quiet scholars or lordly bishops. Towards the end of his life, hearing that a new prophet had appeared at Mecca, Zayd hurried back across the desert only to be taken and lynched by brigands a few days short of his destination. Zayd had been born before his time. He is the very model of a Dervish, those wandering sufi mystics who would later crisscross the Muslim world in their search for a direct encounter with the divine.

Muhammad was close to many of the principal *hanif*. Waraqa in particular seems to have been an intimate and trusted friend. We know that he shared their interests, principles and desires. We know that he had travelled on the caravan trails through many of the landscapes they had also investigated. We cannot know, nor is it right to guess, or even to suggest, whether or not Muhammad explored the religions and beliefs of the Middle East in the same methodical way as 'Ubayd Allah, Waraqa, 'Uthman and Zayd had set out to do. It seems probable that he did not share their physical search but that he might have learned much in discussions and shared spiritual exercises. Muhammad was certainly a passionate propagandist of learning throughout his life. Of this his sayings leave no doubt:

'Go in quest of knowledge even unto China.'
'An hour's contemplation is better than a year's adoration.'
'Who so honoureth the learned, honoureth me.'
'Seek knowledge from the cradle to the grave.'
'One learned man is harder on the devil than a thousand ignorant worshippers.'
'The ink of the scholar is more holy than the blood of the martyr.'
'He who leaveth home in search of knowledge walketh in the path of God.'

Some Western scholars treat the whole subject of the *hanif* with intense suspicion. To their minds it seems too neat a prologue to Muhammad: that four men set out on four quests that ultimately lead them individually to the north, to the south, to the east and to the west, seems suspiciously like a mythological construct of sacred geometry. However there are *hanif*-like characters active in every generation.

Far from being a literary construct the stories about the *hanif* seem refreshingly familiar and contemporary. Even their facial expressions can be imagined – drawn from a tangled blend of modesty and vaunting spiritual ambition, just as their outwardly anarchic lives mask hidden traits of loyalty and tenacious dedication. Their desire for revelation combines with a natural suspicion of public knowledge and a fascination for the hidden, the rare and the occluded.

☾

No one can hope to understand the birth of Islam, nor fully appreciate the achievements of Muhammad, without understanding the religious beliefs of pre-Islamic Arabia. This is a difficult task for it was a culture dominated by public listening rather than by private study. The inhabitants of Mecca would have been familiar with a whole body of traditional tales and inherited beliefs that are now completely lost, not to mention the gospels, letters, prayers, commentaries and sermons from this age that have also perished. Our knowledge of the period is necessarily based on the chance survival of written documents and inscribed stones, most of which belong to the wider world of the Middle East rather than specifically to sixth-century, central Arabia.

Of all the religions within pre-Islamic Arabia it is clear that Muhammad must have been most intimately aware of Jewish belief and practices. There were Jewish communities spread throughout the oases of central Arabia, at Yathrib (Medina), Fadak, Khaybar, and Tebook. Most fundamentally of all Muhammad shared their passionate belief in the supremacy of the One God, the God who had spoken to Abraham and Moses. Muhammad revered all the heroes of Jewish history, all the Jewish prophets as well as King David and King Solomon with the same passion as any Jew. Jerusalem was for most of his life the spiritual lodestone of earth, the touchstone to heaven. Only a few years before Muhammad's death would Mecca nudge Jerusalem into second place. The habits that he would later teach to his followers – such as paying a charitable tithe, fasting for a month, honouring the day of atonement, existing within a living community (rather than a monastery) and remaining within the comforts of family life – can all be linked to existing Jewish habits. However, there were limits to the influence of Judaism on Muhammad. He was illiterate and thus could not read the existing languages of the Arabs such as Syriac, let alone Hebrew. Although Muhammad had no access to the written histories of the Jews, he must have been aware of their beliefs. The Qur'an is full of stories that complement, correct or add details to the traditional accounts of the Torah.

Late antiquity had been an exceptionally dynamic period for Judaism. Instead of obliterating Judaism the Roman destruction of Jerusalem and the Jewish national identity had served to liberate the Jewish faith. Instead of a religion dominated by a central temple, by sacrifices and by a landed aristocracy of high priests, Judaism had been reborn in local families and communities across the diaspora. Synagogues emerged as the new focal centres of Jewish life, of liturgy and education, directed by the rabbis. These were the lineal successors of the Pharisees, observant Jews who had pored lovingly over the Torah, who had collected the oral traditions and then led interpretative sessions in the synagogue. They cherished a new ambition, aspiring to raise all of Judaism to the old exalted standards demanded of the priests. They aspired to sanctify everyday life with ritual, to turn a whole nation into a priesthood. The rabbis remained a scholarly class, trained up by such academies as Beth Midrash. They were equal to any intellectual challenge posed by the Christians, but stopped safely short of becoming a priesthood. The Jews were also protected from the odd behaviour of the celibate Christian monks, for they insisted that their revered scholars live within the community of the faithful. The Jewish rabbis led a people without fear of the future. Muhammad's career may be reminiscent of that of Akiba ben Joseph, an illiterate shepherd boy who had become a self-taught authority on religious law. It was Akiba who had started the great commentary on the Torah, which would mature into the Mishnah. Further summaries were added so that, by the time of Muhammad, the Jews were in possession of a whole new code book for life, the Babylonian Talmud. This voluminous tome bound the Jews in exile together as a people more effectively than loyalty to any temple or King. The Jews were working on perfecting their religion by adapting the stories about the old prophets to current conditions. In a sense that is exactly what Muhammad would do, though instead of following in the Jewish tradition of literary scholarship he would cut to a direct revelation from God.

Although the Jewish Mishnah and Talmud would be treated by many early Muslims as holy books, not every Jewish document from this period was given so much respect. It is clear above all else that Muhammad would have no truck with the thinking behind the Toledoth Yeshu. This popular and well-distributed document, compiled around 170 C.E., was a Jewish counter-offensive to the attacks of the Christians. It claimed that Jesus was no more than a sorcerer and that, far from a divine being, he was actually the bastard son of a Roman auxiliary soldier named Panthera.

Throughout his life Muhammad always treated the Christians and their beliefs with great affection. The Qur'an goes out of its way to honour both Jesus and his mother, Mary. Indeed, Mary gets much more of a mention in the Qur'an than in any of the four canonical Gospels. Only the non-canonical gospel of James, with its detailed account of the childhood of the Virgin, can match the Qur'an in its detailed description of Mary.

Muhammad's revelations would also be quite emphatic about the status of Jesus. His birth from a virgin mother was miraculous and had been at the bidding of God working through his messenger, the Archangel Gabriel. Jesus was a prophet, a miracle worker and a great teacher, however he was not the son of God, nor did he die on the cross. At a single stroke Muhammad removed the essential belief behind all mainstream Christianity: that Jesus had died and on the third day risen again from the dead. Without his death there could be no redeeming sacrifice, no washing away of sins, no need for the mystery of the mass.

Seen in this light the scholarly debate about the possible influence of this Christian Church or that Christian Church on Muhammad seems irrelevant. The furious debates about the nature of Christ that divided the Orthodox Church from the Nestorian Church, and the Nestorian Church from the Monophysite Church, could have absolutely no relevance for Islam. In the eyes of Muhammad and his followers they are all equally misguided. Nor would Muhammad have been impressed by the curious schisms of Christianity that took refuge in the desert. The Ebionites angrily rejected all Gospels other than that of Matthew, while another group replaced the symbolism of the life-giving cross with that of a phallus. Marcion of Sinop was a passionate follower of Paul the Apostle. He quoted from a gospel that had much in common with Luke but seems to have rejected the entire Hebrew Bible.

However, with every passing year the growing body of archaeological evidence makes it clearer and clearer that the Christian presence in the pre-Islamic Arabia of Muhammad's time was substantial. There was an entire chain of Christian monasteries down the Persian-dominated eastern coast of Arabia. This was the missionary territory of the Nestorian Church, which was based in Persian Iraq and backed by the Lakhmid kings. The Nestorian

Church was a vigorously missionary church and believed in using the language of the people. It was the first to use Pahlavi (the language of Persia) as well as the universally understood Aramaic of the Middle East. During the life of Muhammad the Nestorians also began sending missionaries to India and into Central Asia. Muhammad may have listened to a Nestorian preacher sometime during his manhood, perhaps somewhere on the eastern leg of the caravan route or at one of the great annual fairs. The Nestorians did not, of course, see themselves as a schismatic breakaway group but as the one true Holy Apostolic Church. It is only outsiders who have labelled them as the Assyrian, or Syriac, Church. A century after Muhammad's death they had even become established in Mandarin-speaking China. By the twelfth century they were the largest Church in the world.

Mecca, the Red Sea coast and central and southern Arabia were in the missionary sphere of the Monophysite Christians. This large group includes the Coptic Church of Egypt, Abyssinia and Armenia, and the Jacobite Church of Syria. Their dispute with Greek Orthodoxy and the Nestorian Church was over the exact composition of God and man in the nature of Jesus Christ. The arid subject of Christology is best understood in terms of wine, water and olive oil. The Nestorians are "olive oil and water" Christians. They believe in two natures that cannot mix. The Monophysites are "wine and water" Christians. They also believe in two natures but argue that the mix is impenetrable to theological analysis.

The Ghassanid kings were great supporters of the Monophysite Jacobite Church. They had established a whole chain of monasteries and hermitages the length of the Red Sea coast and were well established in the Yemen. Najran, Dhufar, Aden, San'a, Socotra and Marib are all confirmed Christian sites within pre-Islamic Arabia. The story about the Christian hermits of Bostra – Bahira and Nestor – recognising Muhammad as a prophet almost certainly involved the Jacobite Church in Arabia. They also had a useful patron in the Abyssinian Negus who supported their activities. It is almost certain that Muhammad would have listened to Jacobite preachers on a number of occasions. Indeed, there is some evidence that Jacobite missionaries were in attendance at the great annual fair of Ukaz held outside Mecca. They would have spoken in whatever tongue they needed to address their audience. Some scholars have even suggested parallels between the language used by these Christian missionaries to describe the torments of hell and descriptions in the Qur'an. Across time and space, prophets and visionaries have used the existing imagination of humankind to describe spiritual realities that are literally unworldly. Pieter Brueghel's visions of hell in the sixteenth century were fuelled by the massacres and torments he had witnessed. Surely the massacre of the Christians in the Yemen by the Jewish king Dhu Nuwas who despatched them in a furnace influenced the conception of hell in this period. There is also an enduring tradition, cited by Isfahani, that the young Muhammad had been very impressed by the passionate oratory of Quss ibn Sa'ida, Bishop of Najran. Indeed, he was known to have memorised part of a sermon that began,

> Oh people, assemble,
> listen and pay heed.
> All who live die
> and all who die are lost
> and everything that is coming will come.

What of the Christians of Abyssinia? Could they have influenced Muhammad in any way? Clearly not in matters of theology but in other ways they might have been an inspiration to him. Like the pagan Arabs the Abyssinians were a people apart from the old centres of power and culture in the Middle East, locked into the mountains of Africa, yet they had succeeded in developing a heritage that linked them with the prophetic tradition of the Hebrew Bible. The traditions of Abyssinia turned the biblical meeting of King Solomon and the Queen of Sheba into a tale of national and spiritual identity. The Queen of Sheba returned to her own land with a son by Solomon, Menelik (in Arabic ibn al-Malik, 'son of the king'), who as a young man would visit his father in Jerusalem and then return to Abyssinia and teach the worship of the one God to his people. Indeed, the Qur'an describes details missing from both the Bible and the Abyssinian accounts to enrich further the story of Solomon and Sheba (referred to in the Qur'an as Bilqis). At such times there seems to be an almost innate empathy between Islam and Christian Abyssinia. Many traditions were shared, such as styles of dress, male circumcision, the taboo of eating pork, the habit of remov-ing shoes before entering a place of worship and complete prostration at prayer.

The conversion of Abyssinia to Christianity in the fourth cen-tury is an astonishing tale of adventure that reveals the amazing cross-cultural connections that could cut across political bound-aries. It is also fascinating to see how the connection between trade and philosophy (invisible in terms of archaeology) can inspire and transform a world.

A Christian merchant-philosopher from the university city of Tyre took two students (Aedesius and Frumentius) with him by ship to India to visit the great schools and markets of the East. On the way back they stopped off on the Red Sea coast of Abyssinia for water, unaware that some tit-for-tat war had been declared against the Roman Empire over a broken treaty. Their ship was confiscated and the entire crew slaughtered except for the two young students who were presented as slaves to the King of Abyssinia. The students became trusted servants of the king and after his death served his widow (acting as regent for her infant son) with even greater authority. Assisted by those foreign merchants who passed through the land, they set up the first churches around the capital city of Aksum. When the prince came of age, Aedesius and Frumentius took their leave, the former returning to Tyre, the latter travelling on to Alexandria. Once there Frumentius delivered his report to the Patriarch Athanasius on the embryonic state of Christianity in Aksum. The Patriarch pressed Frumentius to return, for 'what other man can we find than you, who has already carried out such works?' Frumentius accepted and was consecrated bishop. This tale was written down by a contemporary of his, the historian Rufinus, who declared 'These facts I know ... from the mouth of Aedesius himself who had been Frumentius's companion and was later made a priest in Tyre.'

Excavations into the trading centres of the Red Sea are still in their infancy but already a picture is emerging of an extraordinary fusion of cultures. At the current American excavation at the Egyptian Red Sea port of Berenike evidence has been discovered of twelve written languages (including Sanskrit and Tamil as well as Coptic, Aramaic, Abyssinian and Greek) and two completely unknown scripts. Whether assessed in terms of the textiles, teak, peppercorns, beads or coins found at the site, it is clear that the important long-distance trade with India drew many cultures together. There is, however, no indication of trade with Western Europe – not so much as a shard. By the middle of the sixth century Berenike had silted up but it seems fairly clear that this cosmopolitan trade would have moved to the great Abyssinian port of Adulis during the lifetime of Muhammad. Even among the many deities of Hindu India there is a monotheistic unity in the supreme God Brahman who can never be depicted, yet is all-pervasive.

One of the greatest losses from this period of religious history is the teaching and writings of Mani, the founder of the Manichean faith. Mani (217–277 C.E.) clearly had a strong appeal to his contemporaries. He was a universalist, who honoured the old prophets of every creed and nation but who created a new spirituality from elements of Christianity, Mithraism and Zoroastrianism. At the root of Manicheism was the ancient dualistic Persian philosophy that the universe was divided between two antagonistic powers, darkness and light. The god of darkness was the ultimate ruler of the material, earthly world. The god of light ruled a higher spiritual dimension. It was the duty of the worshipper to help to develop the powers of light by prayer, ethical conduct and a freedom from material possessions and desire. To this end Mani elevated music and painting as a form of prayer. He taught that all creation contained an element of the divine spark imprisoned within a frame of flesh, in much the same way that the Qur'an would affirm that God fashioned humankind from earthly matter: 'Allah is the light of the heavens and the earth . . . light upon light! Allah guides whom He will to his light' (surah Nur, no. 24, verse 35). However, the unworldliness of Mani's doctrine, its innate opposition to all forms of earthly authority and its toleration of sexual activity that did not lead to conception, brought with it an unending catalogue of persecution. Mani was protected as an enlightened sage by the old Persian emperor Shapur I but was ultimately executed by Shapur's son, Bahram I, in 277. Some of his doctrines re-emerged in a quasi-socialist religious movement led by the Persian high priest, Mazdak. This was violently suppressed during the reign of Chosroes I (531–579), which must have witnessed another generation of refugees fleeing into Arabia. The *hanif* of Mecca must have listened to these creeds just as attentively as had St Augustine who first began his spiritual path as a Manichean 'hearer'.

To whom or to what religious teaching Muhammad might have listened as a young man we can never know. It is still an important belief within Islam to acclaim Muhammad as the unlettered prophet, untainted by reading and writing. It is also a popular concept within Islam to view the forty-year-old Muhammad as a blank sheet of paper waiting to receive the imprint of God's revelations. It used to be thought that Arabia at the time was a backward, isolated, pagan world cut off from the main avenues of religious thought. It was also taught that the old monotheistic religions of the central Middle East were tired and discredited after centuries of persecution, war and tithe collecting. These are no longer valid concepts. Indeed, it becomes ever clearer that the sixth century was in many ways an exceptionally dynamic one. It was a time of great confidence and renewal for Judaism, a time of great missionary activity in the Jacobite, Abyssinian and Nestorian Churches while the Arabian coast was also washed by the influence of Persia and India.

5

Muhammad's
First Revelations

Muhammad was to be born twice in Mecca. Forty years after he first entered the world as a human being he pierced another dimension and entered sacred space. It was as terrifying and unexpected an experience as the first.

His sacred second birth took place in a cave on the slopes of Mount Hira, one of the many hills overlooking Mecca. It was the seventeenth night of the month of Ramadan in 610. Muhammad was then a middle-aged merchant, a happily married forty-year-old and proud father, with a good reputation in the city of his birth, built up over thirty years' experience of the caravan trade. During the pilgrimage season it was his habit to take a break from the claustrophobic atmosphere of Mecca and decamp with his family to a cave on the mountain side. Only a few of his closest friends knew that beneath the exterior of this calm, trustworthy man of business there was a passionate searcher after enlightenment. He prayed, he fasted, he gave food to the poor and followed the path of righteousness. All his life he had searched after God. What he was not prepared for now was that God had searched through him and had now come to take possession.

He awoke suddenly on that first night in the cave in abject terror, his whole body, his whole inner self, caught in a vice-like grip that seemed to hold him within a massive pressure field. Later he would try to explain the sensation: it was as if an angel had gripped him in a terrifying embrace that threatened to squeeze the life and breath out of him. As he lay there, shattered, he heard the commandment, 'Recite!'. This he could not do: he was no trained poet, no soothsayer, no bard with a thousand well-turned lines ready on his lips. Indeed, as he protested, he was completely illiterate. The angel closed in upon him, possessing him again with such force that he felt he would burst. 'Recite!' he again commanded.

'Recite! in the name of the Lord thy God; who created man from a drop of blood. Recite! Thy Lord is most bountiful, who by means of the pen, taught man what he knew not' (surah Ignaa, no. 96, verses 1–5). There was no room for refusal. The first revelation burst from the lips of Muhammad, like breath being exhaled.

Thus were the beginnings of the Qur'an, which translates literally as 'the recitation'. It is the word of God through the mouth of Muhammad. If you believe this you are a Muslim; if you do not you cannot be one. At first Muhammad did not believe. He felt as if he had been possessed by a spirit, by one of the innumerable jinn. He had seen enough of the confused madness of spirit possession to be appalled at the idea: the lonely woman cajoled out of her black moods of depression by drums; the shaman poets rolling in the dust, spitting out their verses in a shower of blood and phlegm; or the exorcising healer, a figure of necessity but also one to be feared, who inhabited the outer edges of society. Was this where his piety had led him? Was this where meditation took a man? Was this the reward for all his fasting and prayer? Still shaking, still fearful but resolved, he left the cave and the still-sleeping members of his family. He climbed swiftly but steadily towards the peak of Mount Hira. He had self-murder in his heart. Halfway up he was halted by an angelic voice, and the vast, all-embracing form of the Archangel Gabriel filled his vision, no matter which way he turned, dominating every horizon, every perspective, vast, continuous and inescapable. 'I raised my head to look at the sky, and lo! I beheld Gabriel in the shape of a man with extended wings, standing in the firmament, with his feet touching the ground . . . Then I turned my face away from him to other parts of the sky, but in whatever direction I looked I saw him in the same form.'

Muhammad staggered back to the cave and crawled to the comfort of his wife, whom he implored, 'Cover me, cover me'. Khadijah embraced him, covered his exhausted body with her cloak, settled him and listened to his story. After he had told it, she stole quickly down into the city to talk to her spiritual guide, her well-respected cousin Waraqa ibn Nawfal. Assured by Waraqa's advice, she returned to the cave and was the first to acclaim Muhammad as a prophet of God.

It was a second birth into the world of the spirit. All that he had assembled in the first half of his life – property, a good name, a family life and a respected position within Meccan society – would now have to be sacrificed. When Muhammad had recovered sufficiently he walked back into Mecca and made the ritual circuit of the Kaaba. There he was confronted by Waraqa, who warned him of what lay ahead: 'You will be accused of lying, you will be persecuted, shunned, exiled and attacked.' The old sage then bowed before the Prophet and kissed his brow.

The Muslim world commemorates the holy night on which the Qur'an was first revealed as the festival of Kadir. No one can be absolutely certain of the date. The seventeenth and twenty-seventh nights of Ramadan are the most popular choices and are celebrated as festivals throughout the Muslim world. It is an important night to get right for it is believed that prayer on the night of Kadir is better than that of a thousand months. Holy men have learned to be evasive about enquiries concerning the correct date for prayer, and tend to answer 'treat each night of Ramadan as Kadir; only then can you be certain'.

☾

The first blinding revelation in 610 was followed by two years of complete silence. The divine spirit that had possessed Muhammad so suddenly left him just as immediately; it was as if he had been possessed by a tormented sea, only to be abandoned, beached on the shore. It was a tense period for Muhammad who was thrown into what might today be labelled depression – it was a time in which he felt forsaken and abhorred. Then, like the agonisingly delayed note of a great choral recital, came a second revelation, aptly named 'daylight'.

> By the light of day, and by the fall of night, your
> Lord has not forsaken you, nor does He abhor
> you.
> The life to come holds a richer prize for you than
> this present life. You shall be gratified with what
> your Lord will give you.
> Did He not find you an orphan and give you shelter?
> Did He not find you in error and guide you?
> Did He not find you poor and enrich you?
> Therefore do not wrong the orphan, nor chide away
> the beggar. But proclaim the goodness of your
> Lord.
>
> (Surah Ad-Dhuha, no. 93, verses 1–11)

The recitation had begun again. The experience would never be quite as terrifying as it had been on that first night, even though further recitations were just as unpredictable. Muhammad explained, 'Never once did I receive a revelation without thinking my soul had been torn away from me'. The process was so debilitating that afterwards he often had to be covered with a blanket and left to shiver and shake under its protective darkness. On other occasions eyewitnesses talked of a great heaviness appearing to fall upon him and a look of grief that seemed to transfigure his face, before his head slumped between his knees. A similar position would be adopted by some Jewish mystics when they prepared themselves for a meditation on the throne of God. It was the selfsame attitude later taken by Christian monks as they repeated the Jesus prayer. In Muhammad's case it seems not so much a spiritual technique as physical exhaustion.

Nor did the revelations follow exactly the same pattern. Sometimes they were as clear and articulate as if an angel was dictating a text behind a veil. More often than not they were perceived as images or emotions that Muhammad had somehow to articulate into a language. The Prophet described them as, 'sometimes coming unto me like the reverberations of a bell, and that is the hardest upon me, the reverberations abate when I am aware of their message'. Nor could he hurry the process: as he recalled in another self-reproving description 'move not thy tongue with it to hasten it; Ours it is to gather it, and to recite it. So when we recite, follow then its recitation'. This must have been enormously challenging, for sometimes the message was intensely visual. Aisha, one of his wives, recalled the 'first sign of prophethood vouchsafed to the prophet were true visions, resembling the brightness of daybreak'. Very occasionally a Qur'anic verse replaced or amended an earlier one. One can only guess that the same divine vision had been repeated but this time Muhammad had better 'gathered it'.

Even to contemplate this process is exhausting. No wonder the Prophet declared that the only miracle he had ever performed was the reciting of the Qur'an.

Muhammad's energies were taken up in reciting the revelations, in preaching, in leading a pious life. He never directed that his Qur'anic recitations should be collected in a standard edition or be preserved in any particular order. They were, however, committed to memory by his followers. The early believers would meet for all-night vigils during which the verses would be collectively chanted.

There is an interesting parallel here to the way Buddha and Jesus presented their divine teachings. Like Muhammad, they called for the creation of spiritual and just societies, setting an example by living simple and God-centered lives. They saw themselves as prophets, not as the founders of what would so soon become institutionalized religions.

The Qur'an remained in an oral state during the lifetime of the Prophet. It was always meant to be recited and it was only finally edited from written and oral sources some years after the death of the Prophet. To read the Qur'an in Arabic, rather than to recite it from memory, is to lose nine-tenths of its power. To read a translation is to remove oneself even further from the power of its words. The sound of its verses should be allowed to envelop the body, to course down into the very heart and soul of the individual. They are not just a plaything for the mind. This verbal strength of the Qur'an has always been carefully preserved and today there are colleges in the great theological universities of Islam where the seven approved types of recitation are taught. Here the young scholars sway as they recite the verses, their Qur'ans open before them, although they may already know them by heart. The sound of their voices drifts around the enclosed courtyards, echoed by the dancing lines of script carved by long-dead craftsmen into the cedar beams of the roof, into the pale plaster walls and into the ceramic tiles. No one knows for certain the origin of these seven variant readings. Some trace it back to the seven early reciters of the Qur'an: Nafi, Ibn Kathir, Abu 'Amir, Ibn 'Amir, 'Asun, Hanza and Kisa'i. Others claim it represents the dialects of the seven Arab tribes around Mecca: the Quraysh, Hudhayl, Thaqif, Hawazin, Kinanah, Tamim and Yaman. Some argue that they are merely a by-product of the furious theological disputes of ninth-century Baghdad.

The Qur'an was always Muhammad's ultimate, unanswerable weapon. Again and again, Arabs who were intensely hostile to his doctrines were seduced by its sound. Some of the pagan Quraysh, however, concluded 'this is nothing but tales of the ancients', as the Qur'an itself attests. Other hostile listeners complained that it was not a continuous narrative, like the epic odes or even the gospels, but that each verse returned to the same themes. This is indeed one of the great features and glories of the Qur'an. For each verse can stand on its own, as a separate call to the divine. Each surah takes the believer on a journey, towards the divine source of life and the purpose of existence. Many warn of the punishments that have befallen humankind in the past for ignoring the words of the prophets of old and those that await all humankind on the Day of Judgement. But there is always, amidst the many stern warnings, a ray of hope. God is also Ar-Rahman – 'the Kind' – and Ar-Rahim – 'the Merciful' – who at the end of days offers forgiveness even to Satan. He is also intimately present, in those haunting words of the Qur'an, 'We created man . . . and are closer to him than his jugular vein' (surah Qaf, no. 50, verse 16).

☾

Muhammad remained a shy man. For three years after the revelations had resumed he restricted the recitation of the new verses to a domestic circle composed largely of his immediate family, converts from disgruntled young members of Meccan society and its weakest, most needy members. Muhammad's aunts were ardent supporters, although his uncles remained firmly aloof. His first important non-family convert was his friend and fellow merchant Attiq ibn 'Uthman, known better to history as Abu Bakr. They would contemplate the great gift of God – the miracle of everyday life – and try to reflect this in their daily conduct. The small group of devotees would meet for organised prayer in the morning and in the evening. Their distinctive prayer ritual had three stages – standing, kneeling, and bowing down to God, greeting him as a friend, a servant and a slave – and was an important element of this new faith from its very first days.

In 615 Muhammad's reticence was interrupted by a Qur'anic command that he should go out and preach publicly. Undoubtedly a time of great anxiety for him, it would get rapidly worse. Muhammad's first inclination was to speak to his own Beni Hashim clan. He invited the forty leading men of his clan to dine with him, but instead of making an occasion of it – slaughtering a camel or at least a fat sheep or two – he shared with them a leg of lamb and a bowl of milk. Though admirably modest, if not ascetic, his was not the way to win the support of an audience in tribal Arabia then, any more than it is now. The evening ended before it had really begun when one of the most important guests stormed out as soon as Muhammad started to speak. The gathering of forty clan elders was repeated the very next evening. This time his guests stayed long enough to hear Muhammad's message. His exposition was followed by an unbroken silence. Not a single clansman offered him a word of support. The silence was finally broken by Ali, Muhammad's thirteen-year-old adopted son, who had helped to serve the food. That this gawky adolescent should be Muhammad's only follower among the Beni Hashim was considered a great joke.

The distinguished company collapsed in merriment and made their way into the night.

☾

For Arabs of a traditional mindset there were many problems with the Prophet's message. They could accept his warning that they should give more thanks to Allah, the High God of Mecca. They could also acknowledge that they had responsibilities to others, especially members of their own clan. Indeed, blood loyalty was one of the cornerstones of Arab nobility. What they could not accept was the Qur'anic declaration of a continued form of existence after death. They felt that to believe in life after death was inherently beneath their dignity. It was something with which to console widows, grieving mothers, the poor and downtrodden slaves. But for an Arab, a proud clansman of the Quraysh? A thousand times no. It went against the grain of the old Arab ideal of nobility, of a stoic acceptance of one's fate combined with a proud self-sufficiency. This concept, defined by the word *staqa*, lay at the heart of Arabic pagan culture. The Day of Judgement, when all the world's dead are gathered and judged, features very strongly in the Qur'an. It is no less explicit about the excruciating tortures of the wicked and the heavenly reward of the godly. Because the traditional men of the Quraysh could not accept this, they saw the idea of judgement after death, with its offer of a divine reward or punishment, as a delusion. Live piously by all means, they agreed. Respect the gods while you are alive, for you need their help to survive and prosper in life. They considered death to be the end of all existence. Only the gods lived for ever. To the pagan Arabs the art of life was to relish this present existence, with all its pride, desire, love and glory. The only form of immortality was the kind offered by poets, whose verses in praise of great heroes would continue to be recited over the generations. That was the only form of afterlife pagan Arabs aspired to. They scoffed at the very notion that those dry old bones, lying half-exposed in the sand and gravel burial grounds around Mecca, could ever be brought back to life.

The word for the pagan opposition within Mecca is often translated into English as the 'unbelievers', a term which would never have been used by the Prophet, who fully understood that they believed; he just wanted them to believe much more. A more accurate translation of the original Arab word would be 'one who is ungrateful to God'.

There were other matters standing between Muhammad's fledgling Muslim community and the pagan Arabs. The Prophet had explained that on the Day of Judgement none of the traditional virtues – wealth, fame, lineage, position in society, friendship with the poets, the beauty of the women in a household or the number of descendants – would be of any consequence. What mattered was an individual's behaviour; feeding the poor, caring for orphans, sheltering widows and protecting the weak. This overturned all the fundamental values upon which Mecca's society was based.

Nor could the proud Quraysh come to terms with the idea of prayer. They were used to making circuits of the Kaaba, to offering blood sacrifices of animals while they appealed to the gods for help; they were accustomed to pouring libations of wine and milk at domestic altars, to using the sanctuaries as a witness to a solemn oath. These, however, were all contractual deals, of the 'I-do-this-so-that-the-gods-might-do-that' nature. The Prophet offered a much closer relationship with the divine, as revealed by the very word 'Islam' which means to 'surrender yourself [unto God]'. The final attitude of prayer, with the individual kneeling and his head touching the ground in prostration, expresses this in perfect physical form. The pagan Quraysh, however, saw this as a further degradation of their stoicism. Indeed, Abu Talib, the Prophet's revered uncle, is remembered as having expressed his distaste at any attitude of prayer that raised his backside above the level of his face.

In 616, Muhammad's mission became even more difficult. From 612 to 614, the new faith had been something of a private, family affair. Muhammad had been instructed to start public preaching in 615 – as he had done to disastrous effect while entertaining the elders of his clan – but now he was told to condemn the worship of idols. The effect was immediate. From being a curiosity that was merely tolerated, Islam was now directly challenging the old order. The first clashes occurred between rival groups of Muslim believers and pagans. Blood was spilled. Many who had been quietly interested in Muhammad's preaching now fell away, refusing to turn their backs so completely on the religion of their ancestors. The fertility cult of the Near East went back far beyond the reaches of history. It was part of the nature of life, reflected in the seasons, the calendar of lunar months and dozens of sacred sanctuaries. The Quraysh were also deeply concerned lest they be considered impious by the Bedouin tribes, who might unite and turn against them. Among the clan leadership there was a growing consensus that Muhammad was no longer simply a nuisance but a danger.

It was a terrible period for the Prophet. Any support and sympathy he had painstakingly built up over the past four years in his beloved Mecca evaporated almost overnight. He yearned to unite Mecca around his divine warnings. The last thing he wanted was to be the leader of a schism within the Quraysh.

It was around this critical period that the incident known to the Western world as the Satanic Verses may have occurred. Of the four early biographers of the Prophet, only two mention it. Pious Muslim scholars seldom make reference to it, but, after Salman Rushdie's 1988 novel *The Satanic Verses*, it is impossible to ignore.

According to one of the biographers, al-Tabari, the Prophet

was meditating in the environs of the Kaaba when he first uttered surah 53, the verses known as 'the Star'. In this surah there is mention of the great heavenly Sidrah tree that stands at the summit of the seventh heaven, a boundary marker beyond which even the angels do not proceed. It is sometimes referred to as the Lote tree of the extremity. Muslims saw this heavenly Sidrah tree as being thronged with an angelic host. Surah 53 makes an oblique reference to this: 'when that tree was covered with what covered it'. The Qur'an then moved from this image of the sacred Lote tree, full of a myriad chattering angels, to the three goddesses of pagan Arabia: 'Have you thought on Al-Lat and Al-Uzzah, and thirdly on Manat?' This linking of imagery is important for it was in this way that the Qur'an chose to explain the gulf that separated the spiritual world of angels, spirits and jinn from the all-encompassing power of the one God. Imagining the goddesses as three birds among the host of angels perched on the sacred Lote tree was a brilliant way of leading a pagan people gently towards the right conception of divinity. Islam has never disputed the existence of the spirit world. The Qur'an is full of references to the invisible jinn, 'created from a subtle fire', to spirits and angels.

Muhammad then followed this Qur'anic vision with: 'these are the exalted birds whose intercession is approved'.

As a gesture of compromise it worked; the pagan Arabs were delighted with this reference to the intercession of the goddesses. In political terms it could be conceived of as an outstanding strategy. However, in terms of prophecy it was a failure and Muhammad knew it. He had slipped up in his preordained task of bringing the message of God to man. He had 'moved his tongue to hasten' the recitation and in the process had not produced the correct 'reading of the revelation' in verses 19 and 20. A few days later the revelation would be repeated, verse for verse, until the familiar lines: 'Have you thought on Al-Lat and Al-Uzzah, and thirdly, on

Manat? Is He to have daughters and you sons? This is indeed an unfair distinction! They are but names which you and your fathers have invented: God has vested no authority in them. The unbelievers follow vain conjectures and the whims of their own souls'.

The amendment is testimony to Muhammad's remarkable personal honesty. It is an incident that ranks with the temptations of Jesus by the devil in the wilderness. Muhammad could not live with two false phrases in a sixty-two-verse revelation, even in circumstances when he knew that to do so would bring ease to his life, and heal the discord within Mecca.

The issues raised from the utterance of the Satanic Verses are immensely important. Conservative theologians considered the Qur'an to be a document that had existed throughout all eternity, graven like the tablets of Moses by the hand of God. They saw Muhammad as little more than God's scribe and even considered the classical Arabic of the Qur'an to be created by God and the eternal language of heaven. This belief is attractive to those who aspire to make an immutable law code out of their religion. It is not so useful for those wishing to understand the individual's relationship to the divine. It is more enlightening to see the illiterate Prophet grappling in an attempt to place the sacred revelations within a human language, with all its limitations. It was a task into which he poured all his energy and abilities. Muhammad testified, 'Never once did I receive a revelation without thinking my soul had been torn away from me.' He constantly strove towards ultimate perfection in this task of recitation. Perhaps he knew he had succeeded when the recitations no longer sounded within him as clear as a bell, but he could hear them as if they were dictated by an angel standing 'at a distance of two bows – or even closer'. To take this one surah as an example, some authorities believe that verses 26–33 were added at an even later date, and that verses 34–42 were perfected at a fourth stage, probably at Medina. This can be seen as Muhammad's ever-increasing assuredness in giving the complex divine revelations their truest possible expression in human language.

Muhammad's final recitation of surah 53 finished the controversy. A delegation of Quraysh sheikhs approached Abu Talib requesting him to remove the protection of his clan from his troublesome nephew. Their words have survived: 'your nephew has cursed our gods, insulted our religion, mocked our way of life . . . you must let us get at him . . . and we will rid you of him'. As a devout pagan Abu Talib probably sympathised with their complaints, but he would not consider breaking his blood loyalty to his kinsman.

By the time the delegation next approached Abu Talib they had dropped their appeal and now began to threaten the entire clan of the Beni Hashim, promising all kinds of woes if they did not bring Muhammad under control. Abu Talib tried to arrange a compromise with his nephew. It was an impossible task. Muhammad confessed that he was prepared to die rather than forsake his God and his mission. Even 'if they put the sun in my right hand and the moon in my left on condition that I abandon this course . . . I would not abandon it'. In the face of such utter conviction, Abu Talib assured his nephew, 'go and say what you like, for by God I will never give you up on any account'. It was a brave statement. Abu Talib did not agree with Muhammad but he was prepared to defend his right to speak. He also knew that his entire clan would suffer as a result.

Some of the finest men of the Quraysh of Mecca now stood ranged against the Prophet: honest men like Suhayl ibn 'Amr, the sheikh of the 'Amir clan, whose devotion to the old pantheon of Arabia had led him on spiritual retreats every bit as sincere as the Prophet's; and Abu Sufyan, the sheikh of the 'Abd Shams clan, another fine leader amongst the Quraysh who had in earlier days numbered himself as one of the friends of Muhammad. They were supported by the best of the young noble lords of Mecca, men of the calibre of Khalid ibn al-Walid and 'Amr ibn al-'As.

Two less admirable characters, even more violent in their opposition, were Muhammad's own uncle, Abu Lahab, and a sheikh of the powerful Makhzum clan of the Quraysh, who was nicknamed by the Muslims 'Abu Jahl' – the 'Father of Ignorance'. Abu Jahl was born ambitious and saw that Muhammad's prophethood would grow into leadership unless he was checked. He was also, like many of the pagan Quraysh, sincerely devoted to the old gods and troubled by the new religion that split families apart over matters of belief, pitting brother against brother and son against father. Abu Jahl directed the campaign against the Muslims. Powerless converts and slaves would be picked out and beaten up by gangs. Those Muslims of Mecca who were safe within the protection of one of the clans would be scorned, accused of betraying their heritage, their ancestors and their reputation. The most powerful tool of these men was the trade boycott. There was hardly an individual in Mecca who was not a merchant and a trader at heart. To be cut out of the spring and winter caravans, to be barred from the markets, to be excluded from the deals, business partnerships and trade banter was punishment indeed.

Muhammad was protected from harm by his own direct experience of the divine. He was, despite the violence of party feeling, revered for his strength of character even by his enemies. He was also protected by his uncles, who, although they might remain pagan, would not tolerate the physical abuse of such a close kinsman. In any case nothing that humankind could throw at Muhammad could dampen his religious zeal. However, even he could at times be driven to fury by the petty savageness of the attacks. One neighbour in particular, who had shouted insulting couplets at Muhammad's back, while his wife had once scattered thorns on the path frequently used by the Prophet, won the only known personal denunciation in the Qur'an: 'he shall roast at a flaming fire and his wife, the carrier of the fire-wood, upon her neck a rope of palm-fibre'.

Muhammad, who could do nothing to alleviate the suffering of his small, embattled community of believers, was appalled at the privations that they were forced to endure.

At last, he advised some of his followers to leave Mecca and take refuge elsewhere. Nowhere in Arabia – not in the Yemen, not on the Syrian frontier – was thought to be safe from the Quraysh. Muhammad was familiar enough with the powers that existed beyond Arabia to select the most likely secure place of refuge and the one he chose for them was Abyssinia. In the words of a much repeated tradition he said to them, 'If you were to go to Abyssinia, it would be better for you until such time as God shall relieve you from your distress, for the king there will not tolerate injustice and it is a friendly country.' It is a proud testimony to Abyssinian hospitality, and Muhammad was not alone in his high opinion of that country. In the *Iliad* Homer speaks of the 'blameless Ethiopians' while Diodurus has it that even the gods were 'awed by their piety'. The Book of Psalms, not normally very forward in its praise of nations other than Judea, has it in Psalm 68, verse 31, that 'Ethiopia shall soon stretch out her hands unto God'. Muhammad may also have had a practical motive in sending his followers to Abyssinia. The Quraysh embargo was impoverishing the Muslims and the Prophet and his followers may have hoped to recover the losses imposed upon them by playing a greater role in the trade to Abyssinia.

☾

The first group of Muslims, twelve men and five women (including the Prophet's daughter Ruqayyah and her husband 'Uthman), rode west out of Mecca to the port on the coast. From there they took passage on a boat heading south down the Red Sea, through

the coral reefs and the rock-littered shores of the Dahlak archipel-
ago to reach Adulis, the principal port of the Abyssinian Empire.
Adulis was an entrepôt that had been trading with Egypt for two
thousand years. It lay astride the main trade route to India and at
the crossing between Africa and the Yemen. A babble of tongues
was spoken there by traders acquiring such essential goods as ivory,
gold, incense and tortoiseshell. In exchange, bolts of worked cloth
and wrought metals were imported while deals were easy to cal-
culate as the coinage of Aksumite Abyssinia neatly dovetailed with
the Byzantine weights in gold, silver and bronze.

The refugees next travelled inland, up from the familiar hot, dry
coast into the comparatively well-watered mountain plateaux of
Abyssinia. Their eight-day journey took them past great conical
mountains capped with monastery churches and dotted with hermits' caves to the capital city of Aksum. This first group sent back
such favourable reports that the following year another group of
refugees left Mecca to join them, led by a cousin of the Prophet.
This Muslim community thus grew until it numbered some
eighty-three families.

Rather than celebrate the departure of these refugees, however,
the Quraysh of Mecca were furious and despatched a delegation to
the Negus, the ruler of Aksum and the Emperor of Abyssinia.
Arab historians recall the ruler as being Ashama ibn Abjar, perhaps
Armah of the Aksum king list, who also gloried in the title of the
Emperor Ella Sahem. The Quraysh delegation intended to slander
the new faith in the eyes of the Christian king, and so expedite the
expulsion of the refugees. They therefore petitioned for an audience with the Negus.

Aksum was vast but it had little in common with modern-day
assumptions of what a city looks like. It was a stone encampment,
comprising dozens of scattered palaces, each associated with a
royal necropolis marked by towering granite obelisks. In between

these great complexes, fixed like so many stars in the sky, were meadows which were filled with thousands of tents and huts when the tribes were drawn to Aksum at the time of the great markets and annual festivals.

Before one of these vast stone palaces the delegation of the Quraysh presented their tribute to the Negus. It was recalled that they brought gifts of leather for they gave 'the most excellent of what they produced'. An eyewitness account of a Byzantine ambassador from this period depicts the Negus approaching a foreign delegation on a wheeled platform, bound around with golden leaves, and drawn by four elephants. 'He wore a gold and linen headdress, with fluttering golden streamers. His collar, armlets, and many bracelets and rings were of gold. The king's kilt was of gold on linen; his chest was covered with straps embroidered with pearls. He held a gilded shield and lances, while around him musicians played flutes and his nobles formed an armed guard.'

In addressing the Negus, the Quraysh accused the Muslims of wrecking the unity of their city, of blaspheming against the ancestral gods and, most tellingly, of denying the divinity of Christ. The Negus, surrounded by his court of monk-bishops and clerics, was clearly appalled that he was harbouring such heretics in his land and commanded the Muslims to explain themselves. Ja'far (a cousin of the Prophet and son of Abu Talib) stepped forward and answered, 'We were folk immersed in ignorance, worshipping idols, eating carrion, given to lewdness, severing the ties of kinship, bad neighbours, the strong among us preying on the weak; thus were we till God sent to us a messenger of our own, whose lineage, honesty, trustworthiness and chastity we knew. He called us to God that we should acknowledge his Unity and worship him and turn away from the stones and idols that we and our fathers used to worship beside Him . . . And when persecuted and oppressed, we came forth to thy land, and chose thee above all others, and sought thy protection, and hoped we should not be troubled in thy land, O King!'

The Negus considered this and then asked for an example of Muhammad's message. Ja'far chose well when he chanted surah Maryam, no. 19, verses 17–26, about Mary, the mother of Jesus:

> Then we sent unto her Our spirit in the semblance of a perfect man. And when she saw him she said: Lo! I seek refuge in the Merciful One from you, if you are God-fearing. He said: I am only a messenger of thy Lord, and have come to give you a faultless son. She said: How can I have a son when I am a virgin, untouched by man? He said, So it will be. Thy Lord saith: it is easy for Me. And it will be that We may make him a revelation for humankind and a mercy from Us, and it is a thing ordained. And she conceived him, and she withdrew with him to a far place. And the pangs of childbirth drove her unto the trunk of the palm-tree. She said: Oh, would that I had died ere this and had become of naught, forgotten! But a voice from below cried out to her. Grieve not! Thy Lord has placed a stream that runs at your feet, and if you shake the trunk of the palm-tree it will drop ripe dates into your lap. So eat and drink and be consoled. And if you should meet any mortal, say: Lo! I have vowed a fast to the Merciful, and may not speak this day to any mortal.

It is said that when Ja'far had finished the Negus and his entire court were in tears. They were the first Christian court to hear how the Qur'an so greatly honours the Virgin. The Negus turned to the delegation of the Quraysh: 'If you were to offer me a mountain of gold, I would not give up these people who have taken refuge with me.' But the Quraysh were not entirely unsuccessful. It is thought they persuaded the merchants of Abyssinia that the Muslims did not represent Mecca, and were a powerless and persecuted minority. The Abyssinia trade remained safely in the hands of the Quraysh.

Back in Mecca, between 616 and 618, the boycott of the Muslims organised by Abu Jahl was tightened up. Neither they, nor the clan of Beni Hashim, nor the descendants of 'Abd al-Muttalib, who continued to protect the Prophet Muhammad, could intermarry, trade or even buy food from the markets of Mecca. All the other clans swore to uphold this ban. It is said that Abu Bakr's trading capital deteriorated from 40,000 dirhams to just 5,000. The ban did not, however, make the Muslims submit. Rather, they built a ghetto for themselves in the streets around Abu Talib's house. The pattern of friendships and intermarriage between the clans ensured that, while the Muslims went hungry, they were not starved into submission. Their fortitude slowly began to impress the other clans.

☾

In the meantime, the beauty of the Qur'an was slowly working itself into the hearts and minds of even the most powerful and determined opponents of the Muslims. Verse upon beautiful verse was revealed, clarifying the doctrines of Islam. Some of them reiterated even more plainly the spiritual reality that had to be embraced. There was no escaping the threat of hellfire or the reality of Satan in the Qur'an, but this was balanced by a constant repetition that God is 'mighty and forgiving', that God is 'forgiving and bountiful in his rewards'. Other verses seemed to answer the questions of doubters, while yet others tried to open up the imagination of the Arabs to the vast, all-encompassing power and mercy of God: the God who did not just reign over Mecca but had made the world; the God who held together the universal laws, who had charged that we were all to be created from a single drop of man's seed. The single animating force of God could not be challenged by anything that our minds could even consider testing him with. As the Qur'an says, 'Who will give life to rotten bones? Say "He who created them at first will give them life again: He has knowledge of every creature . . . Has He who created the heavens and earth no power to create their like? That He surely has. He is the all-knowing Creator." When He decrees a thing He need only say: "Be" and it is. Glory be to Him who has control of all things. To Him you shall return' (surah Ya-Sin, no. 36, verses 78–83). (This command to 'Be' has ever since been a source of poetic inspiration. The Mevlevi Dervishes begin their rituals with a single note of a flute. This is the 'Be', that gentle breath of divine command that begins all their symphonies and dances.)

The hidden power of the Qur'an was to claim an unexpected convert. 'Umar ibn al-Khattab, the nephew of Abu Jahl, came from impeccable pagan stock. It was his father who had expelled his own half-brother, Zayd (one of the four *hanif*), from Mecca many years earlier because of his apparent lack of respect for the old gods. 'Umar was a prince among the Quraysh, a man who liked his wine as much as his hunting and was educated enough to read with ease. He was infuriated to find that even his own sister and cousin (the son of Zayd) had secretly gone over to the Muslims. In a fury he knocked his sister to the ground one day and snatched the parchment she was reading from her hands. He read, 'It was not to distress you that we revealed the Qur'an, but to admonish the God-fearing. It is a revelation from Him who has created the earth and the lofty heavens, the Merciful who sits enthroned upon high.' It is the beginning of surah Ta-Ha, no. 20, verses 2–5; on reading it, 'Umar found that it had stormed his heart.

☾

By 619 the two-year boycott of the Muslims and the Beni Hashim clan had fizzled out. For a month or two things looked quite promising, as Mecca settled back into her familiar ways. Then fate struck a series of punishing blows against the Prophet.

First Khadijah died. For twenty-four years she had been Muhammad's beloved wife, friend, companion and counsellor. She had shared with him the joy of their four daughters, as well as those mournful trips to the cemetery when they had buried their two infant sons. She had been the first to recognise him as a Prophet of God; it was she he had turned to when confronted by the first revelation. Muhammad was able to comfort his four daughters and the adopted boys, Ali and Zayd, that Khadijah had been assured a place in paradise. While she was alive Muhammad never took a second wife. As an older woman Khadijah may also have filled some of the empty corners of Muhammad's orphaned heart. She was in many ways his equal. From the stories lovingly recounted about his life by his companions, subsequent wives and friends there was clearly a gaping hole in his heart left by Khadijah's death.

After she died, over the course of several years, the Prophet took ten wives; none of them bore him any children. Part of this continuous quest for women may have been an attempt to ease his aching heart after the death of Khadijah. Certainly the favourite among his later wives, Aisha, confessed at the end of her days that she 'was not jealous of any other wife of the Prophet as I was jealous of Khadijah, for his constant mentioning of her . . . many a time said I unto him: It is as if there had never been any other woman in the world, save only Khadijah.'

Shortly after Khadijah had been buried, Muhammad's revered old uncle Abu Talib fell ill. It was clear that he too was dying. The Arabs have always honoured the opinion of the dying, freed as it is from the passions and ambitions of mortal life. The old clan leaders of the Quraysh put aside their differences and came to Abu Talib's bedside, both to honour this courageous old sheikh and to ask him, once more, if he could arrange a compromise deal between them and Muhammad. They asked that 'he [Muhammad] should let us be, and we will let him be'. Muhammad was all for peace but provided only that the Quraysh would declare, 'there is no god but God, and I renounce all worship apart from Him'. The meeting failed and broke up.

When the clan sheikhs had gone, Abu Talib whispered to his nephew, 'Son of my brother, you did not, as I saw it, ask of them anything out of the way.' Muhammad's heart soared at the thought that his protector might be on the point of accepting Islam. 'Uncle,' the Prophet whispered, 'say those words' (by which Muhammad meant the *chahada*, the Muslim confession of faith, that 'There is no god but God and Muhammad is the Prophet of God'), for he knew that only then would he be able to intercede for him with heaven. The proud old man could not, for he did not want anybody to think that he had converted merely from the fear of death. He would die as he had lived, fearless of any man or god.

When death finally stole upon Abu Talib he was heard to whisper a few words. A cousin, thinking to please the Prophet, claimed that it was the *chahada*. With a slow shake of his head, Muhammad uttered a strangled 'I heard it not'. He could not agree to this pious invention, however well intentioned.

The death of Abu Talib closed another door. Muhammad and the Muslims were no longer under the protection of a clan leader. Leadership of the Beni Hashim passed to Abu Lahab, one of Muhammad's most violent opponents. The effects were immediate. Dirt was publicly thrown in the Prophet's face, rotten offal was hurled into his private courtyard and once, while he was praying, someone threw a shit-smeared sheep's uterus over him.

In his desperation Muhammad thought of leaving Mecca himself.

He rode out to the walled town of Taif, surrounded by its orchards, palm groves and ripening fields of barley. It was an odd choice, for Taif, as an agricultural settlement, was even more deeply wedded to the ancient fertility cults. The shrine of the goddess al-Lat stood at the centre of life there, just as the Kaaba did in Mecca. The temple and its surrounding sanctuary were guarded by the Thaqif, the dominant tribe of Taif. It was a long shot to try to seek help from such a quarter but this is exactly what Muhammad did. He rode his camel up to the house occupied by the three brothers who served the goddess as her temple guardians and there followed a frank and full exchange of views. One brother shouted, 'Let me never speak to you', another 'Could God find no one else but you?', while the third declared that 'If God really sent you, I will tear down the hangings in the Kaaba'. Muhammad left, but on his way out of Taif he was chased down the street by a jeering crowd. Here was a fall from grace indeed, and to escape the mob he took refuge in one of the walled gardens on the edge of the oasis. He tethered his camel to a palm tree and hid beneath the shade of a vine. It was a moment of deep humiliation. Typically, his first thought was of prayer: 'O God unto you do I complain of my weakness, of my helplessness and my lowliness before men. O most merciful of the merciful, you are Lord of the weak. And you are my Lord. Into whose hands will you entrust me? Unto some far off stranger who will ill treat me?'

Later he started the two-day journey back to Mecca and stopped overnight in the valley of Nakhlah. As night fell Muhammad performed his prayers and then chanted a chapter of the Qur'an. Before long he realised he was not alone. Around him had clustered a group of spirits, seven jinn from Nasibin, who were listening attentively. He had won no converts that day among his fellow men, found no tribal lord as his protector, but that night he heard the jinn confess that they had heard a 'wondrous recitation which guideth unto rightness, and we believe in it'.

The next day was critical. News of his visit to Taif would soon reach Mecca, and with no clan to protect him his days would surely be numbered. His first thought was to appeal to his long-dead mother's clan, the Zuhrah: 'Will you give me my protection, that I might deliver the message of my Lord?' While he waited outside the city boundary, a passing horseman gallantly offered to take a message and return with an answer. The answers he received were not encouraging. The chief of the Zuhrah would not commit his clan to the dangerous nature of Muhammad's request. A second request to the chief of the 'Amir clan was also declined. Rather than enter the city without protection, Muhammad decided to spend the night on the slopes of Mount Hira. The following morning a third petition, addressed to Mut'im, the head of the Nawfal clan, was accepted at once. The chivalric chieftain of the Nawfal rode out with his immediate kin and escorted the Prophet back into the city in safety. They wore full battle armour, which was not a mere gesture. Even his gallant protectors felt that the time of knives was not far away.

It was during this time of his life that the Prophet went out to dine in the house of one of his first cousins, Umm Hani, daughter of Abu Talib, one evening. After dinner they performed the night prayer together and the widowed Prophet accepted the invitation to stay the night. He could not sleep that evening, so he wandered into the sacred sanctuary around the Kaaba, and settled down under a roofed shelter that stood in the north-west corner.

During the night, Muhammad was kicked awake three times by the Archangel Gabriel who took him by the arm and led him out through the sanctuary gate to where Buraq, a Pegasus-like winged beast, awaited him. The milk-white Buraq is a favourite subject of Muslim artists, who often depict this fabulous winged creature with the head of a woman. Buraq took the Prophet on his back above the caravan trails of his youth and manhood, over that familiar trail studded with oases and ruined cities, to the ruined terraces of the old temple at Jerusalem, where a great company of prophets greeted Muhammad before joining him in prayer. Here he was offered three goblets – of wine, milk and water. Symbolically he chose the milk, the measured middle way between the paths of asceticism and indulgence. From Jerusalem, Muhammad was taken beyond our conceptions of space and time, up through the seven circles of heaven. The milk-white Buraq was transformed into a chariot of fire to take him to the mystical Lote tree rooted in the throne of heaven, which marks the end of knowledge. Here the Prophet was granted a sublime vision of the creator.

Sympathetic modernising commentators feel more comfortable in referring to what is known as the 'night journey' as a mystical experience. They interpret it as a metaphysical journey, one not so much of the body as of the soul. It was Muhammad's longed-for reward of recognition in a heartless world. It was an embrace by the great company of the prophets to compensate for the rejection of his own time. Deprived of his wife Khadijah, the love of his life, and the last protective figure within the adult world, Abu Talib, he now had to stand alone. This was his reward. Those who have read the mystical visions of great saints or the soul journeys of shaman-healers leaving their bodies will recognise many similarities with Muhammad's night journey; indeed, he freely acknowledged that he followed a path of prophecy that had been trodden many times before. However, before translating this experience into a modern idiom one must also accept that the Prophet treated it as a physical, corporeal reality. It had been a number of years since he had been seized by the first recitation. He knew the full power of divine revelation, its different moods and intensities. This was clearly an experience that he deemed completely 'other'. Nothing like this had ever touched him before or would touch him ever again, not even at the hour of his death.

Muhammad's cousin Umm Hani, a devout believer, begged him not to repeat the ecstatic experience he had so excitedly related to her the next morning. She knew instinctively that such precious mystical pearls should not be thrown before jeering swine. Muhammad would have none of it: 'By God I will tell them.' He did, however, listen long enough to his cousin to refrain from telling the hostile public of his journey through the heavens.

Both Umm Hani's and Muhammad's instincts were correct. Without the challenge of the mystical night journey, Islam would have become a very different religion in later centuries. The night journey would inspire generations of mystics to seek a similar experience of the divinity. It was a precious door that the lawyers, legalists and commentators – who would later interpret Islam for the masses – could never close. It kept the faith open to the mystics, the Sufis, who followed in the steps of Muhammad, men such as al-Ghazzali, Ibn Arabi, Sidi Belhassan and Rumi Mevlana, who for generations would explode the stuffy legalism that threatened to constrict Islam and recharge the creed with light, love and a divine scent that came not from this world.

That said, the Prophet's enemies were exultant as they listened open-mouthed to the tales of Buraq and Jerusalem that morning. Now at last, they thought, his followers would see him as a deluded man. Indeed, when Abu Bakr first heard the tale, he accused the town gossips of lying to him, although he accepted it without reservation once he had heard that it had been told by the Prophet. His daughter Aisha always considered that it had been a journey of the mind rather than the body. Ishaq quotes her as saying, 'The Prophet's body stayed where it was, but God transported his spirit by night.' Even the Qur'an remains enigmatic,

'We made the vision that We showed you only as a test for the people' (surah Beni Israel, no. 17, verse 60).

The hostility of Mecca to Muhammad was now fixed. Even before the death of Khadijah and Abu Talib, he had made it his practice to preach to the crowds of pilgrims who came to Mecca each year. It was always an ordeal, as the Bedouin invariably heckled him and reviled his message. Now it became even more important for the Prophet to seek out a new protector, or a new home, if his message was to survive. In the summer of 620 he had an unexpected success amongst a group of six pilgrims from the oasis of Yathrib. Instead of deriding him as the other camps of the Bedouin had, they listened to him with grave respect and lapped up the words of the Qur'an. They returned to Yathrib to spread the word and promised to meet the Prophet at the following year's pilgrimage. In 621 this Muslim cell implanted in Yathrib duly returned under the cover of the pilgrimage. Twelve men now made a covert oath of loyalty to the creed. The Prophet sent one of his trusted followers, Mus'ab ibn 'Umayr, to return with them to Yathrib to instruct them in the correct attitude of prayer and to recite to them surahs of the Qur'an.

Certain political reasons help to explain this breakthrough in conversion. Yathrib was in the process of destroying itself. Unlike Mecca and Taif, it was not a concentric town but a network of hamlets scattered over twenty square miles of palm groves and gardens. There was no identifiable nucleus, simply a complicated grid of murderous local factions. The once-dominant tribe of the oasis, the Beni Qaylah, had split into two rival factions – the Aws and the Khazraj – who had just fought their fourth battle against each other in an ever-escalating round of civil wars. A clear victory by either of these equally balanced factions seemed unlikely. The situation was further complicated by the presence of three clans of Jewish Arabs, the Beni Nadir, Beni Qurayzah and Beni Qaynuqa, in the oasis. They are referred to here as Jewish Arabs because, whatever their ethnic origins, these Jewish clans were thoroughly Arabic. They spoke Arabic, they took Arab names and were fully integrated into the system of alliances that linked the rival hamlets and clans of Yathrib with rival tribes of Bedouin in the desert. It is a mistake to think of them in terms of ethnic Judaism, or as some ghetto in the desert. The Jews of Yathrib were clearly quite a force to be reckoned with. It was they who had sent the two rabbis south to Yemen in the fifth century to convert a Himyarite king, Abikarib As'ad (383–433), to Judaism.

Recent archaeological work has also uncovered something about which literary sources have remained completely silent: the mines of old Arabia. More than a thousand sites have now been positively identified, some of which were in full operation in the early seventh century, such as the silver mines of Qabaliyya and Juhayna outside Yathrib and that of Radrad, near San'a, in the Yemen. In this period the Arabs still remained suspicious of all metal-working and it appears that even the itinerant black-smiths and jewellers of the tribes were outsiders, which in practice usually meant they were either Persians or Jews. Indeed, there is a slightly derogatory reference to 'pit-Persians' in the correspondence of one of the kings of the Yemen. It seems likely that the development of mining in Arabia had been of great benefit to the Jewish Arabs, for not only would it make them richer, more confident and more capable of forging alliances with the Bedouin tribes but it also might go some way towards explaining why the Persian Empire backed the Jewish insurrec-tion of Yusuf Dhu Nuwas in the Yemen back in 520–525. If all this is true – and it is no more than supposition – it would give extra weight to the concerns of the Aws and the Khazraj. It may have been growing fear of the political ambitions of these Jewish Arabs that made the more sensible Aws and Khazraj regret their murderous blood feud and look for some unifying figure. This is where Muhammad fitted into the picture. An outsider removed from the jealousies of the Yathrib clans, widely acknowledged as a pious, God-directed, God-fearing prophet, might be the only figure who could save the community.

In 622, after eleven months in Yathrib, Mus'ab ibn 'Umayr returned to make a confidential report to the Prophet. He had done his job well and a few weeks later a delegation of seventy-three men and two women from Yathrib met the Prophet in secret during the pilgrimage month. They met, as before, on the edge of the valley of Mina as it rises towards the hills that surround Mecca. This place is known as Aqaba. On the third night following their arrival the new Muslims of Yathrib crept forward – as quiet as a sandgrouse – to their secret rendezvous. By the light of the moon, Bara, a chieftain of Yathrib, advanced and took the Prophet's hand. He swore, 'By Him who sent you with the truth, we will protect you as we protect them [our wives and children]. So accept the pledge of our allegiance, O Messenger of God, for we are men of war, possessed of arms that have been handed down from father to son.' The Prophet replied, 'I am yours and you are mine. Whom you war against, him I war against. Whom you make peace with, him I make peace with.'

So it was done. The bonds with Mecca were loosed and new ties bound the Prophet and the oasis of Yathrib. The Prophet's uncle Abbas, a well-respected banker, had come to witness the ceremony. Abbas was not a Muslim but he wanted to be sure that his nephew was in safe hands.

That summer of 622, the Muslims of Mecca began quietly to make their way north to Yathrib. Their departure began not a moment too soon, for Mut'im, the chieftain of the Nawfal who had become the Prophet's protector, had died, which once more opened up the prospect of violence. Abu Jahl had also perfected a plot to murder the Prophet. Each clan would put forward one stout-hearted young warrior who would together form a team of assassins. They would strike the Prophet as one, thus sharing the responsibility and blood guilt equally amongst all the clans of the Quraysh. Abu Lahab was not privy to this plot though it was highly likely that, as a known opponent of Islam, he would settle for blood money.

By the lunar month of Safar, Mecca was virtually empty of Muslims. Only the households of Abu Bakr and the Prophet remained. The conspirators surrounded the house of Muhammad but when they heard the voices of the women inside they reconsidered their plan. Despite the importance of their mission, they were loath to bring disgrace upon themselves by violating the sanctity of an Arab home. But, having spotted a sleeping figure in the house wrapped up in the Prophet's familiar green cloak, they decided to bide their time. As dawn broke, however, they were infuriated to find that the cloaked figure was young Ali: Muhammad and Abu Bakr had slipped out of Mecca during the night on a pair of camels. For all their piety and prayer, they had lost none of their wits or desert craft. The tracks of a flock of sheep obscured those of their camels and they hid out the first night in a cave on Mount Thawr, which stood above the caravan trail to the Yemen. It was a road that was not likely to be watched by their enemies. They waited in the cave for three days. They would not make their next move until they had found out what the Quraysh were planning. The leaders of Mecca had offered a reward of one hundred camels to whoever could bring back the Prophet. The city and its surrounding hills were seething with Bedouin scouts and bounty hunters.

On the afternoon of the third day, Muhammad and Abu Bakr heard a search party making its way around the slopes of the mountain. Six men approached the threshold of the cave, their steps echoing down into its dark interior as they entered. But a spider had sealed the cave entrance with her web, while a rock dove rocketed off her nest, providing graphic proof that no one could possibly be hiding in the cave. The search party moved off. That night Abu Bakr's young son and daughter made their way to the cave. They brought provisions and in the valley below a Bedouin guide waited with a string of three of Abu Bakr's camels. Even at this critical moment the Prophet insisted that he be permitted to buy one of the animals, especially as he noticed that Abu Bakr was offering him Qaswa, by far the best mount of the three. To foil the search parties watching all the known routes between Mecca and Yathrib, they rode in a diametrically opposite direction, bearing south-west until they hit the coast of the Red Sea. Only then did they start to work their way north again, travelling by night along the coast before branching inland towards Yathrib.

☾

Muhammad's *hijra,* or migration, from Mecca to Medina in 622 marks the beginning of the Muslim era and its calendar. Dates are given as A.H., "After the Hijra." It was a turning point in history in a number of ways. Once the Prophet had arrived in Yathrib in September 622 he began to establish a theocratic community. From this secure base he began to wage war against the non-believers. There should be no mistake about one point in particular: the Prophet was the aggressor in the conflict, even though his forces were much weaker than those of his adversaries. He wished to convert the Meccans to Islam; they essentially wanted to be left in peace with their wealth and their pagan deities. At the very beginning of his prophetic mission Muhammad had obstinately refused to accept a deal that left him worshipping his own God and the people of Mecca worshipping theirs. The Prophet had always made clear that he demanded only one thing, a declaration of the *chahada*, the confession that defines a Muslim. It is the simple rite of initiation with which any person can step over the line from non-belief into the world of Islam – into submission to the rule of God.

6

Muhammad in Medina: The Prophet and His City

It was after midday on Monday. The heat from the black volcanic rocks that surrounded this most southerly outpost of Yathrib oasis, a village called Quba, had become mind-numbingly intense. The lookouts were exhausted and had left their posts, for no one travelled at this time of day, the hottest. A terrible silence had settled over the Muslim refugees. The Prophet was known to have been among the last to leave Mecca but where was he now? By their calculations his arrival at Yathrib was overdue. It was well known that he had escaped from the band of assassins that had surrounded his house. That story had spread like wildfire. But he had still not arrived. This was the time to seek shelter, even if sleep was not possible in the heat.

Distant figures suddenly emerged on the summit of the basalt rocks, shimmering through the haze on the horizon. The small party rapidly descended the rock slope. To Western eyes they would have been indistinct blobs, but to the Arabs of the desert the gait of each camel could be recognised. The first jubilant cry sounded from a rooftop, 'He is come, he is come'. The silence of

the desert was subsumed as wave upon wave of ululations rose
from the throats of the village women. Like Jesus entering
Jerusalem, the Prophet carried all before him that day. His face
wreathed in smiles, he sang out to the welcoming crowds, 'let my
people give each other the greetings of peace', 'feed food to the
hungry', 'pray in the hours when men sleep'. Tears flowed as the
exiles from Mecca were safely reunited with their leader. Despite
the emotion of the moment, the Prophet's political sensitivity
remained as sharp as ever. He accepted the hospitality of a man
from the Aws faction of Yathrib while seeing that Abu Bakr lodged
in a Khazraj household. They were both exhausted from the trek
but not for a moment did they show it. After the customary three
days of hospitality in Quba, they advanced the three miles into the
main oasis of Yathrib.

This time they did not ride alone. The clamorous procession
gained more followers with each advancing mile. This joyous cavalcade, this caravan of hope, included villagers, herdsmen, every
holiday-loving child and household slave as well as a sterner core
of refugees from Mecca. At noon they halted beneath the shade of
palms in the valley of Rahuna, where a clan of Bedouin joined
them in open-air prayers. After sheltering from the mid-afternoon
heat they continued their advance on the dense forest of palm
trees, which constituted the Yathrib oasis. They were greeted by
lines of warriors, all dressed in armour with their swords raised in
salute, glinting in the afternoon sun. The midnight oath at Aqaba
to protect the Prophet was now a reality, this time not for just
seventy-three men and two women stealing through the night as
quiet as sandgrouse, but for the entire community proudly arrayed.
This homage of raised swords was much loved by the Arabs.
The poets liked to conjure up its image, which they compared to
flames in a dark night, stars in the sky, the glow of torchlight and
sunlit glass. After the men, it was the turn of the women to sing

their hymn of welcome: 'The full moon has arrived and grace is upon us, the messenger is with us. He came in accordance with God's order. Welcome the best of messengers to the city.'

From now on, the oasis of Yathrib would be known as Medina, or, more properly, Medinat al-Nabi, 'the city of the Prophet'. Although the Arab word 'Medina' means city, in the seventh century the oasis was a scattering of villages and hamlets. Now every village clamoured to be chosen as the home of the Prophet. Muhammad was well aware of the furious local rivalry between the villages as well as between that of the dominant clans. The last thing he wanted to do was to inflame these further by choosing one group over another. It seemed an impossible quandary but he rose to the challenge with an extraordinarily graceful gesture. Combining a wise understanding of human nature with an unworldly holiness, he let no human hand hold the reins of his camel but rather allowed Qaswa, the beast he had purchased from Abu Bakr, to choose her own way. Through the sandy alleys, past the mud and stone houses, through palm-shaded gardens they wandered, surrounded and pursued by an exultant crowd. The evening sun cast a gilded light on the allotments, walls and orchards. Finally the camel came to a halt within an overgrown courtyard overlooked by a few palms, an old cemetery and a ramshackle shed, which was used from time to time to dry and store dates. This unworthy, neglected backwater would henceforth be the home of the Prophet. He would not accept it as a gift, despite the entreaties of the owners – a pair of orphan brothers – and insisted he pay them a fair price. It was now evening. Neither Muhammad nor his camel could be persuaded to move an inch further, or to accept the many invitations to dine and shelter for the night. 'A man must not be parted from his baggage,' protested the Prophet.

☾

The humble courtyard in Medina was to become the focus of life in the oasis and a prototype for Muslim households. From the start it functioned as an open-air prayer hall, the house of the Prophet and as a community centre. However extensive the Prophet's following became, his house never lost its simplicity.

Now the faithful began to work on its construction. To spur them on in their labour, the Prophet divided them into two rival gangs. The Helpers – Ansar – were the local Muslim converts from Medina, while the Emigrants – Muhajirah – were the faithful who had left Mecca. They sang as they worked. The songs were composed as they went along, but two verses became especially popular and were repeated like a refrain:

> O God, no good is but the good hereafter
> So help the Helpers and the Emigrants.

This was balanced by:

> No life there is but life of the hereafter
> Mercy, O God, on Emigrants and Helpers.

Seven months later, the complex was finished. Garden walls as high as a man, built with sun-fired mud bricks, enclosed a square courtyard in which shade was cast by a few fine, single palm trees. Most of the other trees had been felled to clear an open space in the centre of the courtyard. This was used as a mosque and was filled with the faithful at the time of prayer. When the wind was high the sand was wetted to settle the dust, and at festival time the surface was brushed with palm fronds that traced arabesques on the floor. At first, prayers were offered in a northerly direction, towards Jerusalem. A shady area – known as the *zulla* – was subsequently created against the north wall. The trunks of palms formed the vertical columns, supporting a roof made with cross-beams of split palm trunks with palm branches as the thatch. Anyone who has travelled in Arab lands may remember seeing similar structures, and recall the many happy hours spent in their shade watching the dappled light of sunbeams moving across the floor. The noon prayer was often performed under this welcome shelter from the powerful midday sun. Here there was none of the fixtures that later invariably became associated with a mosque. No apse-like *mihrab* indicated the direction of prayer; no *dikka* (raised platform) was used in recitation; no pulpit-like *minbar* stood to the right of the *mihrab*.

Against the south-east wall were a series of huts for each of the Prophet's wives. In the first year at Medina there were just two huts, but the number would eventually increase to ten. Food for the household was stored in one, if not all, of these huts, and cooked and prepared in the open courtyard. Architectural embellishments were unwelcome. It was recalled that when one of his wives, Umm Salamah, was building an extension to her room (to give her privacy from the prying eyes of men) Muhammad had declared, 'Verily, the most unprofitable thing that eateth up the wealth of a believer is building.'

On the wall opposite the shaded *zulla* was a smaller but similar structure, which could be used as a guesthouse for passing visitors. Even now few Arab households make much of a fuss about a spare bedroom. Any space can be converted into a sleeping area by rolling out a mat and covering it with a blanket.

In his lifetime Muhammad designed just one other mosque. This stood on the site of an old sanctuary on the edge of Quba, where he had first entered Medina. Here he established a rectangular sanctuary enclosed by a garden wall, measuring 85 by 100 feet. The mosque was subsequently venerated as the place where the Prophet first rested and first led the prayers upon his arrival.

Its design, layout and rustic simplicity must have met with the Prophet's approval, for, after it had been damaged during the wars with Mecca, he restored it in 629.

The call to prayer – that haunting cry of faith that rolls across the Muslim world to this day – was established by the Prophet less than a year after he moved to Medina. The oasis was still full of Jewish and Christian Arabs existing in comfortable proximity to the Muslim exiles from Mecca, so Muhammad needed to find a distinctive way of calling the faithful together, one that was different from that of his neighbours. At this time the Jews were summoned to prayer by horns, at once reminiscent of the practice at the old Temple at Jerusalem. The Christians used bells, though outside the big cities they could seldom afford to cast them in bronze, and so in practice they made frequent use of wooden clappers. In Abyssinia the Coptic Church played drums during services, but would summon the faithful by lithophone, menhir-like stones suspended in pairs from trees so that their natural resonance could sound once they had been struck.

The Muslim call to prayer did not come out of a revelation. It was decided in a public meeting where the young Muslim community chose the human voice. It is typical of the Prophet's humanity (and antipathy to racism or snobbery) that he should have selected a freed Abyssinian slave, Bilal, to be the prayer caller. Bilal had been well tested in the faith; he had had an especially miserable time during the persecution in Mecca for he had no protection of an Arab clan. No doubt he had a good and powerful voice.

The call to prayer is known as *adhan*, so the person making it became known as *mu'adhdhin*, which has been corrupted into the more familiar muezzin. *Adhan* is used for the five daily prayers and, though it is recommended, it is not obligatory nor is it considered part of the actual prayer. On his own initiative Bilal added

'Benediction and peace be on you, O Prophet of God, and the mercy of God and his blessing' to the morning call. After Muhammad's death, Bilal would continue the habit, addressing Abu Bakr (the leader of the community and his former master) as *khalifat Rasul Allah* – caliph (successor) to the Prophet of God. Later caliphs were also to be blessed in the morning, but as *amir al-mu'minin* – commander of the faithful.

What of the minaret, the slender turret of the mosque – that architectural exclamation mark on the horizon, that most emblematic of all symbols of Islam from which the muezzin calls? The first purpose-built minaret was erected in 673, some fifty years after the death of the Prophet. Before that the muezzin simply made use of a rooftop. Simplicity was everything in early Islam. It is one of history's ironies that those fabulous early surviving mosques, those venerable sanctuaries that glorify Islam at Cairo, Damascus, Kairouan, Medina, Samarra, Mecca and Cordoba, and have sent generations of travelers into ecstasy, would have appalled the Prophet. His innate personal modesty and love of simplicity are nowhere to be seen in such constructions. He would not have been able to forgive their architectural magnificence, which he would have considered to obscure the direct contact between worshipper and God. In 707, the people of Medina cried up to the heavens in horror when the Umayyad Caliph Walid, ruling from Damascus, decreed that the House of the Prophet and the First Mosque of Islam should be pulled down. After the dust had settled, armies of Christian workmen brought down from Syria and Egypt laboured for two years to raise a magnificent testament to the world domination of Islam, a temple of cut stone, polished marble and gilded mosaic. Well did the Prophet say, 'Verily, of things which I fear for you, after my departure from the world, is this: that the ornaments and goods of the world may be pleasing to you.'

Muhammad always lived his heartfelt prayer – 'O Lord! Keep me alive a poor man, and let me die poor; and raise me amongst the poor' – and this helps to explain the extraordinary success of his mission to the Arabs. His most compelling personal conduct was a continual sermon, putting the tenets of the Qur'an into practice, and at times it seems that the personal qualities of the Prophet brought in almost as many converts as the words of the Qur'an.

☾

The Prophet's manners were based, very simply, on an innate respect for the equality of individuals. The years spent at Medina were the true test of this, for it is surely easier for a man to be graceful and fair when he needs to win approval than when he has been placed amongst the high temptation of authority.

Muhammad never hid behind ushers, doormen or bodyguards. In times of war two brothers volunteered to sleep across his doorway but this was always an exceptional measure. He always remained accessible to whoever wished to speak to him. There was a daily opportunity for public intercession where any of the faithful could make a statement immediately after prayers.

After the morning session, it was the Prophet's habit to inquire if anyone was sick, and to go and visit those who were. If anyone had died he helped to wrap the corpse and would conduct the funeral prayer; or if anyone had been upset by a dream he would sit down, listen and interpret it for them.

When men stood up as he walked by, he would ask them to remain standing only if that was their way of showing respect for all humankind. If they were simply standing up for him, however, he told them they should sit down. Muhammad would declare, 'I am a man like you. I eat food like you and I also sit down when I am tired – like you!' He put this habit into practice himself, sometimes greeting new arrivals on his knees or even embracing friends while sitting on the ground with his knees up.

Muhammad would never sit down while others worked. When moving through the desert one day together with three friends, they came to a stop. One of his companions offered to butcher a sheep, the other to skin it, the third to cook it, whereupon he rose up and started gathering wood. They pressed him to remain seated. He replied that he knew they could do everything without his help, but that he did not wish to sit apart from his friends.

To this end Muhammad would always assist his servants with their work. Anas ibn Malik, who served the Prophet for the last ten years of his life, claimed that 'he served me more than I served him. He has never been angry with me. He never treated me harshly.' When his attendance was requested by someone's servant or child, he never insisted on assuming the dominant role but allowed the servant the dignity of leading the way. Indeed, in Medina he followed the local custom and walked hand in hand with the messenger. It became an accepted maxim of the Prophet, 'that the dearest one in a society is the one who always serves others'.

The Prophet was a shy man who seldom looked anyone in the eye. He never created for himself a forceful, charismatic gaze, never adopted a rhetorical stance. He waited his turn, smiled and spoke briefly, repeating himself word for word if his audience failed to hear him. Muhammad would never allow a seat to be reserved for him when attending a meeting but would sit wherever there was an empty space.

He also turned his back on the old Arab stigma about superior mounts and would cheerfully ride on the back of a donkey or a mule, or share his camel or horse with someone. This was a deliberate decision, for we know that from boyhood he had been taught the etiquette of camel riding as thoroughly as any desert Arab and delighted in the company of his favourite animals.

The Prophet had also been well trained from boyhood in the grooming and care of animals. Like any good stockman he ensured the animals were fed before he himself ate. He would patiently hold up the water bucket until they had drunk their fill. He often wiped the face and the eyes of his horse. As he grew older he increasingly allowed others to do these tasks, just as he had helped his foster-father, grandfather and uncle when he was young.

It has become traditional within Islam to list things in groups of five, such as the five daily prayers. Even animals can be listed in this way. The favoured animals of Islam are the camel, the horse, the cat, the goat and the sheep. Amongst the unclean animals of Islam are the snake, the rat, the pig, the fly and the dog. Muhammad's love of cats is well known; indeed, he once cut a hole in his cloak so that he could remove it, rather than disturb a cat that was asleep on it. Muhammad's reputation among dog-lovers is not so well remembered, however, for he once ordered the destruction of stray dogs around Medina. Anyone with first-hand knowledge of the packs of feral dogs that scavenge the rubbish tips and wastelands on the fringe of an oasis will realise that this prob-ably had something to do with maintaining public order (and a desire to sleep through the night undisturbed) rather than dislike of the animal.

☾

The rulers of Muhammad's day ate in fine vaulted halls from mag-nificent gilded silver services. He, however, preferred to eat on the ground in the open air. There was no table, no tray, no carpet, simply a woven palm mat spread out on the ground. The sharing of food, of God's plenty, was a sacred duty to the Prophet. He mem-orably declared: the food of one is enough for two, the food for two is enough for four, and the food of four enough for eight. This attitude prompted occasional resentment from his wives, for he never put aside more than a year's supply of barley and dates and even this 'reserve account' was constantly diminished by gifts to the poor and the feeding of strangers. The ease with which food is shared and hospitality is offered remains one of the most conspicuous differences between a traditional Muslim society and the Western world. On this issue all the grace and generosity belongs with Islam, all the cold-heartedness with the West. All the familiar excuses the Western world gives for excluding a guest from their table – not enough warning, not enough room, not enough food, the wrong numbers – simply cannot be translated into an Islamic context.

It was the Prophet's practice to eat only once a day. Like all Arabs he used his right hand, reserving the left hand for personal hygiene. He never developed a taste for luxurious food, preferring bread made from barley flour to the more expensive sifted wheat flour. Dates, milk, soup (especially mutton broth) and bread dipped in olive oil were his daily staples. He liked to shop in the bazaar for food and carry it back home to his wives himself. He was, however – like every desert dweller one has ever met – passionate about meat and would eat any of the five desert meats: camel, rabbit, gazelle, chicken or mutton. He was fond of chewing meat off the bone, especially the shoulder, which he would eat with his fingers. There is no other way. Outsiders often wonder why pumpkin is so often served up in the stews and bowls of couscous in Muslim homes. It is another of the foods of the poor in which the Prophet delighted, and so it occupies a special place in Muslim family meals. His favourite fruits were melons, grapes and he loved cucumbers, which also remain staples of the diet in a Muslim household.

One fruit more than any other is associated with the Prophet: the date. Muhammad often fasted for two or three days at a time and when the time came to eat he would always break his fast with dates. Throughout the world the Muslim daytime fast of Ramadan ends every evening with the eating of dates. Similarly in many prayer halls, dates and milk are always served first, before the main dishes. This link between the prayers that Muhammad taught to the world and the food he loved seems to offer a direct physical connection. The Prophet's wives were instructed never to turn away a beggar from the door, even if they could only offer half a date.

He never pointed out the food he did not like, but simply ate that which pleased him. He was also acutely aware of overpowering breath and always avoided eating too much garlic and onion, though he tried to keep these personal habits from being considered as doctrine. Similarly, if asked for something he never said 'I do not have it'. He would give if he had it; if not he would remain silent. This policy extended to gossip, which he disdained. He was always careful to preserve a person's honour, never to expose someone's fault to their face.

When he had to meet an ambassador or envoy, he would dress up for the occasion in a fine cloak and a robe. In all other instances he declined to wear, or accept as a gift, anything luxurious. Gold, in his mind inextricably linked with the pride and cruelty of the royal courts, was almost repugnant to him.

He wore simple white clothes, often woven from a mixture of wool and cotton. Many of these had been spun, washed and woven by the women of his household, although the Prophet liked to mend and patch his own clothes. It is said that he preferred cloth that he could wrap around himself rather than sewn garments with buttons. He customarily wore a long shirt, a robe covered by a thick blanket-like cloth (*ihram*) that was wrapped around like a toga, and a white, black or green turban. (No real significance can be seen in the choice of these colours, any more than it can in his fondness for yellow leather slippers.) The turban is an essential part of desert life: it protects the wearer from the sun and has folds that can be pulled down to cover the eyes, ears and mouth against dust storms. It is made from a three-metre length of cloth wrapped around the head several times with one end looped over to shield the head and tucked in with a flap extending down to shield the neck. The turban has also acquired an external wrapping of symbolism. It is a robe that honours the head, the temple of the intellect. It can also double up as the funeral shroud of a good Muslim, a constant reminder of all that he will leave the world with, as well as a convenience to his companions should he die in some far-off field. Under his turban, in keeping with the habits of his time, Muhammad always kept his hair oiled and when it grew long it would be braided.

The Prophet was a great proponent of cleanliness and he established clearly the ritual of washing as a vital preliminary to prayer. The face, forearms, feet, toes, nose and ears all had to be cleaned before prayer. This was the little ablution. If there was no water, clean sand could be used. After sex, or prior to the more formal weekly Friday midday prayer, you were required to clean your entire body. The correlation between sex and bathing remains deeply established in Islamic practice.

Scent was one of the Prophet's great passions, one of his few luxuries, which he listed beside women as the sensual loves of his life. He would rub musk and perfumes on his face, head and hands while his body and clothes were scented with aloe wood oil and camphor. It is a habit that still remains amongst the devotedly religious of the Islamic world. He also used to tinge his eyes with kohl, powdered stibium. This once-ubiquitous practice has all but died out except in the more traditional mountainous territories of Islam in Central Asia – it is supposed to offer protection against dust and other irritants.

The Prophet used the desert toothbrush, a twig variously called *siwak* or *mswak*. Even when dying he continued to keep his teeth clean with a *siwak* twig, for, as he was fond of explaining, 'Purify your mouths, for they are the channels through which you utter praises to God.'

The Prophet seldom opened his mouth to give a belly laugh, though we do know that he smiled a great deal. He liked to joke, mostly with outsiders in the community or visiting foreigners, the very young and the very old. For him laughter was a rare treat. When once questioned about his gravity and sobriety he gave a famously chilling reply: 'Among you I am the person who has understood God the best and fear him the most. If you had seen what I saw, you would laugh less and cry more.'

It is said that the Prophet could sleep anywhere: out on the sand like a good Bedouin, on a mat of felt, or of palm leaves; or on a wooden bed strung with leather straps. In Medina it was his practice to sleep by strict rotation in the different chambers or huts of his wives. If they owned a mattress, it would be stuffed with date fibre. Once his favourite wife Aisha offered him a mattress made of soft beaten wool and he immediately rejected it. 'If I need luxury, God will send me down beds of gold and silver,' he chided her.

Possessions meant nothing to the Prophet. He happily accepted presents and would often give gifts in return. On other occasions he preferred to mask his generosity as a business deal (though one that often might be deeply unprofitable). His early followers were astonished at how the fortune in camels and trade goods that he later amassed in the war against Mecca was immediately given away again, as gifts to the newly converted. His cousin and son-in-law Ali and his daughter Fatimah, possibly the most saintly of all his followers, once broached the subject of their wealth, or rather their complete lack of it, while everyone else seemed to be the recipients of endless gifts from the Prophet. Why, they asked, do we alone of all your followers never get given anything? Why are we, the first of the Muslims, also the poorest? At that time Ali was drawing water from wells while Fatimah was grinding corn for her better-off neighbours. The Prophet replied that he had nothing of material benefit for them but later that night he came to their hut and gave what he valued most, prayer.

☾

The Prophet Muhammad loved women. He freely confessed, 'It has been given to me to love perfume and women, and coolness hath been brought to mine eyes in prayer.' We know from the anguished admission of Aisha that he never stopped thinking and talking about his first wife Khadijah. In the Muslim hierarchy in heaven, there are four women of the first rank: Khadijah, Fatimah (the Prophet's daughter), the Virgin Mary and Asiye (Moses' step-mother).

Muhammad adored every aspect of his women: their company, their wit and advice, their wisdom and artistry, their chatter, even their complaints and squabbles were music to his soul. He often liked to bring one of them along on expeditions. At times it seems that only their presence could repair the damage done to his body and mind by the exhausting process of divine revelation. His delight in them, in their different natures, beauty and virtue, does much to explain why the Prophet kept increasing his number of wives. He strongly disapproved of celibacy and looked upon marriage as both a pleasure and a social obligation. He was a man, not an angel. In his own words, 'I go into women and I eat meat.'

Muhammad's wives had plenty of work to do. As the Prophet's standing grew beyond Medina, so did the demands on his household. There was a continuous stream of visitors to be greeted and fed. Destitute refugees were housed in a shelter in one corner of the courtyard while the poor could always be sure of receiving something at his door. The Prophet's home was the functioning headquarters of Islam and it was staffed mainly by his wives. So Muhammad had need of his women for a number of reasons, and they seem to have enjoyed his high regard for them.

It must have concerned the Prophet deeply that he had no surviving sons. The two boys born to him by Khadijah had both died in their infancy. Despite that, one of the most honourable ways of addressing Muhammad was as Abu Qasim – the father of Qasim. The failure to father male descendants is still a cause for great concern in the Middle East of today. In more traditional Arab societies it is tantamount almost to dishonour, and can lead to couples having large families, pursuing fertility treatment of dubious efficacy and, more often than not, divorcing each other. Men used customarily to divorce their wives for failing to produce a son. This cult of masculinity was even stronger in pagan Arabia where a man, his clan and his tribe could only be assured of a future existence through his male descendants. They needed warriors too. The whole Arab nomenclature system, based on both ibn/ben – son of – and Abu – father of – rested on a proud recital of the male patronymic. Without a son these lines of descent lost all their meaning; they were like fine cloth that had become unravelled. An Arab man without male offspring ranked low in society, while a man such as Muhammad's grandfather 'Abd al-Muttalib, the father of ten sons, acquired enormous additional respect. One of the critical questions the pagan Quraysh used to level at Muhammad was why, if God had chosen him as a prophet, had he not thought to favour him with any sons?

Once Muhammad had established himself at Medina, the people of the oasis were in a continual frenzy of expectation that he would be blessed with the birth of a boy. One of the reasons

Muhammad took one wife after another might have been the hope of fathering a son. He was far too kind and affectionate a man ever to consider divorcing a wife simply because of her failure to produce an heir. The Prophet gave allowance for divorce as an expression of human failing but he also declared, 'of all things licit the most hateful unto God is divorce'.

There were also the needs of tribal and clan politics to consider. The easiest and most effective way of cementing an alliance was through marriage. With each new marriage of the Prophet, a new set of relationships was established that bound tribal Arabia closer to Islam. But in this one instance of multiple marriage, the Prophet's example was not set as a standard for others to follow. Indeed, he decreed that no Muslim should have more than four wives, but even this carried an injunction that men could only take additional wives if they treated them equally. Many doubted their ability to do this. Abu Bakr, for instance, remained content with one wife.

After Khadijah's death the Prophet's household and his daughters were cared for by Khawlah, the wife of one of his loyal followers. After the first period of mourning had passed, Khawlah suggested that he should find another wife. She herself put forward two candidates: the very beautiful Aisha, daughter of Abu Bakr, and Sawdah, a motherly thirty-year-old. Muhammad chose both of them. Sawdah, one of the Muslims who had taken refuge in Abyssinia, had recently been widowed. She was therefore immediately available and moved in to take charge of the household. Aisha, then still a pre-pubescent virgin, was betrothed by her father but did not physically become Muhammad's wife until she was considered sexually mature, after her first menstruation. Even then the age disparity was considerable: she was only nine while Muhammad was fifty-three. On the morning of marriage Aisha remembered being taken from her seesaw to be made ready, to be adorned with jewelry, and to be clothed in a fine red robe that had been imported from Bahrain. The ritual of marriage was simple: she shared a bowl of milk with Muhammad before they went to bed. She had known him all her life and was aware that he was held in the highest regard by both her mother and father. Despite their new relationship her childhood continued unchecked. Sawdah ran the house while Aisha's girlfriends were allowed to come and go as they pleased.

The relationship between Muhammad and Aisha was tender and loving. Of all his women, she was the closest to his heart but there would be moments of acute tension. She took great pride in her position as the daughter of Abu Bakr and the Prophet's only virgin bride. She was furiously jealous of each new wife if she felt the woman rivalled her own beauty. Despite this, she gradually befriended most of them. Aisha was priviledged to be the only one of the Prophet's wives present during a revelation. It was also in her company that he eased many of his earlier prohibitions and permitted singing and dancing at festivals and marriages. For her part, Aisha joked that if she died before him it would be only a matter of days before Muhammad started to look for another wife.

When Muhammad first left Mecca for Medina, he went without Aisha and Sawdah. Such was the honour in which Arabs held women that not one of his enemies tried to molest any members of his household after he had escaped from the city. Only when, seven months later, the new house at Medina was ready did Muhammad send a messenger to fetch them. They completed their journey without interruption. The old standards of Arab chivalry and clan pride also survived undiminished in Medina. For instance, although Sawdah had been a passionate convert to Islam, this did not stop her berating one of her pagan cousins from Mecca for not fighting hard enough against the Muslim army! She poured scorn on her relation for leaving the Battle of the Wells of Badr before he had been wounded. It was in the aftermath of this battle that Muhammad took a third wife. He asked one of the new war widows – the eighteen-year-old Hafsah – to come into his household. His fourth wife, Zaynab, also joined the household as a young widow. As she was the daughter of a Bedouin tribal chieftain, Zaynab's marriage to Muhammad also had political implications.

Muhammad gave his own daughters in marriage only to his most intimate supporters. It is clear that both he and Khadijah had thought long and hard about the most suitable husbands for their children. Zaynab, the eldest, had been married in Mecca to a maternal cousin who was also Khadijah's favourite nephew, Abu l'As. This particular son-in-law remained obstinately pagan, though he was later to be reconciled with the Prophet through the patient advocacy of his wife. The child of this marriage, Umamah, was certainly greatly cherished by her grandfather. It was said that she made her second home on the Prophet's shoulders. Muhammad's second daughter, Ruqayyah, was married to the gentle 'Uthman, of a noble Quraysh clan. After her death, 'Uthman went on to marry another of the Prophet's daughters, Umm Kulthum. When she herself subsequently died, Muhammad tried to comfort his grieving son-in-law by saying that had he another daughter, he would give her unto him. Fatimah, the youngest daughter of Muhammad, had married her cousin and childhood friend Ali, but not before the Prophet was safely established at Medina and she was twenty years old. She gave birth to al-Hasan, 'the Beautiful', just a year after her marriage, in the month of Ramadan 625. The Prophet came to greet his newborn grandson, whispering into his ear the call to prayer before he named him. A year later his brother was born, al-Husayn, 'the Little Beautiful One'. From these two children descend all the

Muslims who claim to be *shorfa*, of the bloodline of the Prophet. (Amongst the modern representatives of this lineage is the young Hashemite King Abdullah of Jordan and the Alaouite King Muhammad VI of Morocco.) More contentious in their sacred claims to power through this bloodline were the medieval dynasties of the Shiites, the line of hidden Imams and the Fatimid caliphs who would rule over a Muslim Empire from Cairo.

Muhammad adored his daughters and was always pained by the traditional reaction to the birth of a female child. He deplored the behaviour of the typical Arab father: 'when a daughter is announced to one of them his face becomes dark and full of anger. He hides himself from the people because of the evil of that which is announced to him. Shall he keep it with disgrace or bury it in the dust?' The allusion to burying it 'in the dust' comes from the pre-Islamic practice of a father burying alive his unwanted newborn daughter in the sand. It is not certain if this was a form of pagan sacrifice, or simply a way of avoiding the expense of feeding another mouth and having to provide another dowry. Muhammad is also reported to have said, 'Whoever has a female child, and does not bury her alive, nor hold her in contempt, nor prefer his male child to her, shall enter Paradise.'

☾

Muhammad had always included Jews and Christians amongst his friends. Indeed, while he lived in Mecca he might have had more in common with them than his own pagan cousins, the Quraysh, who persecuted him. The hospitality shown to the Muslim refugees by the Christian Emperor of Abyssinia had only served to intensify his regard for Christianity, while the mystical experience of the night flight made it seem natural that praying should be undertaken facing in the direction of Jerusalem. When he arrived in Medina, he expected to make converts from the large resident Jewish population. Muhammad was proud of the handful of converts from Judaism. There is even a Qur'anic verse to testify this: 'Think if this Qur'an is indeed from God and you reject it; if an Israelite has vouched for its divinity and accepted Islam . . .' (surah Al-Ahqaf, no. 46, verse 10). However, these individuals were the exception; the vast majority of the Jews of Arabia rejected Muhammad's teaching. In fact, he was faced with critical inquiries from their leaders and his lack of a detailed literary knowledge of the Torah and gospels was soon made apparent. It was made clear too that the vast majority of Jews, while they were prepared to accept new prophets, expected them to be both Jewish and highly literate in the scriptures.

Muhammad was remarkably quick to make the necessary adjustments. Just seventeen months after arriving in Medina (ten months since the completion of the first mosque) he changed the direction of prayer. Now the faithful no longer faced in the direction of the old Temple at Jerusalem, but knelt towards the Kaaba of Mecca. Since the open area for prayer at Quba was so basic, it was a simple enough matter for the Prophet himself to move the *qibla*, the stone marking the direction of prayer, from one side to the other. This was how the prayer hall of Quba won its unique name Masjid al-Qiblatayan – the mosque of two *qiblas*. In the Prophet's house and prayer hall at Medina there was a little more work to be done. The shaded rest area, the *zulla*, was dismantled and reassembled on the other wall.

Early Islam and the two older monotheistic religions can be likened to an energetic young nephew and his two devout great-aunts. Muhammad would respect them but he was determined to live his life according to his own precepts. The Qur'an states, '. . . we believe in God and that which is revealed to us, and in what was revealed to Abraham, Ishmael, Isaac, Jacob . . . ; to Moses and Jesus and the prophets by their God. We make no

distinction between any of them, and to God we have surrendered ourselves.' It is also full of clear directions that the Jews and
Christians – collectively known to the Muslim world as the *ahl al-
kitab*, People of the Book – must be left undisturbed.

However, in Medina Muhammad gradually reveals the Islamic
version of the Christian story. The Qur'an is emphatic that Jesus
did not die on the cross: 'They killed him not, nor crucified him.
But it was made to appear so' (surah Al-Nisa, no. 4, verse 157).
Muslim tradition would later add the story that Yehuda (Judas)
took his master's place and died on the cross full of remorse for his
treachery. According to surah Al-Nisa, at the end of his life Jesus
was transferred to heaven, 'For of a surety, they killed him not.
Nay God raised him up to Himself' (verse 158). There, according
to a widespread Muslim tradition, he remains one of the four
living prophets who watch over humankind and can be appealed
to in prayer. Idris (the Jewish Henuh) and Jesus guard humankind
from heaven, while Khidr and Elias wander the earth. It was also
believed that the arrival of the Prophet had been clearly predicted
in the gospels. In the Gospel of John (chapter 16, verse 7) Jesus
speaks of his successor, 'Nevertheless, I tell you the truth; it is
expedient for you that I go away: for if I go not away, the
Comforter will not come unto you; but if I depart, I will send him
unto you.' All Muslims accept that this 'Comforter' is the Prophet
Muhammad. Just as John the Baptist prophesied the coming of
Jesus, so did Jesus alert the world to the Prophet Muhammad.

The Qur'an is full of references to the prophets who came
before Muhammad. There are twenty-five prophets named in the
Qur'an and it is clear that there are many others. According to one
Muslim tradition there are ninety-nine prophets buried at Mecca
alone, while later commentators came up with a figure of 124,000
prophets in the world. Some of the most liberal-minded interpreters of Islam would include in this number all the spiritual

heroes of humankind, from the Buddha and Zoroaster to the shamans of Siberia. This enlightened viewpoint has it that they all come from God.

What is much more important to Muslims, liberal and fundamentalist alike, is the belief that Muhammad is the greatest and the last of the Prophets. Whatever the history of religion, the Qur'an is believed to have rewritten the prophetic tradition for all time. A Muslim considers that the Qur'an contains all you need to know from the previous history of revelation. There is no need to look at the Hebrew Bible or the gospels. Few would deny that the Holy Books of Judaism and Christianity are honest attempts to remember the work of the great prophets of the past. It is just that ever since the lifetime of the Prophet Muhammad they have become obsolete in the eyes of Muslims.

The Qur'an, combined with the sayings of the Prophet, effectively created a new Muslim version of the Torah, which augments some accounts, adds new chapters and introduces new prophets (such as the prophet Hud), who had not previously been recorded. For instance, it was recalled that when Adam was expelled from heaven, he was given the softest possible landing on the island of Ceylon. Eve was allotted the port of Jeddah on the Red Sea. They sought each other out and were finally and tempestuously reunited at Muzdalifah, outside Mecca.

These intimate details, adding names and incidents not mentioned by the traditional Jewish accounts, are in the Qur'an, vouchsafed by an ageless council of the jinn. 'Our people!' these spirits said, 'we have just been listening to a scripture revealed since the time of Moses, confirming previous scriptures and directing to the truth and to a straight path' (surah Al-Ahqaf, no. 46, verse 31). The veil that keeps past and present clearly separated was at times made transparent to the eyes of the Prophet. Once on the way from Medina to Mecca he stopped his companion Abu Bakr in an empty valley and asked, 'do you know what happened here? The prophet Hud passed here on his way to Mecca, he was riding on the back of a female camel, red in colour and young in age.'

Essential to Muslim belief are Abraham and his son Ishmael. In the Qur'an they are the ancestors of the Arabs who together established Mecca's unique spiritual status. Every ritual action of the Hajj pilgrimage can be seen to have been initiated by these great patriarchs. In the Muslim account Abraham has two separate families. His Jewish descendants come from his marriage to his cousin-wife Sarah. His Arab descendants come from Hagar, his Egyptian concubine. Hagar had been given to Sarah as a gift from Pharaoh's sister and, although Sarah had initially allowed her husband to sleep with her, Sarah became furiously jealous when she remained barren while Hagar became pregnant. When Hagar gave birth to Ishmael, Abraham was forced to separate his two women. He took Hagar and her baby across the Arabian desert and left them with just a bag of dates and a jar of water in the empty valley of Mecca. As he climbed out of the valley he stopped on the plain and prayed to God to care for them. As their supplies dwindled, Ishmael began to cry out with thirst. Hagar ran distractedly up first one hill and then another (these two hillocks, the hill of Safa and the hill of Marwah, stand just outside the Kaaba sanctuary) searching desperately for water. She ran between these hillocks seven times (the origin of the oldest of the practices of the Muslim pilgrimage) before finally collapsing. The Archangel Gabriel then appeared to her and dug down into the earth in order to expose the *zemzem* spring, whose waters bubbled out to save both mother and son.

Many years later Abraham returned to find his son Ishmael grown into manhood and Hagar presiding over the town of Mecca. His joy was great but his dismay even greater when God tested him by calling upon him to sacrifice his first-born. Ishmael, like his half-brother Isaac, was of course spared this terrible fate. Instead father and son built the Kaaba as an altar to the One God. In the process they discovered the foundations of an earlier altar built by Adam but which had been washed away in the flood. They instituted a three-day festival, which culminated in the sacrifice of a ram to commemorate God's mercy. This is the original Aid el Kebir, the feast of sacrifice. It is the single greatest festival of the Islamic year. Male circumcision was also instituted at this time by Abraham, then aged eighty.

☾

The Qur'an, the word of God as revealed to humankind through the Prophet Muhammad, is of the most absolute primacy to a Muslim. However, for a Muslim the words and deeds of the Prophet Muhammad are like a complementary text to the holy word; the "sayings" of Muhammad, enshrined in the large body of literature called Hadith, are second only to the Qur'an in sacred authority. The life of the Prophet is the role model to which Muslims constantly refer and with which they instinctively compare themselves. There is no detail too small that it will not have some ramification upon the way a Muslim behaves. It is also the template for the way all successful leaders of the Islamic world should behave: they will only be loved and obeyed if their conduct follows this 'true and straight path'.

7

War with Mecca

Muhammad's war against the city of Mecca was not a struggle for empire, wealth or personal domination; it was a war for the survival of God's word. The Qur'an defines his war aims: 'fight them until persecution is no more, and religion is all for God' (surah Al-Anfal, no. 8, verse 39). He was in a uniquely strong position to do so, for being of Mecca he knew exactly how to hit them hardest.

The Prophet started operations within months of his arrival in Medina in 622. He knew that the Meccans had one particular weakness – caravans. If he could halt the flow of wealth, if he could seize their camels and merchandise, they would be forced to make peace. He knew the routes they were likely to choose, the wells that they had to pass, the seasons in which they had to operate.

The following autumn he received an early warning that the great Syrian caravan comprising two thousand five hundred camels was returning home. His scouts assessed that the armed guard, excluding Bedouin guides and cameleers, was a hundred strong. Muhammad rode out at the head of two hundred warriors but, despite crisscrossing the desert trails, they failed to make contact. Three months later this same war party was back in the desert searching for a north-bound caravan to Syria, but once again the practised manoeuvres of a Quraysh-led convoy escaped the raiders.

The first successful Muslim raid was on a much smaller scale. A handful of local traders, carrying bales of leather and panniers of raisins, was attacked in their camp just a day's ride from Mecca. It was a chance encounter, for the Muslim party was actually on a scouting mission looking out for the Yemen caravan. It also turned out to be somewhat self-defeating: the Muslims had attacked on the last evening of the sacred month of Rajab, a time when all fighting, even blood feuds, was traditionally prohibited. The Muslim community lost a great deal of respect from the Bedouin tribes by its abandonment of traditional law. At first Muhammad was in a quandary as to how to deal with this act of impiety, but at length he decided it was his duty to back his men in the field, right or wrong.

The southbound caravan from Syria was due to return to Mecca sometime in March 624. That season Muhammad was better prepared. Muslim scouts had been posted along the Red Sea coastal route and they were able to report back to Muhammad in time. He proceeded to march out with a force of three hundred and fifty warriors to intercept the caravan at a vital halt, the Wells of Badr. He rode out under a white banner while the Emigrants – the refugees from Mecca – and the Helpers – the men of Medina – were marshalled in their own squadrons under black banners. As Muhammad knew full well, he was threatening the very lifeblood of the merchant society of Mecca. The Quraysh (who were not without their own spies in Medina) moved quickly to protect their wealth and their pride, summoning an army of one thousand men from the city of Mecca to ride north and escort the caravan to safety.

The Muslims approached the Wells of Badr cautiously. They could not be sure (especially with their record of near misses) if they had arrived in time. They were very poorly mounted, with just seventy camels between three hundred and fifty men, and they had not been able to move nearly as fast as they had hoped. At dawn two scouts crept up to eavesdrop on the conversation of the young women drawing their daily ration of water at a well-head. One of the Bedouin girls was overheard promising that she would soon be able to repay her debt, as there would be plenty of paid work watering the camels of the caravan, which was due two days hence.

Muhammad and the Muslim army were delighted at the news. The trap now seemed well set. But in fact the Muslim scouts had themselves been spied upon. Or, rather, the peculiar dung of their camels, rich in date-stones, had been spotted by an alert man of the Quraysh and identified as the camel-fodder of Medina. The caravan was immediately diverted away from the Wells of Badr. Now, instead of a vulnerable caravan, the Muslims faced the one-thousand-strong relief force of Mecca.

Muhammad was to learn this soon enough from two warriors from Mecca who had been captured as they innocently watered their camels at a well. As they were being questioned, and roughly manhandled by their captors, Muhammad interrupted and, with his courtly greetings and concern for the prisoners' welfare, managed to slip in one or two oblique questions himself. When he learned of the number of animals that were being slaughtered each evening – 'sometimes nine, sometimes ten' – he was able to estimate that the Meccan army numbered between nine hundred and one thousand men. The Muslims were outnumbered by three to one. Should they stand and fight, or retreat to Medina? The army was insistent that the time to fight had come. During the discussion, one of Muhammad's men tactfully asked if their present campsite had been chosen by Muhammad the man or Muhammad the Prophet, as part of a revelation. If it was the former, he had a better proposition. There were several wells in the area: if they blocked the peripheral ones they were presently guarding and moved on to watch over the central wells, they could be certain of controlling the entire water supply in the region. The Meccans would either have to attack them or retreat in disgrace.

On March 17, 624 – the ninth month of the year 2 A.H. (After the Hijra) – the two armies faced each other, in the age-old tradition of Arabian warfare. Then, out of the ranks of the Meccans rode a warrior whose brother had earlier been slain by the Muslims. He began to tear at his clothes while lamenting his murdered kinsman. This was the established practice of the blood feud and it served to excite his fellow warriors in their desire for righteous vengeance. Then, as if in the first steps of some murderous ballet, three champions advanced from the ranks of both armies and began hacking away at each other with broadswords. As the battle lines moved forward, each came within bow-shot of the opposing army. Arrows rained down into the massed ranks. Then, with a cry of *'Ya mansur amit'* (God's ordained warriors will slay), the Muslims rushed upon the Meccans.

Perhaps the Meccans had never taken the small, poorly equipped, badly mounted group of desert raiders as much of a threat. They were, after all, the same group of men they had persecuted and reviled for years. The discipline, passion and fury of the Muslims caught them completely off-guard. The line of the Meccan army broke. The rest of the day was given over to vengeance. Abu Jahl, paramount lord of the Quraysh and persecutor-general of the Muslims, found himself at the mercy of a poor young Muslim shepherd whom he had once publicly struck in the face. Before the sword blows severed his head from his shoulders, Abu Jahl was able to declare, 'Thou hast climbed high indeed, little shepherd.' Bilal also exacted vengeance that day when he spotted his old master and persecutor among the prisoners. Huge ransoms could be expected for such men, but the most notorious enemies of Islam were dragged off to their execution, their corpses flung into a pit with those killed in battle. Fifty Quraysh were buried in the pit and another fifty taken captive.

In the aftermath of the battle, Muhammad assured his comrades that those Muslims who had fallen were martyrs who would be received in paradise. He silenced the disputes about the spoils of battle with a revelation: 'They will question thee concerning the spoils of war. Say: the spoils of war are for God and the messenger.' Having ended the bickering and established a precedent, he finally distributed the spoils when they were just three days from Medina. It was an exultant and heroic force that returned.

☾

After a year in Medina, Muhammad came to realise that the three powerful Jewish tribes – the Beni Nadir, Beni Qurayzah and Beni Qaynuqa – in the oasis of Yathrib posed a deadly threat to the young Islamic community and he determined to rout them. They had failed to accept Islam, and though they were bound by personal treaties to Muhammad, he knew that they would always try to diminish his authority. By their very unbelief they questioned the truth of his revelations and his role as a Prophet. They were also a military threat, for they were rich, well-armed, numerous and accustomed to making their own decisions and pursuing their own interests. Nor were the Jews scattered amongst the oasis so that they could gradually be integrated into the mores of the new community. They dwelt in distinct villages where their cluster of fortified houses appeared like so many castles.

It was vital, however, that the Jewish tribes of Medina should not feel under threat or be allowed to unite. Even individually they were still more than a match for Muhammad's small Muslim army. Collectively they enjoyed overwhelming superiority. They had also established a network of alliances with the surrounding Bedouin tribes. If they had the opportunity to call up their allies all would be lost. If he was to overwhelm the Jewish clans, therefore, Muhammad would have to strike suddenly, without warning and with decisive confidence.

Such an opportunity first presented itself shortly after the victory at the Wells of Badr. A riot in the marketplace outside the fortified village of the Jewish Beni Qaynuqa tribe led to the death of two people. It seems the dispute had begun with a row between a Muslim woman and a Jewish gold merchant. By the clauses of their treaty with Muhammad, he should have been called in to arbitrate the affair, but the Beni Qaynuqa preferred to use the old network of tribal alliances. Muhammad used the incident as an excuse to immediately blockade the entire village with his army. Had they trusted in the force of their own arms, the Jews would surely have held their own. They could muster seven hundred fighting men, half of whom were fully armoured. This was twice the size of the force Muhammad had commanded at Badr. However, the Jewish clans within Medina were too ingrained in the old habits of clan politics to ever confront Muhammad head-on. Instead of trusting in their own strength they called upon a mediator – Ibn Ubayy. Before the arrival of Muhammad, Ibn Ubayy had been the leading figure in Medina. He had embraced Islam but could still pull many strings within the tribal network of the oasis. As a respected chieftain, Muhammad was bound to listen to Ibn Ubayy's appeal on behalf of his old Jewish allies. Muhammad granted the Beni Qaynuqa their lives, but all their property was confiscated.

It was a bold coup. At once Muhammad was seen to be the effective power within the oasis. At a stroke he had equipped his army with weapons and armour. By handing over to them the confiscated houses and gardens of the Jews he also provided the penniless Muslim refugees from Mecca with a means of subsistence.

☾

After the Battle of the Wells of Badr the young Muslim shepherd had been able to present Muhammad with the severed head of Abu Jahl. In Abu Jahl's place Abu Sufyan had emerged as the paramount leader of the Quraysh. Although the Quraysh had lost many men, the Syrian caravan had come through entirely unscathed. At a meeting of the clans it was decided to use the profit from trading to recruit a large army and wreak revenge upon the Muslims. Abu Sufyan's wife Hind set the mood for this studied vengeance by vowing to chew upon the liver of Hamzah, Muhammad's heroic uncle, whom she blamed for the death of both her brother and father at the Wells of Badr. She added a new slave to her household, Washi, an expert huntsman from Abyssinia. He was a renowned marksman, especially adept with the javelin. Hind promised Washi his freedom if he would kill Hamzah for her.

Abu Sufyan decided to switch the routes of the trade caravans. Future caravans would avoid the tracks near the Red Sea and strike out north-east across the desert. To this end Abu Sufyan strengthened the traditional Quraysh alliance with the great Ghatafan tribal confederation and with the Beni Salaim, who grazed the lands between Mecca and Medina. As well as protecting the caravan route the tribes were urged to raid Medina and keep the Muslims on the defensive.

Abu Sufyan also made use of the voice of Ka'b ibn al-Ashraf, a notable Arabic poet who was, through his mother, descended from one of the Jewish tribes of Medina, the Beni Nadir. Ka'b had left

Medina after the Battle of the Wells of Badr in order to offer eulogies to the noble Quraysh who had fallen that day. He fanned the flames of vengeance in Mecca, declaring that since that day there was more honour amongst the fallen than the living, that 'the inside of the earth is better than the outside'. He later returned to Medina and from the safety of the Beni Nadir fortress village issued further verses satirising and lampooning the Prophet and some of his leading companions. Muhammad was infuriated. Ka'b's verses were too well composed, and too pointed, to be ignored.

It is possible that the extreme Muslim sensitivity about the story of David and Bathsheba dates from this time. King David had deliberately sent Bathsheba's husband to his death in the front line of battle, thus leaving Bathsheba free for him to claim. Ka'b might well have used the Prophet's own marriage to Hafsah, widowed at the battle at Badr, to draw unfair parallels between the two men. Years later, Muhammad's son-in-law Ali was still threatening one hundred and sixty lashes to anyone who so much as mentioned the story of David and Bathsheba. The details of Ka'b's clever libels have long been forgotten, but the Muslims would have found such an insult unworthy of an answer, let alone a denial. The stain could only be wiped out in blood. Muhammad prayed, 'O Lord, deliver me from the son of al-Ashraf [Ka'b] however thou wilt, for the evil that he declareth and the poems he declaimeth.' Then he addressed his people, 'Who is for me against the son of al-Ashraf, for he hath done me great injury . . . he wrote poetry against us and none of you shall do this but he shall be put to the sword.' The next time Ka'b left the safety of the fortress of the Beni Nadir, an assassin's knife put an end to his verses for ever.

The caravans of the Quraysh continued to evade the Muslim raiding parties but their luck changed in the fall of 624 when the

Prophet's adopted son Zayd, at the head of a hundred horsemen, seized an entire Iraq-bound caravan at the waterhole of Qaradah. This disaster spurred the Quraysh to take the offensive. Finally, in the new year of 625, Abu Sufyan's preparations were complete. In March (the tenth month of the year 3 A.H.), he led an army of two thousand foot soldiers and two hundred cavalrymen out of Mecca, all mounted on camels for the ten-day crossing to Medina. The Thaqif tribe of Taif contributed a further regiment while the whole host was escorted by Bedouin of the Kinanah tribe.

Muhammad called a council of war. Ibn Ubayy, the old chieftain of Medina, declared, 'Our city is a virgin that has never been deflowered.' He meant to protect the oasis with his three-hundred-strong tribal levy but the more militant of the Muslim warriors were all for leaving the safety of the oasis and repeating their first victory in combat on the open plains. One of them confidently declared, 'We face two things: either God will grant us the mastery over them or else God will grant us martyrdom. I care not which – for there is good in both.' It was just such faith and determination in their cause that had won the day at Badr. In the event Muhammad brokered a compromise deal of sorts, for he had some knowledge of the size of the army that they would face. The Muslim army was to occupy the upper slopes of Mount Uhud which stood to the north of the oasis. From there they could defend Medina, and, if the opportunity presented itself, engage the enemy.

On March 23 at dawn Muhammad, mounted on one of his most sure-footed horses, led the seven-hundred-strong Muslim army out of Medina. He was dressed in full battle armour with a shield across his back and a bow on his shoulder. Muhammad had no love for militarism but he was an excellent judge of character. He awarded his personal sword to a fearsome warrior named Khazraj, who wore a red turban. Even though he had selected this man to be his champion for the day because of his murderous skill with the sword, he could not resist an aside aimed at Khazraj's swaggering pride: 'that is a gait which God detests, save at such a time and such a place'.

A swift march in the light of the early morning gave Muhammad possession of the higher ground. Here he made his dispositions. The army was divided into three divisions and each leader was awarded a great spear from which hung a flag of command. In addition Muhammad ordered that the fifty best archers be formed into a square to guard the rear.

For his part Abu Sufyan called upon the men of Medina to leave in peace, for he had no dispute with them. He declared that his war was with the Muslim exiles from Mecca and with them alone. He had almost certainly heard of the difference of opinion between Ibn Ubayy and Muhammad and now wanted to weaken his enemy by encouraging further division. Even without these tactics the pagan army from Mecca already enjoyed a formidable advantage in numbers.

Next it was the turn of the women of the Quraysh, who struck up a battle hymn from their position in the rear:

> Advance and we embrace you
> And soft carpets spread
> But turn your backs, we leave you,
> Leave you and do not love you.

This was accompanied by drum-beats that matched the determined advance of their men. As the two armies moved ever closer, the women's song was drowned by fierce cries from the ranks: '*Amit amit*', kill, kill. The two armies clashed, and once again it seemed as if the Muslims' impetuous charge would carry the day. The Meccans were pushed back down the hill towards their camp.

In the excitement of battle the fifty Muslim archers the Prophet had so carefully held back rushed down to join in the fray. This was immediately spotted by Khalid, the brilliant young commander of the Meccan cavalry. He wheeled his squadron and fell on the now unprotected rear of the Muslims. The Muslim warriors panicked. They broke rank and fled for the protection of the upper slopes of Mount Uhud. A Qur'anic verse would later chide those warriors who had championed glory in council but had fled the field of battle: 'You wished for death until you met it.'

Great was the slaughter. In the melee of hacking blades stalked the figure of Washi with his javelin. Muhammad's uncle Hamzah was always a conspicuous figure, whether out hunting or as a boisterous drinker, and that day he wore a plume of ostrich feathers on his helmet. Once he had identified a target Washi never missed his mark. With a single javelin throw he won his freedom and then quietly removed himself from the slaughter.

An even greater danger now threatened the Muslims, as the leaders of the Quraysh, in their hour of victory, sought out Muhammad. Twenty valiant men guarded the Prophet with their lives but at one point their ranks were broken and Muhammad was struck down. As he lay sprawled upon the ground it seemed the end of all hope. The Quraysh were jubilant as the news spread around the battlefield.

However, although Muhammad had been knocked to the ground, he had only received a glancing blow, though one strong enough to force a ring in his helmet deep into his cheek. Thought to be dead, but his body protected by the drawn swords of his last remaining bodyguards, he was taken to the safety of the mountain top. The fighting was over by noon, at which point the Quraysh women swarmed on to the battlefield. Hind was led by Washi to the javelin-impaled body of Hamzah. In fulfilment of her vow, Hamzah's abdomen was cut open. She groped around amongst his entrails to identify the liver and then deftly removed the organ, slicing off a mouthful to chew. Hind handed over her necklace as additional reward to Washi and then fashioned for herself the ornaments of vengeance. Hamzah's nose, ears and other bodily extremities were hacked off and strung together to form a necklace of flesh. Elsewhere on the battlefield, other stooped figures were creating their own gory tributes.

Meanwhile, the Muslim force was regrouping on the summit of Mount Uhud. Abu Sufyan rode up to the foothills and bellowed to the vanquished Muslims, 'War goeth by turns – and this is a day for a day. Exalt thyself O Hubal, make prevail thy religion.'

To the Muslims it seemed a miracle that the Prophet had survived, and this did much to raise the army's crushed morale. Then it was noticed that the enemy were abandoning their camp. Muhammad called to a keen-eyed watchman, 'are they riding their horses and leading their camels, or riding their camels and leading their horses?' If they were riding their camels it meant they were heading back to Mecca; if they were riding their horses they were heading into the oasis of Medina. Fortunately for the future of the new faith, the Quraysh were returning to Mecca, probably believing that the Prophet was dead, and the war was therefore over. If Abu Sufyan had attacked Medina at that stage, it is difficult to imagine that anything could have stopped him. He was never again given such an opportunity.

As dusk approached the Muslims were aghast at the carnage, the butchery that had been played upon the bodies of their comrades. Muhammad was so overcome that he promised to revenge each mutilation, blow for blow, upon the Quraysh, though a Qur'anic surah would later supersede this personal cry for vengeance with a call for mercy. Each of the fallen was buried with the Prophet's prayers and the promise of heaven until it seemed that the martyrs laid to rest below Mount Uhud were the true victors of the day.

After the Battle of Uhud there was a lull in the fighting, though later that year a skirmish left the Quraysh in possession of two Muslim prisoners, who were taken back to Mecca. The captives were tied to a cross. Boys whose fathers had been slain at Badr were then given the opportunity to exact their vengeance on the captives. The first prisoner was pierced with forty spear cuts before falling to the final thrust of a lance. Mu'awiya, one of the sons of Abu Sufyan, later remembered being hurled to the ground by his father so that he would not be numbered among those cursed by the dying breath of the tortured prisoner.

However, any Bedouin tribe that tried to take advantage of the defeat of the Muslims soon learned that it had been but a temporary setback. A militantly anti-Islamic chieftain of the Hudhayl clan was struck down by one of Muhammad's assassins and the Beni Asad, confidently planning their own raid on Medina, were struck first by Muslim horsemen. A march in force through the territory of the Ghatafan similarly put a stop to any plans they might have been hatching themselves.

In Medina, meanwhile, Muhammad bided his time. While meeting with the clan leaders of the Beni Nadir one day, the Prophet, who had been leaning against a wall, suddenly stood up and left the company. He had been warned (or felt an intuition) that they were about to attempt his assassination. It may well have been some blood feud lingering from the affair concerning Ka'b, the poet. Whatever the cause of the rumour, the Prophet acted with decisive speed.

He ordered his Muslim forces to surround the fortress village of the Beni Nadir so that it was cut off from the rest of the oasis. Just like the Beni Qaynuqa before them, the Beni Nadir put their trust in the old system of tribal alliances rather than in their own resources. They were unaware that a new order had quietly replaced the old. Once their tribal allies proved unable to relieve the three-week-long

Muslim siege, the Beni Nadir sued for peace. They were allowed to carry away all their portable possessions and livestock, though they agreed to abandon all their property, houses and lands, their weapons and armour to the Prophet.

To compensate for their losses, the Beni Nadir elected to leave Medina in style. Their women paraded all their finery, dressed in layers of embroidered robes set off by sparkling jewels and twinkling anklets, to the sound of fifes, tambourines and lilting song. No one could remember ever having seen so much glittering wealth in a single day. On the other hand, the Beni Nadir were forced to leave substantial resources behind them. Once again the Prophet was in a position to reward his followers with gifts of gardens, houses and well-tended orchards.

☾

The fifth year after the hijra, the summer of 626, was a difficult time for the people of central Arabia. Drought left the grazing grounds parched and the herds depleted. Nevertheless Muhammad responded to a public challenge to meet the Quraysh in another battle and led his army out to the old battlefield at the Wells of Badr. The Muslims gained some credit in the eyes of the Bedouin tribes for facing the challenge. The tribes also noticed that the Muslims had increased their army to a force of fifteen hundred well-armed men who held their camp with admirable discipline for eight days. The Quraysh, although they had marched out of Mecca, unaccountably never showed up. Abu Sufyan publicly blamed the drought. This was only half convincing, though in truth the Muslim army still possessed only a fraction of the camels that the army of the Quraysh travelled with and so were more capable of coping with the lack of grazing. Whatever the reasons, the Quraysh felt some shame, which meant that war was inevitable the following year.

Around this time Muhammad took another wife. Unwittingly entering the house of Zayd, his adopted son, one day the Prophet saw for himself the beauty of his forty-year-old daughter-in-law, Zaynab. As he hurried away Muhammad was heard to murmur, 'Glory be to Him who disposeth of men's hearts!' Zayd soon divined that Muhammad had become entranced by Zaynab's beauty and at once offered to divorce his wife. They had not been getting on well but in truth Zayd would have done anything to please his adopted father. The prospect obviously interested Muhammad, though he refused again when Zayd repeated the offer. The Prophet was known to disapprove of divorce. There was an additional problem – Zaynab was Muhammad's daughter-in-law and therefore could not lawfully be married to him. In addition, the Qur'an prohibited men from having more than four wives, and demanded that all wives be treated equally.

It was then that a revelation came upon Muhammad that swept away all obstacles: 'We have made lawful to you . . . women who give themselves to you and whom you wished to take in marriage. This privilege is yours alone, being granted to no other believer . . . You may put off any of your wives you please and take to bed any of them you please' (surah Al-Ahzab, no. 33, verse 50). The same revelation also specifically changes the rules of adoption; and it instructs that the Prophet's wives be addressed by believers from behind a curtain, that no one shall 'wed his wives after him', and that they should 'draw their veils close around them'. These verses were meant to give the Prophet's wives protection from the unending stream of visitors, but later generations of clerics and rulers took these verses out of context and applied them to all Muslim women.

This revelation can be interpreted as showing the intimate concern of God for his Prophet and how the day-to-day dilemmas of early Islam allowed for the creation of practical rules for future ethical behaviour. But to modern Western eyes this incident is often the point at which their personal sympathy with the Prophet falters. It is as if finally, Muhammad's egalitarianism found its limits, as he allowed himself a dispensation not offered to all the other believers. In every other detail of his life he retained the habits and generous nobility of the poor and could truly assert that 'humility is my pride'. Women were his one great pleasure as a man. Muhammad, of course, never claimed to be anything more than a man. Indeed, compared to some of the great prophets of the past, like Solomon with his courts filled with concubines, his marital behaviour was quite modest.

Muhammad always insisted on the absolute spiritual equality of the sexes. The Qur'an often uses inclusive words like *insan* – human being – and *bashar* – humankind – or concepts like Children of Adam that specifically include both sexes. This is emphatically reiterated in many individual verses such as 'I do not allow your deeds – be you male or female – to go to waste. You are of each other' (surah Al-Imran, no. 3, verse 195), 'Whosoever, male or female, does good deeds and is a believer We will give unto them a good life' (surah Al-Nahl, no. 16, verse 97) and 'O people we have created you of a male and female, and made you into nations and tribes that you may get to know one another' (surah Al-Hujurut, no. 49, verse 13).

On the question of married life, the Qur'an is emphatic that a husband is the head of the family – but with that came a financial obligation to provide food and clothing. The clause 'that one extra degree that was granted to man' may be a reference to the traditional chivalric duty of an Arab man to protect his women – even at the cost of his life. Most famously Muhammad assured Muslim women of their right to hold property, and to recover their dowry should they divorce.

☾

Abu Sufyan's preparations for an assault on Medina in the spring of 627 (the eleventh month of the year 5 A.H.) were meticulous. He had been in contact with the exiled Beni Nadir, who were prepared to mortgage all their jewels in order to regain their lands in Medina and exact revenge upon the Prophet. Their fortune, combined with that of the Quraysh, helped to marshal an impressive army of tribal allies. The Beni Asad and the Ghatafan offered two thousand warriors; seven hundred more came from the Beni Salaim; the Quraysh and their local allies fielded an army of four thousand warriors and three hundred cavalrymen. Though the Muslim force had grown stronger in numbers and equipment, they would be swamped by this vast army. Abu Sufyan's emissaries had also been unusually discreet. News customarily leaked across Arabia with extraordinary speed, but in this case the Prophet had just ten days' warning of the expected attack and of the vast numbers that had mustered. This time there were no tactical arguments within the Muslim ranks. Defence seemed the only possibility. But how could the vast perimeter of the oasis be guarded?

Fortunately for the Muslims a military engineer emerged from within their ranks. Salman al-Farisi had been born outside the great Persian city of Isfahan to a devout Zoroastrian family. He had converted to Christianity (presumably within the Nestorian Church) and had pursued his studies by travelling from region to region. On one such journey he joined an Arab caravan but was seized by his guides and sold as a slave to one of the Jewish landowners of Medina. The moment the Prophet arrived in Medina, Salman had been immediately drawn, like a moth to a flame, to Islam, although he remained a slave. The Prophet organised a collection amongst the Muslim community to ransom Salman. The price his owner had demanded, forty ounces of gold and an orchard of three hundred newly planted palms, was deliberately inflated but the Muslims matched it. And now they were able to reap the reward for their sacrifices.

The engineer Salman al-Farisi designed the defence of Medina, a moat that encircled the central belt of the oasis, and in doing so became greatly honored. Everyone acclaimed him: the Meccan Emigrants, the Medina Helpers, even the household of the Prophet. Salman's defence made use of every feature of the land within Medina's boundaries, turning the existing fortress-like houses of the villages and outcrops of rock into watchtowers. Every man in Medina laboured on its construction, working in shifts for six days on end. Muhammad enthusiastically took his turn in the digging, and the sight of their Prophet labouring away in his distinctive red cloak, his head covered in dust, always redoubled the energy of his companions. The Prophet ordered all the outlying crops to be harvested and the evacuation of any districts not protected by the moat. Three thousand men watched over the defence of Medina, while a force of hand-picked cavalry patrolled the streets. These men kept a watch for any potential defectors, maintained morale within the oasis and were prepared to race to the support of any section that needed it. The Prophet commanded from the front, pitching his red-leather campaign tent in a strategic position on the foot of Mount Sal, so that his men would be inspired by his presence.

Thus the vast army led by the Quraysh was stalled outside Medina. At night their camp, with its hundreds of campfires dotting the outskirts of the oasis like the stars in the sky, looked awesome and irresistible. However, the actual fighting that took place was desultory, restricted to one or two attempts to storm the moat at its weakest point. Reports of the large number of horses wounded during these attacks may testify to Salman's use of stakes in a vertical inner wall or to spikes buried in the sandy floor. Although the descriptions are sparse, Salman's moat may have borrowed many technical details from Persian frontier defences. We know that both the northern Persian frontier (against the nomads of Central Asia) and part of their southern Arabian frontier were most efficiently guarded in this period by great sections of moat.

In the end the siege became a test of endurance. The Quraysh were quickly running out of provisions, while the Muslims were well supplied by the oasis. After two weeks a storm blew in from the east, an extraordinary gale that flattened the tents of besieged and besiegers alike, and then soaked the combatants with driving rain. Morale on both sides hit rock bottom. The Bedouin allies of the Quraysh were the first to leave, though the lords of Mecca were not far behind them.

Muhammad, aware that his own men were also near breaking point after weeks of work followed by ceaseless garrison duty through day and night, also gave the order to break camp. As soon as he had given the command his men abandoned their stations beside the moat and began streaming back to the welcoming arms of their wives. Suddenly Muhammad was seized with a terrible suspicion. What if the enemy had only pretended to withdraw? They might suddenly reappear on the horizon. He gave a counter-order for his soldiers to return to their posts at the moat but the Muslim soldiers only had thoughts of home. The Prophet then understood the limits of military authority. Rather than rage at the ill discipline of his men, he broke into sympathetic laughter, sharing their feelings about the grimness of war. To Muhammad, necessary conflict was never to be avoided, but the goal of war was always peace.

Once the Muslims had rested a while, there was work that needed to be done. During the siege the Beni Qurayzah, the last of the three great Jewish clans of Medina, had behaved like an independent third party, receiving foreign agents from the Bedouin tribes and sending out emissaries to the enemy. They had threatened the very safety of Medina with their equivocal status. It was true that they had not actually gone over to the army of the Quraysh, but it had been a dangerously close thing. The Prophet now ordered his army to place their fortress village under siege. For twenty-five days they held out. Like the two other Jewish communities before them, they seem to have been paralysed by Muhammad's decisiveness, neither capable of fighting for their liberty nor converting to Islam. They wished to retain their status as a free and wealthy clan, independent of any authority, but the Muslims had determined that those days were over. The Beni Qurayzah offered to pay tribute. This Muhammad refused. They were asked to embrace Islam. This they refused. Having secured neither good terms nor the assurance of a glorious death, they eventually decided on an unconditional surrender, leaving themselves entirely at the mercy of their conqueror. First the men were led out, their arms tied behind their backs, and they were marched to a guarded camp. Then the women and children filed out and were marshalled to a different site. Next their goods and armour were taken out of the village and neatly stacked. Their jars of wine, rare vintages fermented from the raisin-like grapes of the oasis and the season's cloudy brew of date sap, were poured into the parched earth. It would not be the only liquid of the Beni Qurayzah that the dry soil would soak up.

Muhammad was fully aware of the traditions of war. If a fortified place was stormed in battle it was normal practice for the men to be slaughtered, the women to be enslaved and the victorious soldiers to seize all movable property. In a negotiated surrender the terms could vary enormously. In the past, while the Beni Nadir swaggered out with all their possessions, the Beni Qaynuqa had just escaped with their lives. Both Jewish clans had left Medina to become staunch allies of the Quraysh. Indeed, the Beni Nadir had played an important role in assembling the vast army that had recently threatened Medina. If the Muslims spared the Beni Qurayzah, they too would only go on to strengthen their enemy the following year.

However, the clan of the Aws of Medina, old pre-Islamic allies of the Beni Qurayzah, now petitioned Muhammad on their behalf. He at once acceded to their request, asking them if they would be satisfied 'if one of yourselves pronounced judgement'. It was a generous offer, which was at once taken up. The Prophet sent for one of the earliest Muslim converts from the Aws clan, Sa'd ibn Mu'adh, who was being nursed in a tent that had been pitched in the Prophet's courtyard. Sa'd had received a mortal wound during the defence of Medina, and being a dying man made his words doubly honourable. As a devout believer Sa'd also knew that he too would soon be judged. He had no hesitation in condemning the men of the Beni Qurayzah to death and the women and children to slavery. The next morning narrow trenches were dug along the breadth of the old marketplace. Then, one by one, the seven hundred bound men were led down, decapitated with a sword stroke and their bodies thrown into the trenches. The slaughter continued all day and the last batch was executed by torchlight. The brutality of this act sent shock waves throughout Arabia.

The body count in the pitched battles of tribal Arabia seldom mounted to more than a dozen. Even in the ferocious battles fought between the Muslims and the Quraysh the dead on both sides had numbered only around a hundred. Individuals might perish, but the clan always lived on to fight another day. Sa'd's sentence had completely obliterated an entire clan. Nor was Muhammad displeased with the result – he responded to Sa'd's decision with the valedictory, 'thou has judged with the judgement of God'.

With the massacre of the Beni Qurayzah in May 627, the Muslims suddenly revealed themselves to the world as an implacable enemy. They were a force to be reckoned with, a power at once honourable to its friends and terrible to its enemies. There is also the politics of mercy to ponder on. For by the inescapable logic of human nature, mercy is only really appreciated if it has first been combined with fear. If the Prophet had not revealed at least one instance of implacable judgement the clemency that he would later show (at Mecca, for instance) could have been mistaken as weakness.

In Medina that night there was, to borrow the words from the gospel of Matthew, 'but one voice heard, lamentation, and weeping, and great mourning'. The women of the Beni Qurayzah were weeping for their men, 'and would not be comforted, because they are not'. Even as they lay bound before the trenches, the men of the Beni Qurayzah were aware that conversion to Islam would have saved them from the executioner's sword wielded by Ali but they all found death preferable to forsaking the inheritance of their forefathers. Zabir ibn Bata, one of the leaders of the Beni Qurayzah, found that he alone of his clan had been pardoned. A Muslim whose life Zabir had saved many years before had returned the debt by interceding on his behalf with the Prophet. Zabir first made certain that this pardon extended to the women of his family, then demanded that he be led down to the bloody trenches of the old marketplace and executed. He had no wish to live after the death of his clan, 'for now they are gone, there is no good in life'.

After the slaughter Muhammad took Rayhanah, a beautiful widow of the Beni Qurayzah, into his household. Although she converted from Judaism to Islam she begged to be kept as a concubine rather than enter his house freely as a wife. She felt easier being a captive, albeit one resigned to her fate, than entering as a free woman the household of the man who had presided over the destruction of her clan.

The Prophet now ruled Medina in both body and spirit.

☾

Five months after the siege of Medina had ended, a small Muslim raiding force of a hundred and seventy horses, once more under the command of Zayd, the Prophet's adopted son, seized an entire caravan returning from Syria to Mecca. With every passing month, the Muslims seemed to gain in standing amongst the Bedouin tribes of the desert. Mutual respect was a vital ingredient. A Muslim force captured Juwayriyah, the daughter of a powerful Bedouin sheikh, and she was ransomed by her father. Only after this exchange had been honourably settled would the Bedouin sheikh contemplate discussing a political alliance with the Prophet; this soon extended into kinship, when Juwayriyah was returned to Medina as a new wife for Muhammad.

On another raiding expedition, the speed of the military column was slowed somewhat by the presence of Aisha who dropped behind the line of march and became lost. Fortunately she was found, but much was made of the fact that her rescuer was a handsome young man named Safwah. Tongues wagged in Medina and from mere gossip this incident became a scandal. Aisha found herself in disgrace, though she was never formally accused of adultery. Fortunately Muhammad had implicit faith in young Safwah – 'he knew naught but good of the man' – and though Aisha was much too affronted to say anything on her own behalf, a Qur'anic revelation eventually cleared her of any impropriety. She later recalled the incident: 'he was seized with the pangs that seized him at such times, and as it were pearls of sweat dripped from him, although it was a wintry day. Then, when he was relieved of the pressure, he said in a voice that vibrated with

gladness: 'O Aisha, praise God, for He hath declared thee inno-
cent.' Something of Aisha's unquenchable spirit can be divined by
her response to her mother's advice that she go and thank the
Prophet. 'No by God, I will not rise and go to him, and I will
praise none but God.'

This surah, while solving a particular personal crisis, was also
typical of the revelations at Medina in that it established rules for
future conduct. Any subsequent accusations of adultery (which
was a grave offence) had to be substantiated by the sworn evidence
of four eyewitnesses, while false or malicious accusations were to
be punished with a whipping.

This was also the time when early Islam turned its back on
alcohol. An earlier revelation urged believers not to pray while
drunk (traditionally believed to be a reaction to the behaviour of
the Prophet's bibulous uncle, Hamzah). Later revelations, while
showing an understanding of man's attraction to wine, were even
more specific. Surah Al-Maidah states that, 'wine and intoxicants
and gambling and the arrow game [of divination] are unclean
devil's work. Keep clear of them that you may meet with success'
(no. 5, verse 90). The Qur'an also declares 'they will ask you concerning wine and gambling. Say, "There is great sin and profit in
them for man. But their evil is greater than their utility"' (surah Al-
Baqarah, no. 2, verse 219). Ever since, if alcohol is consumed in
the Muslim world – it is officially forbidden – it is done in private.
Whenever possible wine is avoided (owing to a strict loyalty to the
letter, rather than the spirit, as it were, of the Qur'an) and beer or
some form of grain spirit consumed instead.

☽

Muhammad had become a powerful ruler. Despite the concerns of
diplomacy and leadership, however, matters of the spirit always
remained an absolute priority to him, as he dramatically proved in

the spring of 628 when he embarked on what looked like a reckless gesture of faith.

Muhammad decided to march into Mecca, with the hope of
enduring hostilities once and for all. He was determined to perform the three-day pilgrimage. This was not part of Mecca's annual
Hajj festival but part of Umra, the lesser pilgrimage, that could be
performed at any time of the year. Muhammad marched not at the
head of an army but with a thousand of his most devout followers,
protected not by armour but by two pieces of unstitched cloth.
They carried their swords, but no lances or bows, and so were
essentially defenceless against a determined foe. Ahead of the
Muslims walked seventy unsaddled, garlanded camels, marking
them as destined for sacrifice. They set out during Dhu al Qaada,
one of the months of the sacred truce that governed all the tribes
of Arabia. Despite this protection there were many reasons for a
determined pagan to exclude them from its provisions. Not only
had the Muslims broken the truce once but arguably their whole
break with the old deities put them outside the pagan traditions.
This fear was one that was shared by many of the more recent allies
of Muhammad, especially the Bedouin. They had all made their
excuses for not joining this march of faith. They expected no plun-
der from it and saw only danger.

Indeed, the Quraysh were determined that he should not pass.
At the way station of Usfan, Muhammad learned that a solid
screen of Meccan horsemen barred the road eight miles to the
south. Rather than force an early confrontation, he decided to
take a detour, leading his pilgrims across the barren rocky slopes to
reach a little known wellhead in the valley of Hudaibiya, about
eight miles from Mecca. Here he pitched camp. His head was
now firmly in the lion's mouth and he waited to see if it would be
bitten off.

Muhammad was visited in his camp by Hulais, a chieftain of

the Beni Kinanah tribe, and by Urwah, of the Thaqif tribe of Taif. Both were key allies of the Quraysh, but were less personally involved in the war and could put matters in perspective. Not for a second did Urwah show any deference to the Prophet (indeed he tried to clasp him by the beard as if he were an equal sheikh) but his alert, court-trained eyes took in a thousand telling details. He noticed how the followers of Muhammad fought over the dirty water in which the Prophet had washed and how they lowered their eyes in his presence. The Muslims might have been recruited from the poor of many tribes, but when Urwah returned to the Quraysh he reported: 'I have visited Chosroes, King of Persia, at his court, the Roman Caesar in Constantinople and the Negus of Abyssinia in his own country, but never have I seen a king treated by his subjects with the veneration which Muhammad receives from his companions.'

Muhammad had sketched out a possible peace deal to Hulais and Urwah but he also decided to send his own ambassador to Mecca. He named two candidates, but for once his followers had a better grasp of political reality. They advised Muhammad that of them all only 'Uthman ibn 'Affan would be acceptable to the Quraysh. Not only was 'Uthman a man of peace, but he was of noble stock, and was in fact a second cousin to Abu Sufyan, as well as son-in-law twice over to Muhammad. They were right: 'Uthman was received in Mecca with every mark of respect, but he was also assured that the Quraysh would not let Muhammad enter the Kaaba. The Quraysh issued a personal invitation to 'Uthman to visit the Kaaba but he declared 'I maketh not my rounds of the House until the Messenger of God maketh his.'

During 'Uthman's absence Muhammad decided to confirm his relationship with his followers. He knew that any treaty he now made with the Quraysh would sorely test them. Muhammad sat against the trunk of an acacia tree that was just coming into leaf so that it cast a dappled shade on the ground. One by one the believers clasped his right hand and declared, 'O Messenger of God, I pledge thee mine allegiance unto that which is in thy soul' – a beautiful vow that was made up on the spur of the moment by the first believer to step before him.

Thus fortified, the Prophet agreed to sign a ten-year truce with the Quraysh, since known as the Truce, or Treaty of Hudaibiya. His followers ground their teeth as ambassadors of the Quraysh refused to sign any document that addressed Muhammad as the Prophet of God. The Muslims were forbidden from taking in any fugitives from Mecca, but the Quraysh were allowed to harbour refugees from Muslim lands. This accord was immediately put to the test. A young Muslim who had just escaped from years of imprisonment in Mecca to the safety of the camp of the Prophet had meekly to be surrendered to his captors. The pilgrims were also appalled that the Prophet had agreed not to enter Mecca that year. 'Umar, one of the most loyal and faithful of followers, faced his master in a potentially ugly confrontation: 'Are you not God's Prophet . . . Are we not in the right and our enemies in the wrong . . . Then why yield in such a lowly way against the honour of our religion?' These were exactly the questions being asked throughout the Muslim camp.

When the Quraysh ambassadors had departed, the Prophet rose and commanded his followers: 'Rise and sacrifice your animals and shave your heads.' They were being asked to perform the holy rituals of the pilgrimage as if their campsite at Hudaibiya was the sacred landscape of Mecca. But they remained seated; not a man moved. Again the Prophet ordered them: 'Rise and sacrifice your animals and shave your heads.' Again, no one moved a muscle. After a third command had failed, Muhammad turned and, in sorrow, entered his tent. Fortunately, the Prophet benefitted from a woman's council. One of his wives, Umm Salamah, had travelled

with him in a howdah, a canopy raised over a camel, and now sat
in the privacy of his tent. She advised Muhammad to go out
immediately in silence past the seated Muslims and perform the
very actions he had commanded. Muhammad thus descended
into the valley and approached his own camel, garlanded in readi-
ness for the sacrifice. He prepared the noble beast for the knife
with the blessing 'In the Name of God, God is most great' (*Bism-
Allah, Allahu Akbar*). The spell of mutiny was broken. Every single
man rose to follow the example of their leader, just as Muhammad
had echoed the example of Abraham.

8

Victory and Magnanimity: Muhammad Converts Arabia to Islam

After the sacred rituals had been completed in the valley of Hudaibiya, the Muslims broke camp. The column of weary pilgrims turned their backs on the road to Mecca and took the trail north to Medina. It was March and the brief but intense springtime in the desert would normally have lightened their mood. Instead, there was a sullen air about the caravan. Since the signing of the ten-year truce with the Quraysh there was no longer any threat of an ambush or a pitched battle. The scouts still rode out ahead of the main party, but no one now feared the sudden descent of horsemen from a gully, or a shower of arrows falling from a rock face. They should have felt relief. Instead they felt exhausted and irritated. It had been a time of great tension; it was as if the life force had been drained from them.

As they marched they were able to reflect on the true nature of this pilgrimage. They had been deserted by all their new converts and allies amongst the Bedouin tribes, but it was little wonder. It must have looked as if the Muslims marching towards Mecca were going as so many lambs to the slaughter. As they searched further into their souls, they realised that they too had not been sure they would survive the pilgrimage. Deep down they had expected some violent confrontation, some resolution that would either have seen them as masters of the Kaaba or striding after their beloved master, the Prophet of God, as he led them as martyrs into heaven. Instead they had never got near Mecca and now had to endure the insulting language of this wretched treaty. Who wanted a truce, a truce that would allow the rich caravans of the Quraysh to pass by Medina unmolested, that would put an end to the thrill of raids and missionary expeditions deep into the desert?

Muhammad was travelling apart from the main caravan. When the caravan was about halfway back to Medina a messenger was spotted galloping back from the Prophet.

This man diligently sought out 'Umar from the ranks and escorted him away. Ever since 'Umar's outspoken defiance of the Prophet, some sort of confrontation had been expected. All eyes followed the pair as they made their way forward. 'Umar, a man of incorrigible strength, a titan among warriors, whose convictions were as firmly held as the hilt of his sword and who was acknowledged as one of the chief adornments of Islam, now looked abject and powerless.

But when the caravan eventually caught up with him 'Umar appeared radiant. The Prophet had uttered a new revelation, a new gift from God. They heard the thirty verses of the victory surah for themselves after the evening prayers. This surah expressed all their collective fears, desires and dissent. To hear it must have been an extraordinary but deeply disturbing moment for the common believer. It began: 'We have given you a glorious victory, so that God may forgive your past and future sin' – a powerful definition that a truce, even if it brought only partial peace, must be saluted by Muslims as a victory and that the object of all warfare must always be the creation of peace. The surah also expressed a firm confidence in the future: 'He has caused you to do as you have done that He may bring the believers, both men and women, into gardens watered by running streams.' The Muslims should be proud of their ordeal: 'God was well pleased with the faithful when they swore allegiance to you under the tree. He knew what was in their hearts. Therefore He sent down tranquillity upon them.' The word used in the Qur'an for 'tranquillity' is *sakeenah*, which has strong connotations with the Hebrew *shekheenah*, the Holy Presence.

Here was honour indeed. To have been present at Hudaibiya was later to become the proudest boast that a veteran Muslim could make. It had been a testing time indeed: a test of fortitude as well as faith, of forbearance and of trusting in fate.

By the time the pilgrims returned to Medina their spirits had soared, though they were physically exhausted. Even the Prophet was affected. A sorcerer in Medina named Labid used this moment of weakness to cast a spell on Muhammad. He acquired some of his hair. This was not a difficult thing to do: the Prophet had had his luxuriant locks shaved off during the sacrifice at Hudaibiya, whereupon they were pounced on by his followers who treasured them as relics and distributed them amongst the faithful. Labid tied a strand of the Prophet's hair into eleven knots while his daughters breathed spells on to the hair as each knot was tied. Thus bewitched, the hair was then enclosed within the pollen-rich male flower of the date palm and flung down a deep and obscure well. The spells sapped the vitality and appetite of the Prophet, and his memory started playing tricks on him. Fortunately he was able to divine the source of the problem, and took to chanting two of the blessings that had been revealed to him during the years of persecution in Mecca.

Say: I take refuge in the Lord of daybreak
from the evil of that which He hath created,
and from the evil of dusk when it dimmeth into night,
and from the evil of the women who breathe upon
    knots,
and from the evil of the envier when he envieth.

                       (Surah Al-Farlaq, no. 113)

Say: I take refuge in the Lord of men,
The King of men,
the God of men,
from the evil of the stealthy whisperer,
who whispereth in the breasts of men;
from jinn and from men.

                      (Surah Al-Nas, no. 114)

These short surahs are the great counter-spells of the Islamic world. They can be recited at any time – while wandering down an empty alleyway at dusk, when entering an ancient cistern, upon overhearing malicious gossip, or when repelling the evil eye unwittingly cast by some ill-considered public praise. Within Islam there is nothing half-hearted about belief in spells, witchcraft and the spirit world of the jinn. They are testified to in the Qur'an. They are known to exist, a parallel universe that is as powerful as it is mortally dangerous to the soul.

Once he had recovered his strength, what did the Prophet do to the sorcerer? Did he torture him on the rack like the Dominicans of the Spanish Inquisition? Did he order him to be walked through four sleepless nights like Cromwell's witch-finders? Did he demand the names of his accomplices under the threat of an *auto-da-fé*? Did he launch a whole-scale purge like that of the puritans of Salem? That was not Muhammad's way.

Having confessed to the Prophet that he had taken a bribe to cast a spell on him, Labid walked away a free man. Muhammad's only action was to order the old well, now poisoned by witchcraft, to be blocked up and a new one dug in its stead.

There were other, more pressing political concerns to attend to. 'Uthman, with the experience of his embassy to Mecca behind him, had reported that there seemed to be a weakening amongst some of the Quraysh in their opposition to Islam. In any case the Prophet now felt it was safe to recall one of the last groups of Muslim refugees from the sanctuary in Abyssinia. He also took the middle-aged Umm Habibah, the widow of one of his cousins, as a wife. Habibah was not only a steadfast believer who deserved a good home, she was also the daughter of Abu Sufyan. The Prophet was building bridges for a lasting peace to replace the truce.

The Prophet judiciously upheld the new truce with Mecca, though it always remained unpopular with his followers. Returning Muslim refugees back to their Quraysh captors was always a loathsome business. In the case of Abu Basir, however, it brought unexpected benefits. Having been faithfully returned to his captors by the Prophet, the young Abu Basir managed to kill his guard and escape. When he reappeared at Medina, the representative from Mecca begged to be excused from the dangers of escorting Abu Basir. While Muhammad had proved himself honorable for upholding every clause of the truce, he had also unwittingly gained himself a guerrilla band, for Abu Basir became a highwayman on the Red Sea coast route.

It was also at this time that the Prophet began corresponding with the great powers surrounding Arabia. There is a certain amount of confusion in the sources about the exact chronology and destinations of these first diplomatic letters outlining the Muslim faith to the neighbours of the Arabs. Correspondence between Muhammad and the Negus of Abyssinia, or at least the

Muslims at his court at Aksum, stretched back over decades. The letter he sent to a governor of Egypt, one Muqawqis, has actually survived. This shrunken scrap of parchment is preserved behind glass in the holy treasury within the third courtyard of the old Topkapi Palace in Istanbul. It reads:

> From Muhammad the servant and Prophet of Allah, to Muqawqis, the leader of the Coptic tribe. There is safety and security for those believers who follow the correct path. Therefore, I invite you to accept Islam. If you accept it, you shall find security, save your throne, and gain twice as much reward for having introduced Islam to your followers. If you refuse this invitation, let the sin of calamity which awaits your followers be upon you. You too are People of the Book; therefore let us come to a word common between us that we worship none but Allah and shall not equalise anything with him. Let us not abandon Allah and take others for lords other than him. If you do not consent to this invitation, bear witness that we are Muslims.

Muqawqis has never been definitively identified, for it might be the Arab version of an administrative title rather than a given name. Some historians consider him to be the viceroy of Egypt, some the Byzantine count in charge of the garrison on the Nile; others see him as the Persian governor who administered Egypt between 616 and 628.

The letter to Muqawqis brought a polite but evasive response, though there was no mistaking the regard in which the Prophet was now held by his neighbours. Accompanying the reply from Muqawqis were one thousand measures of gold, twenty fine robes, a mule, a she-ass and Mariyah and Sirin, two Coptic slave girls accompanied by a eunuch guard. Muhammad, with his usual disregard for possessions, passed these gifts on to his followers though he kept Mariyah as his concubine. She was pleasing to him, so much so that his other wives began to complain that he visited her day and night. Soon Mariyah found herself carrying Muhammad's child.

It is probable that in this period the Prophet also began to correspond with the Persian governor of the Yemen about Islam. There are at least three possible dates for his official letter to the Emperor Heraclius who ruled the entire Byzantine Empire from his headquarters in northern Syria for the seven years between 629 and 636. The year 628 is a possible starting date for this correspondence, though it was a time of confusion in the Near East. A Persian army had penetrated deep within the Byzantine Empire and held Syria and Egypt, while another Persian army sat hungrily looking at the walls of Constantinople from the other side of the Bosphorus. In December 627 Heraclius smashed a Persian army outside the ruins of Nineveh and went on to set afire the Persian imperial palace in January 628. By the summer of 628 the two empires were officially at peace, though the final repatriation of troops would take another year or so.

The synchronicity of events between the world outside Arabia and Arabia itself is uncanny. The struggle between Persia and Byzantium had begun very slowly in 610 with the deposition of the usurper Phocas from the palace at Constantinople and the Persian occupation of Antioch the next year. 610 was the year that the first revelation came upon the Prophet. The years 612–22 witnessed a steady escalation in the disagreements between the Prophet and the Quraysh, just as the relationship between Heraclius of Byzantium and Chosroes of Persia deteriorated. From 622 to 628 was the period of total war between the Persian and Byzantine Empires. This dovetails exactly with the beginning of the Muslim war against Mecca, from 622 – when Muhammad fled to Medina –

to the truce of 628. It is as if these two very different spheres were working together in some hidden harmony, a harmony that worked heavily in favour of Islam. For without the distraction of the six-year war between the two empires, without their mutual destruction of the Ghassanid and Lakhmid Arab kingdoms, the history of conflict between Mecca and Medina might well have taken a very different course. It is difficult to imagine that in a time of peace either the Ghassanids on the Syrian frontier or the Lakhmids on the frontier of Iraq would have tolerated the interruption to the lucrative caravan trade by the six-year war between Mecca and Medina. But it is easy to see which side they would have backed: the respectable Quraysh merchants or the Medina-based raiders? A single military adviser (a young Byzantine captain seconded to the desert front or a Persian military engineer) could have transformed the outcome for the Quraysh after either the Battle of Uhud, the siege of Medina or during the pilgrimage of 628. Instead Arabia was left to work out its own destiny at this crucial time.

Just ten weeks after returning from Hudaibiya, the Prophet announced his intention of attacking the great oasis of Khaybar, known as the garden of the Hijaz. It was a much more substantial settlement than Medina and stood seventy miles to the north, on the edge of a great volcanic massif. No one who had not been present on the pilgrimage march was permitted to join this expedition. The Prophet was consciously trying to balance the tribulations of the spring with the rewards to be gained in the autumn. In doing so he greatly reduced the potential size of the expeditionary force under his command, though he seems to have been charged with an inner certainty of victory. His old enemies in Mecca were less sure. If they had failed to make so much as a dent in Medina with their five-thousand-strong army, how would the Muslims fare with just one thousand men against a much wealthier and more populous oasis?

News of the planned Muslim assault soon reached Khaybar. Keeping absolute secrecy is difficult in Arabia. Before the army left they would need to fill one thousand goatskins with water, sharpen a thousand swords, borrow camels and call in the horses from their grazing grounds. Muhammad led the troops north, but shared some of the military command with Ali, his son-in-law, who had been given a great new battle standard, the eagle, made from a black cloak belonging to Aisha. The army halted in a mountain pass to look down upon a green jewel beckoning on the near horizon, the lush oasis gardens of Khaybar, shaded from the full force of the sun by the rippling fronds of palm trees. Jutting out from this sea of green were the outlines of dozens of hamlets. From this vantage point Muhammad gathered his men and prayed over them: 'O God, we ask Thee for the good of this village and the good of its people and the good of what is in it, and we take refuge in Thee from its evil and the evil that is in it.' Perhaps he was haunted by the knowledge that the old days of purity and simplicity were numbered. Wealth, success and status would now descend upon the nascent Muslim community to replace the years of poverty, persecution and piety. Even in Medina he had watched the slow trickle of the numbers of hypocrites – those whom he perceived to have embraced Islam for the temporal advantages it now gave – with dread. As Islam grew into a stronger force under his canny leadership, this trickle would soon become a stream. Then he added, 'Forward, with God's blessing.'

Khaybar was, like Medina, a disparate group of hamlets dominated by a handful of wealthy Jewish clans. Even forewarned of the Muslim invasion they had failed to unite, either to field an army in defence or to coordinate their tactics. Though the Muslims were not especially competent in siege tactics, they knew enough to concentrate their forces, to cut off water supplies and to batter their way into the walled hamlets, the four-square *ksar* and the prestigious free-standing tower houses, known as *utum*. Unlike those in Medina, however, the Jewish clans here fought back, even issuing challenges to the Muslim heroes to face them in single combat. They knew that if they could hold the Muslims off for long enough the oasis would be saved by the arrival of their powerful allies, the Bedouin Ghatafan tribe. Muhammad was always a greater diplomat than a tactician. Somehow he contrived to ensure that the powerful Ghatafan were put out of action that season. Pious accounts would describe how a voice from heaven warned the Ghatafan warriors that their flocks were in danger, though it seems as likely that the Prophet might also have arranged for one of his Bedouin allies to lead a simultaneous raid into the Ghatafan grazing grounds.

By chance the Muslim forces discovered a mangonel – a war engine used for hurling stones – in the store-rooms of a captured stronghold. This was hauled out and soon put to work battering the mud-brick walls of the fortified hamlets. Eventually just three forts were holding out against the Muslims but, once their secret water supplies had been discovered and blocked, even these were forced to sue for terms. The Prophet agreed that their lives would be spared provided they honestly surrendered all their property. When the discovery of a hoard of newly buried treasure broke the terms, the paramount Jewish sheikh, Kinana ibn Abi al-Huqaiq, was led away to be tortured and executed. One of his widows, Safiya (who had successively lost father, brother and now husband to the swords of the Muslims), was chosen by the Prophet to join the company of his wives.

The gardens of Khaybar had fallen to their new lords by conquest, though their Jewish owners were allowed to continue working the land in exchange for an annual rent of half the annual harvest. At a victory feast a Jewish woman named Zaynab attempted to avenge her fallen people by secretly poisoning the portion of lamb that she knew the Prophet loved to eat best. He sensed something was wrong and spat out the meat. Zaynab was dragged before Muhammad but did nothing to deny the charge. 'You know what you have done to my people,' she said. 'If you were just a tribal chief, I would get rid of you, but if you were a prophet you would know what I had done.'

Muhammad pardoned her, though many, in retrospect, came to believe that the poison administered by Zaynab was the cause of his death three years later. At this point, however, his health did not seem to be affected. Indeed, in the tent pitched after the first day's march back from Khaybar oasis, Muhammad consummated his marriage with Safiya, the widowed Jewish princess. She had agreed to embrace Islam but was mocked for her Jewishness by the Prophet's other wives once they had arrived back in Medina. Muhammad quietened her fears, declaring to the household that they all revered the Jewish patriarchs, 'for Aaron was my father, and Moses my uncle'. The duality of Aaron and Moses fascinated Muhammad. For Moses, the great prophet and leader of his people, had, like Muhammad, never sired a surviving male heir and so it was Aaron who stood at the head of the genealogies of the Jews.

Muhammad's next conquest was Fadak. However, rather than fall before the fury of a similar assault, this neighbouring oasis (a day's march to the north-east of Khaybar) had voluntarily submitted. The conquest of the settlement of Wadi al-Qura completed Muslim control of the region.

Muhammad stayed in Medina for nine months after returning from Khaybar and his new power over the northern oases brought added responsibilities. Over that winter six different expeditions departed from Medina, both to protect the oases from the raids of the Bedouin and to discipline the great Arab tribal confederations, such as the Ghatafan and Hawazin.

In February 629 (the eleventh month of the year 7 A.H.) the elders of the Quraysh looked down from the hill that surrounded their city and watched the dust cloud on the north-west horizon that signalled the advance of the Muslim caravan. Muhammad was leading the pilgrims to Mecca. He alone was mounted, sitting astride Qaswa, the camel that had first carried him safely into exile. Behind him, in perfect order, marched two thousand followers, clothed in the white garments of the pilgrim. In accordance with the truce of the previous year, the Quraysh had agreed to evacuate their city for three days to allow the Muslims free access to the shrine. As thousands of eyes watched him intently from the hilltops, Muhammad's leadership was revealed in an accidental but spectacular manner. As he approached the Kaaba he casually knotted the loose ends of his linen cloak to leave his right shoulder bare. Without so much as a word of instruction that they should do so, the Muslims behind him followed his example – and ever since then this has been the way pilgrims have traditionally worn their cloaks.

Muhammad rode to the Kaaba, touching the revered meteorite (the Black Stone) that had been built into a corner of the wall with his staff. He then dismounted and made the seven circuits of the Kaaba, and the seven runs between the hillocks of Safa and Marwah just outside the sanctuary. At Marwah the Prophet sacrificed a camel and had his head ritually shaved. At noon he asked Bilal to sound the call to prayer. Bilal calmly ascended the roof of the Kaaba, since the Quraysh refused to unlock the sanctuary. As the voice of the muezzin echoed through the empty streets of Mecca, the faithful obediently flocked into the courtyard to stand shoulder to shoulder with one another. As they completed their accustomed cycle, first the standing prayer, then the kneeling prayer and then the solemn prostration, the antagonism between the Muslims and the citizens of Mecca started to clear like morning mist in the warmth of the sun. The Meccans had seen for themselves the discipline of the Muslims, they had seen the respect with which the Kaaba had been treated and they had just witnessed the fact that their city of Mecca stood as the central lodestone of Islamic prayer. Their fears about the desecration of their sanctuary and the destruction of their homes appeared to be groundless. As the Muslims camped out in the streets of the empty city over the next three days, there were endless opportunities for tearful reunions between families and friends who had long been separated by war. At first such reunions were covert affairs carried out at night, but by the third day the fraternisation had broken down all such reserve. The news that the Prophet's uncle, the rich banker Abbas, had just contracted a marriage alliance with his nephew reflected the political shift that was taking place. Abbas was enormously influential in Mecca and known for never putting a foot wrong. His equivocal status as close kinsman of the Prophet and a leading citizen of Mecca had always been respected by both parties and the marriage alliance indicated that he was moving ever closer towards the Muslims.

The leaders of the Quraysh, however, moved to call a halt to any further fraternisation between the two sides. They refused permission for the Prophet to stage a wedding feast in Mecca and instructed him to evacuate the city at the end of the three days granted by the truce. But they were already too late to stop the flood of defections to Islam. Shortly after the Muslims returned to Medina, the Quraysh lost their two most capable battle commanders. The defection of Khalid ibn al-Walid and 'Amr ibn al-'As, who had independently left Mecca to make their submission to the Prophet, completed the decisive shift in the balance of power. These two men, both of whom until now had done everything within their very considerable powers to destroy the Muslims, were greeted joyfully, like prodigal sons. Khalid and 'Amr would quickly go on to win their place within the community, for 629 was also the year in which the Muslims first made direct and disastrous contact with the Byzantine Empire.

The process had started innocently enough in the spring of 629 when Muhammad had sent a number of missionaries to the Bedouin tribes of Syria. Their advances were physically rejected. This was in the nature of Arabian tribal politics. Of a different nature was the messenger who had been despatched to the Byzantine governor in Syria with a personal letter from the Prophet to the Emperor Heraclius. The Muslim messenger, under the age-old sanctity afforded to heralds, took the customary route north from Medina towards the frontier city of Bostra. Here something went wrong. An official, perhaps a military officer, perhaps a pro-Byzantine Ghassanid prince, or the governor himself, had the herald executed. This insult to their faith, to their leader and to the shared manners of humankind enraged the Muslims. Indeed the action may have been specifically designed to cause a dispute. The Prophet immediately despatched an army of three thousand men under the command of his foster-son, Zayd, on a raid of vengeance.

Their arrival in September was anticipated and they were attacked in the desert by a league of pro-Byzantine Arab tribes. Although the Muslims managed to battle their way through, they had now lost any element of surprise. Nevertheless, Zayd led his army deep into Byzantine territory, reportedly to the shores of the Dead Sea. Here they were attacked by the Patricius Theodorus in command of a regular Byzantine field army assisted by his various Arab allies. The fighting was so fierce at the Battle of Mu'ta that Zayd was slain – along with the two other warriors who had automatically succeeded him as commander. The Muslim army retreated back to Medina. Only Khalid ibn al-Walid had gained from the disaster, for after the death of the three commanders he had rescued the Muslim battle standard from the hands of the enemy. He thereafter became known as 'the Sword of God'.

The Prophet rode out on a mule to greet his defeated soldiers returning home but as they entered Medina the crowd turned on them and the women threw dust in their faces and taunted them: 'Runaways. Did you flee from fighting in God's path?' The Prophet tried to deflect this abuse by declaring, 'they are not runaways but returners again to the fight, if God wills it'. He carefully masked his own grief at the death of his beloved adopted son Zayd, but that morning, when he had embraced Zayd's little daughter, his body shook with sobbing. Nor had he felt strong enough to control his tears in the mosque that day and thus had avoided facing the congregation.

The old Byzantine strategy of defence in depth had worked perfectly. There was no time for immediate counter-measures. The Prophet sent 'Amr ibn al-'As to hold the Syrian front with just three hundred men, while he proceeded with his plans for what would turn out to be his crowning achievement.

☾

Very early in the following year, 630 (the ninth month of year 8 A.H.), the Prophet sent out messengers to his allies. They were to assemble all their warriors and gather outside Medina just before the new moon of Ramadan rose. Muhammad had accused the Quraysh of breaking the truce by aiding the Beni Kinanah in an attack on one of his allies. Yet even as the army marched away from Medina in early January 630, they knew neither their enemy nor their destination. Was it to be Taif, the Hawazin tribe, Mecca or the Beni Kinanah tribe? The Prophet remained inscrutable, oblivious to his soldiers' inquiries. It did not matter, for that year they would go wherever he led. With ten thousand men at his back, no power in central Arabia could resist him. They kept the dawn-to-dusk fast of Ramadan until they were within a four days' march of Mecca.

Even with this vast force at his command, Muhammad remained more interested in winning peace by negotiation than in overseeing a triumphant conquest. It seems certain that over the preceding two years he had been preparing for the bloodless conquest of Mecca. He had carefully planned marriage alliances with his uncle Abbas and Abu Sufyan, the leader of the Quraysh. Abbas, the banker, had probably been exchanging political information with his nephew for years, to their mutual benefit. The year before, Abu Sufyan had actually visited Medina. It seems very likely that the Prophet was in direct negotiations with both Abbas and Abu Sufyan to bring a peaceful takeover of his beloved Mecca, the city of his father Abdullah, son of 'Abd al-Muttalib, son of Hashim.

Both Abbas and Abu Sufyan rode out to greet Muhammad as the army camped outside Mecca. Abbas stayed with the Muslims while Abu Sufyan returned to the city with the terms of surrender. They were generous. All the Meccans who remained within their homes, or who took sanctuary by the Kaaba or within the house of Abu Sufyan, would be spared. Mecca accepted its defeat and voluntarily opened its gates. Muhammad split his army into four columns that would simultaneously occupy Mecca from all sides. He continued along the road from Medina to the north-west entrance, while a cousin took the north-east road. Ali advanced from the east and Khalid took the south-west route into the city. Khalid's advance through the ranks of the Muslims had been quick indeed. He was a superbly efficient officer but never one to shy away from conflict. Thus only his column had felt the need to draw their swords and clear a hilltop of 'extremists'.

The Prophet had given orders that the Muslim army should

only fight in self-defence. He surveyed the orderly occupation of
the city from his campaign tent pitched on a hill overlooking the
Medina road. His first action was to make a circuit of the Kaaba.
He then rode in a wider circle chanting a line from the Qur'an:
'The truth hath come and the false hath vanished. Verily the false
is ever a vanisher.' He touched each of the three hundred and
sixty idols arranged in the enclosure with his staff, after which
each was toppled, smashed and the pieces dragged away to be
burned. Only then did he enter the interior of the Kaaba in the
company of Bilal, 'Uthman and his adopted grandson Usamah.
Muhammad raised his hand to protect an icon of the Virgin and
Child and a painting of Abraham, but otherwise his companions
cleared the interior of its clutter of votive treasures, cult imple-
ments, statuettes and hanging charms. The statue of the Syrian war
god Hubal was hauled away, as were the divination arrows that the
Quraysh had been wont to throw before the statue. The idols of
Isaf and Naila were taken away from the summits of the hillocks of
Safa and Marwah. They were thrown into the fire with the other
fallen deities, to which would be added all the lesser idols, the dedicated incense burners, the altars for sacrifice and supplication
that clustered beside the hearth and in the courtyards of the pagan
households of Mecca.

The Prophet then stood on the raised threshold of the Kaaba to
address his army: 'Praise be to God, who hath fulfilled His promise and helped his slave and routed the clans, He alone.' He
advanced to address a crowd of Meccans who had taken sanctuary
within the enclosure: 'What do you say and think to this?' Some
replied boldly, 'We say well, and we think well of a noble and generous brother, son of a noble and generous brother. We are thine
to command.' Muhammad smiled and repeated to them the char-
ity that Joseph had offered to his brothers: 'This day there shall be
no upbraiding of you nor reproach. God forgiveth you and He is

the most Merciful of the merciful.' Muhammad had offered the cup of clemency to his enemies. He now let it overflow. He withdrew to the hill of Safa and sat there personally receiving the submission into Islam of his old enemies. However, no one was forced to convert. The queue stretched back in its hundreds. Hind, the fierce wife of Abu Sufyan who had disembowelled the body of Hamzah after the Battle of Uhud, hid herself amongst the crowd of women making their confession of faith. Only after she had converted and had been forgiven did she reveal herself but the Prophet only smiled in welcome. Nor did his eyes glaze over at the numbers of faces, but he often asked for certain individuals, only to be told that they were afraid to appear. He would demand, 'Bring them to me.' Suhayl, one of his oldest persecutors, could not believe that even he was to be forgiven. Muhammad instructed his followers, 'No harsh looks for Suhayl, if you meet him.'

In Medina a black book containing the names of the enemies of Islam – those people who were to be killed on sight without mercy – had been prepared. At the top of this list was a certain Abdullah ibn Saad, a believer whom Muhammad had trusted so implicitly that he had even allowed him to copy down some of the Qur'anic revelations. Abdullah later returned to Mecca to denounce the entire revelation as a hoax. It was known that the Prophet could never tolerate mockery or personal abuse by professional singers or poets. There could be no forgiveness for such men. Yet the Prophet pardoned even Abdullah. The magnanimity displayed that day turned into a second victory.

Khalid was despatched to destroy the pagan shrine closest to Mecca, the temple to the goddess al-Uzzah at Nakhlah. Tradition has it that Khalid sacked the temple and smashed its idol but was sent back a second time by the Prophet who did not consider that the place had been properly destroyed. Khalid returned and mounted a watch over the ruined temple. Then, from out of the

ruins came a monstrous, dark woman, naked but for a mane of
long hair glistening from the blood of countless sacrifices. Khalid
recalled, 'my spine was seized with a shivering' but he accosted the
goddess shouting, 'al-Uzzah denial is for thee, not worship' and cut
her down with his sword. News of this desecration appalled the
city of Taif which still venerated the goddess al-Lat. When the
Thaqif of Taif had first heard that Muhammad was marching
south from Medina, they had summoned all their allies to defend
the oasis and its ancient temple to the goddess. Now their efforts
were redoubled. All the clans of the great Hawazin tribal confederation had gathered to protect Taif. Instead of pouring in to
reinforce the city they planned to intercept the Muslim army out
in the open country. The clans gathered together in the hills to the
north under the command of their brilliant young chieftain Malik.

Muhammad had but two weeks to enjoy his long delayed
homecoming to Mecca before he knew he had to leave once more
and march out towards Taif. The Muslim army had just been
boosted by the arrival of another two thousand recruits from the
Quraysh of Mecca and the size of this host was very nearly the
undoing of Muhammad. Neither he nor his junior commanders
were used to handling a force of over twelve thousand men.
Communications within the army were stretched and their
progress was ponderous. When the Hawazin launched their surprise attack at dawn on February 1, 630, the Muslim army was
strung out along the length of the Hunayn valley. With their first
charge the Hawazin seemed to carry all before them. Carefully
concealed in a network of ravines, the tribesmen now poured
down on the Muslim column from all sides. In time-honoured
fashion the Hawazin fought as a complete tribe – so at first sight
they seemed to match the Muslims in number. Some parts of the
Muslim army broke and fled back up the valley, causing great
confusion in the rear. The Prophet refused to join this disorderly

retreat and rallied what troops he could around him. The more disciplined section of the army also held their positions and gradually begun to counter-attack. Their superior numbers and training eventually turned the tide but victory that day was a surprisingly near-run thing, as a later revelation confirmed: '. . . on the day of Hunayn, when you exulted in your numbers and they availed you naught, and the earth for all its breadth was straightened for you, and you turned back in flight . . .'

Malik had fought with great bravery and led many of his men back to safety behind the walls of Taif. Some of the Hawazin, however, had not been able to hold their lines and had been pursued and slaughtered all the way back to Nakhlah. There was great exultation in the Muslim camp, for they had seized the entire wealth of the Hawazin, their teeming herds of camels and goats, their women and a hoard of four thousand ounces of silver and jewellery.

Amongst the captives there was a surprise for Muhammad – an old Bedouin woman who claimed to be the Prophet's sister. This fanciful assertion at first caused a great deal of mirth amongst the soldiers but at her continued insistence they brought her to the Prophet's tent. 'O Muhammad, I am thy sister,' she affirmed. 'Have you any proof of that?' he asked. Her reply was to bare an arm to reveal the scars of a bite. 'You did that,' she said, 'when I was carrying you through the valley of Sarar to join the shepherds.' Suddenly the veil of years parted and Muhammad was plunged back to his childhood spent among the flocks of the Beni Saad clan. This was indeed Shayma, one of the elder daughters of his old foster-mother Halimah, the woman who had breast fed and nurtured him through the first six years of his life. In tears he spread out his rug for her and begged her to be seated. They talked for hours of Halimah, of Muhammad's foster-father Haritha, and of Shayma's now large family. He asked her to return to Medina, where she would be assured an honoured position in his household. She gently declined, for her place was with her clan. She would take from him only of his best, the gift of Islam. The Prophet was greatly touched and insisted on adding a little worldly wealth as well. He intended to do much more for her but when he later asked after her it was apparent that she had disappeared. Thus Shayma, having converted to Islam, had returned to the desert, to her flocks and her grazing grounds.

After the Battle of Hunayn, the Prophet next led his army against Taif. The city, though often compared to Khaybar in its fertility, shared none of its weaknesses. It was walled, well supplied and united under the leadership of the Thaqif tribe, which had had sufficient time to prepare for the Muslim assault. The remnants of the Hawazin tribe under the command of Malik now reinforced the defenders and Muslim battle tactics dissolved before this confidently held defensive position. An increasing number of Muslim soldiers fell to the sharp-eyed archers who watched from the battlements of Taif. Muhammad pressed on with the siege but before a month had passed Abu Bakr quietly advised him, 'I do not think that you will gain what you desire.' Advice from such a loyal companion was always to be listened to, and the Prophet gave orders for the siege to be raised. At their departure, his army begged him to curse the place. As they marched away he raised his hands up to heaven and asked, 'O God, guide the Thaqif and bring them to us.'

The various detachments of the Muslim army were reunited at the halt of Jirana. Here they impatiently waited for the Prophet to distribute the spoils of war seized from the Hawazin at Hunayn. Muhammad stood at a pinnacle of personal power: he was lord of Medina, Mecca and Khaybar and everywhere acknowledged as the Prophet of God. He could have dictated a settlement to his troops. Instead he waited until he had gathered together the army at the noon-day prayer and then put to them the issues at hand. He declared that he would give up his share of the Hawazin captives so that they could return to their tribe. Most of the army agreed to follow his example, but those who did not felt free to air their objections. The Prophet listened, accepted their right to differ, but then offered them a generous deal. If they released their share of the captives he would pay them six camels for each captive. It was agreed.

Then it was time to distribute the captured herds. His warriors were so excited and pressed so close to Muhammad that his cloak was torn from his shoulders and trampled underfoot. He took temporary refuge by a thorn tree and laughingly called to the crowd to return his cloak to him. Then, pointing out the thicket of trees around them, he declared, 'By God, if I had as many sheep as there are trees, I would give them all to you.'

When it came to the distribution of camels Muhammad astonished his audience. He presented all the least trustworthy of his new allies with herds of a hundred camels each. The beneficiaries, such men as the Sheikh of the Ghatafan tribe and the lords of the Quraysh, were astounded. It was something of a back-handed compliment, for Muhammad was saying with this gift – you fought on the Muslim side only for booty: here it is. But the Arab chiefs understood so little of the real teaching of Islam that they were flattered and delighted by the gift of a hundred camels. When it was reported to Muhammad that one of the great chiefs, Abbas ibn Mirdas of the Beni Salaim tribe, felt overlooked, he instructed: 'stop his mouth by gifts from me'. This simple statement gives a clear indication of the disdain he felt for any man who valued possessions so highly.

Then it was the turn of the Helpers, the men from Medina, to feel aggrieved that they had been overlooked in the distribution of the herds. This was tactfully pointed out to the Prophet by one of their commanders, who with downcast eyes also confessed that he shared their feelings. Muhammad immediately called them together, addressing them:

> What is this that I hear of you? Do you think ill of me in your hearts? You, who first welcomed Muhammad, a discredited, penniless refugee into the safety of your oasis. You who gave him comfort and honour and had been the first to believe in him – all without any thought of reward. Why then are you now disturbed that I have given away things to win over new people so that they might later become Muslims? It is only because I trust you so highly that I give you nothing other than the way to God. Are you not satisfied that other men take away flocks and herds while you will take back the Apostle of God with you to Medina? If all humankind went one way and you went the other, I would take your way.

He then reached his hands up towards the heavens and called down a blessing upon them, their sons and their sons' sons. When Muhammad looked back down upon the massed ranks of battle-hardened warriors he saw the men of Medina rooted to the spot. They stood and 'wept until their beards were wet'.

On his way back through Mecca Muhammad performed another pilgrimage. Before he left he appointed a governor to rule over the city and a teacher to instruct them in the faith. His generosity to the defeated Hawazin had so impressed them that many, including Malik, hastened to convert to Islam. The tribal lord who had helped successfully to defend Taif was now entrusted with renewing the siege of the city. Malik avoided a formal assault on the city walls and instead subjected the oasis to a series of raids, which effectively isolated Taif from the trade routes. The results were not instant, but the city would soon be forced to realise that it would face economic ruin unless it made peace with the Prophet.

Muhammad returned home to Medina on March 16, 630. There was to be a bitter aftertaste to the triumphal welcome: his infant son, Ibrahim, not yet a year old, died that month. Ibrahim, the child of Mariyah, his Coptic concubine, was the third and last of the infant boys whose body Muhammad would escort to the burial grounds. The Prophet remained in Medina over that summer. In the early autumn he called the army together again. It was a deeply unpopular decision, for the grazing was completely burnt out by the long summer, the wells were low and the date crop was on the point of being harvested. Muhammad was taking the men away from their oasis orchards at the busiest time of the year. They were also concerned about the condition of their animals during and after campaigning in such an arid season. Normally he would have listened attentively to these murmurs of complaint. Unaccountably, however, this time he did not pay much attention. It was as if he knew that the time left to him was running out, that there was so much yet to be done. It was the twenty-seventh military expedition to have been led by the Prophet; he had also organised thirty-eight other expeditions that had been led by junior commanders.

Muhammad and his reluctant army followed the route of the long familiar caravan trail into Syria. It was the last time he would look upon this landscape, which from the age of eight until he was forty had been his life's habitual backdrop. This expedition has often been dismissed as no more than a military gesture, a face-saving parade, for he and his army never penetrated the Byzantine frontier. But this is to misunderstand its objective. The purpose was not to blunder into another military defeat, as at the Battle of Mu'ta, but to pave the way for greater victories in the future.

The Prophet used his army as a negotiating weapon with which to impress and win over the Arab tribes of the Syrian desert. It was these Christian Arab tribes who had thwarted Zayd's army of three thousand men in 629. They had not only harassed the Muslim army under the command of Zayd on its way to Syria but they had provided vital intelligence that had allowed Patricius Theodorus to be prepared. If the Prophet could neutralise these tribes, the playing field of war would become level; if he could win them over to his side he would have achieved a decisive advantage. If he could not, the defeat of 629 was likely to be repeated again and again.

This autumn campaign saw no fighting but instead a series of very interesting meetings. The Prophet halted at Tebook for ten days. Among the local leaders who we know rode over to meet him was sheikh Yahanna ibn Ruba from the Red Sea port of Aqaba. Muhammad was passionately keen to convert these Christian Arab tribes to Islam, but he was also prepared just to make a political deal with them. At the very least he did not want to push them further into a dependent alliance with the Byzantine Empire. Khalid was sent to Dumat al-Jandal (modern Jauf) and such strategic outposts as Jerba and Udrah (once a way station of the 4th Roman legion). According to John Glubb, 'Khalid never could carry out any mission without killing somebody.' He did manage safely to escort Prince Ukaydir of the Arabian dynasty of al-Kinda to meet the Prophet but somehow the Prince's younger brother was killed in the process.

The political static must have been all but visible in the negotiations that took place in the desert in 630. For just on the other side of the frontier the Byzantine Emperor Heraclius had settled down and made the northern Syrian city of Antioch his headquarters. Having personally destroyed the Persian Empire in a series of dazzling campaigns – the like of which had not been seen since the time of Alexander the Great – the fifty-five-year-old emperor was at the very apogee of his power and popularity. Stories revolved around his person; of how he had changed the course of a battle by personally charging a Persian-held bridge, a deed so astonishing in its recklessness that even the enemy general was recorded to have said to a group of Greeks 'look at your Emperor, he fears those arrows and spears no more than would an anvil'. It was also the year that the emperor made his triumphant entry into Jerusalem, returning the True Cross to its rightful home after it had been recovered from the Persians. Heraclius had advanced on the holy city not astride a white horse as a conqueror, but on foot as a pilgrim. He approached Jerusalem from the Emessa road but it is said that his foot never touched the ground. He walked over a road buried under carpets and strewn with fragrant herbs by the jubilant citizens of Byzantine Syria. Once within the city he himself carried the cross up the Via Dolorosa to the doors of the rebuilt Holy Sepulchre where he handed over Christendom's most holy relic to the Patriarch.

Despite Heraclius's popularity, the Prophet Muhammad was able to win over a number of important new Arab allies from the Byzantine fold. Many of these, like Yahanna ibn Ruba, insisted on retaining their Christian faith, though they had to agree to pay a poll tax. For his part the Prophet agreed that it was not just Christian lives he was protecting but also their merchant caravans and trading ships.

More of these vital negotiations would be continued over the next two years, though all future meetings would be held at Medina. It might have been during these years that the Prophet's letter was finally delivered to the emperor. This is a much treasured incident in Arab folk history. The tale records the text of the letter, along with the questions the emperor asked the herald of the

Prophet. At the end of this hearing Heraclius is said to have declared: 'I knew he [the Prophet] would appear, but I did not know he would be from among you [Arabs]. If what you have said is true, he will soon rule the ground beneath these two feet of mine . . .' In the tale, the emperor's personal sympathy to Islam was then drowned out by the clamorous roar of opposition from the assembled bishops, generals and grandees of his court. Whatever the truth of this tradition, the Emperor Heraclius certainly stayed at the city of Antioch during this period. However, it seems that his major concern at the time was to preside over a series of councils where he tried to iron out the differences between the Christian churches.

By December 630 Muhammad was back in Medina in time to meet a peace delegation from Taif. Never had a group of Arabs embraced Islam with more reluctance. They tried to negotiate a three-year period of grace for their goddess al-Lat, or at the very least an adaptation of the prayer ritual, but the Prophet was not the man to move an inch on any position of faith. The first emissary who returned to inform the Thaqif of Taif about the peace terms was lynched by his fellow citizens. Eventually, however, the city had to accept the inevitable. A zealous Muslim hacked the image of their goddess to pieces, shattering the monolithic white stone menhir upon which the devotion of centuries had been poured. Then the ancient treasury of ritual deposits around the hearth altar of al-Lat was dug up. The hidden objects were exposed. The women of Thaqif were loud in their wail. They tore off their veils, ripped their clothes, scratched their faces with their nails and poured dust mingled with tears and lamentations over their wounds. They spat loathing at the cowardice of their menfolk.

☾

In the new year of 631 (the twelfth month of the year 9 A.H.) the Prophet moved quickly to complete the destruction of pagan Arabia. The year's official pilgrimage was the last one an idolater could ever go on. The old tradition of holy nakedness, still followed by some of the pagan pilgrims to the Kaaba, was also banned. In future all pilgrims would be dressed in a simple wraparound white cloth and the pilgrimage to Mecca was to be for Muslims only. The pagans of Arabia were given four months' grace to make their submission, after which they stood outside the law – and could be robbed, killed or enslaved by any believer. If a pagan Arab made the submission to Islam, learned the prayers and agreed to pay the charitable tithe for the feeding of the poor, they were guaranteed not only their freedom but their equality. In the words of Muhammad, 'Know that every Muslim is a Muslim's brother, and that all the Muslims are brethren.'

For months on end a series of tribal deputations rode into the oasis, loudly asking for the House of the Prophet of God. They had come to make a submission or face the consequence of total war but for the sake of their honour they liked to pretend they had sought him out quite independently of any political concerns. The Prophet played his part with unerring grace and treated each new convert with respect. It was, however, not all realpolitik. One story of conversion relates how a proud Arab lord of the desert came to Medina to interview the Prophet. On the way to Muhammad's house, the lord watched as the Prophet was detained by an old woman. He did not brush her aside but listened to her patiently until she had finished her tale. Only when she was finally done did the Prophet proceed on his way. He then instinctively offered his visitor a place on the mat while he himself chose to sit on the dirt floor. This example of grace and humility so impressed the visitor that he embraced Islam before he had heard so much as a single word of the Qur'an.

C

Each region of Arabia treasures the traditional tales of their conversion to Islam. The people of Muscat and Oman (the
south-easternmost corner of Arabia) recall that in year nine after
the hijra, the Prophet sent 'Amr ibn al-'As with a letter to the
brothers 'Abd and Jayfar of the dominant Julanda clan of the Azd
tribe. They had been the chief clients of the Persian Empire within
Oman. Copies of this original letter, a small, elegant rectangle of
bleached parchment covered in big black script, still survive. There
is not much of the world of the spirit in this letter, which contained a veiled threat to bring an army of horsemen into Oman to
eat up and trample over their grazing land. The document reads as
if it was more likely to have come from the mouth of 'Amr ibn al-
'As than the Prophet Muhammad. In any case all of the Yemen and
Oman had been in a political vacuum since the collapse of Persian
power with the death of King Chosroes in 628. At some lush oasis
like Bahla (where a pre-Islamic devil's tower still stands) a council
of sheikhs would have assembled to listen to the ambassador of the
Prophet. They made their submission and in due course received
a second letter. Now one can hear the true accents of the Prophet:
'God guide them and recompense them and provide them with
purity, subsistence and satisfaction with what they are given. God
provide them with fine harvests and successful fishing. God do not
over burden them with enemies.'

The Prophet was not greatly interested in political structures.
He never sent a governor to preside over Oman or interfered in
any way with the existing structure of the tribes. It was enough
that they accepted Islam and paid the annual tithe. For the
Omanis it had an immediate and profound effect. They would
soon start to liberate their own coastline from the dominion of
the Persians. To this day they proudly remember that they sent a

gift of a coat of silk to the Prophet from their port of Sohar while the shroud in which he was to be buried also came from Oman.

There is an alternative version about the first man from Oman to have accepted Islam. Here the honour fell to the pagan priest Mazin bin Ghadhuba al-Tay who destroyed his own idol at the command of God. He recorded his miraculous conversion in verse and then travelled to Medina to receive instruction from the Prophet himself before returning to spread the good word back home.

I broke the Baajir [a stone idol] to pieces when he was a god
And I rested in the shade.
Al-Hashimi [the Prophet] showed us the falsehood of our ways.
His religion was not known before.

Traveller tell Amr and her brothers
That I who once claimed Baajir as my god,
Say that the true God has talked.

The Yemen was converted in a similarly ad hoc manner. The Prophet had replied to letters he had received from the bishop of Najran and the sons of Abid Kulal, a prince descended from the Himyarite kings of the Yemen. He gave them detailed instructions of what was required from a believer. Knowing his people well he put special weight on the payment of the charitable tithe for the support of the poor. 'He who pays this tax to God and his prophet has his security guaranteed . . . but he who withholds the tax is the enemy . . .' He was also explicit that 'if a Jew or a Christian becomes a Muslim, he is a believer with the same rights and obligations . . . those however who hold fast to their religion, whether Jews or Christians, are not obliged to change it. They must pay the poll tax, one dinar for every adult . . . or its equivalent in goods . . .' The correspondence to and from the Yemen was to be an important source for later dynasties. For in these letters, the Prophet went into considerable detail about a number of practical points, from the correct manner of washing before prayers to the different ways of assessing the tithe from irrigated farmland, rain-watered terraces and from the herds pastured on the arid steppe. This would later serve the Arabs as a template for how they should treat newly conquered and converted territories.

It seems reasonably clear that the Prophet had a concept of uniting all the lands where Arabic was spoken and where the Qur'an could be understood. Indeed, there is a longstanding tradition that during the siege of Medina in 627 (when the ter-ritory of Islam had effectively been confined behind a moat) the Prophet had been given a vision of the future of his faith. He foresaw that Islam would spread over all of Arabia to include the Yemen, Persian-held Iraq and the castles of Syria. It is doubtful whether the Prophet ever imagined Islam extending beyond the language frontiers of his people. He had always been proud to define himself as the Prophet of the Arabs. There is no allusion to a worldwide mission for Islam. Indeed, his immediate succes-sors, men who had known him intimately, were at a complete loss as to what to do when there was a massive influx of non-Arab converts to Islam. Their quandary is ample testimony that there was no master plan to extend Islam beyond the Arabic-speaking peoples.

This was also the period when the Prophet rearranged the cal-endar. This act is often misinterpreted, though it is entirely at one with his determined suppression of pagan Arabia. Muhammad deliberately removed the mechanism that forged a connection between the lunar calendar (divided into twelve months of twenty-nine and a half days) and the solar year of 365 days. The lunar calendar lags behind the solar year by eleven days, so it had been the practice within pagan Arabia to add a thirteenth month every three years, in order to align the two calendars. The Prophet abolished this additional month, because it was linked with a popular pagan festival.

The Islamic year was to be based on the twelve lunar months, which made it 354 days long. This meant that every year the Islamic calendar slipped another eleven days back in relation to the solar year and the Christian calendar. The months soon lost any connection with a specific season. In one stroke Muhammad had severed the months from their relationship with the seasons and their ancient link to the seasonal fertility cults. Christianity never achieved this clear severance. Every year pious Christians bewail the fact that their celebration of Easter is undermined by the pagan celebration of spring, with fertility symbols like the rabbit, while the birthday of Jesus has never escaped from the feasting and drinking of the Winter Solstice Saturnalia. Muhammad's calendar reform on the other hand meant that none of the Muslim feast days would ever be associated with the ancient pagan festivals of the seasons. It also allowed Ramadan, the fasting month, to gradually move through the seasons. When it falls during the long hot days of high summer, the fast of Ramadan is a real, debilitating ordeal. When it falls on the shorter days of the winter, it is somewhat less of a challenge. Believers will witness the full cycle of these contrasts every thirty-three years: they can hope to witness the cycle twice if they live long enough, though only the venerable will live to be ninety-nine and see Ramadan pass three times through the seasons. This numerology connects in a profound way with the ninety-nine names of God that can be found in the pages of the Qur'an, thus giving the rhythm of the Islamic calendar a sacred harmony.

By the end of 631 Muhammad was in command of the whole

of Arabia. His rule touched only lightly along the length and breadth of the peninsula, for most of the traditional sheikhs continued to preside over their people. He was not interested in despatching garrisons or governors to consolidate his political authority over these distant regions; instead a steady stream of teachers and letters continually advanced the faith.

☾

In the early weeks of 632 Muhammad decided to return once more to Mecca. On February 20, 632 he led all his wives and a vast host of pilgrims out from the shaded palm orchards of Medina on to the road south, arriving outside Mecca on March 3, the twelfth month of the year 10 A.H. It was only then that the Prophet felt the cold hand of mortality resting on his shoulder. One of the last revealed verses of the Qur'an came upon him at Mecca: 'When God's succour and the triumph cometh. And thou seest humankind entering the religion of God in troops, then hymn the praises of thy Lord, and seek forgiveness of him. Lo! He is ever ready to show mercy.' As Muhammad recited the surah he was also given a premonition of his approaching death.

The actions of the Prophet on this, the farewell pilgrimage, established the ritual of the Hajj for ever. The first night was spent on the plain of Mina followed by the seven circuits around the Kaaba. Then the pilgrims stood in meditation from noon to sunset on the plain before Mount Arafat, a two-hundred-foot granite hill east of Mecca. That evening the pilgrims moved into the valley of Muzdalifah before returning the next day to Mina to throw seven stones at a pillar, representing Abraham's rejection of the devil. The following day was the day of sacrifice, after which the pilgrims' hair was shaved off and they returned to Mecca to circle the Kaaba seven more times and run seven times between the hillocks of Safa and Marwah. The sacred time was concluded on the plain of Mina with a second volley of seven stones.

Muhammad made good use of the premonition of his death to compose his farewell sermon to the massed crowds of pilgrims. This time it was not Muhammad acting as a mouthpiece of divine revelation but speaking as a man summarising his life's teaching before a vast crowd. It does not have the full force of the Qur'an, though it is clear and concise and is imbued with the spirit of doubt. Muhammad seems charged with an anxiety that he has not laboured hard enough to transplant the divine revelations that he had received into the minds of his followers. Some critics doubt that the actual words can be an exact record, for the farewell sermon was only first recorded in the biographies written over a century after the Prophet's death. However, if one is content with the general veracity of the Christian gospels (written at about the same remove) one can also embrace the farewell sermon as one of the great spiritual directives for humankind. It is a pearl without price, and there can be no better general introduction to the Muslim faith. The Prophet's categorical refutation of racism still reads as a shockingly positive and alternative vision for humankind:

O my people, lend me an attentive ear, for I do not know whether, after this year, I shall ever be amongst you again. Therefore listen to what I am saying to you very carefully and take these words to those who could not be present here today.

O my people, just as you regard this day, this city as sacred, so regard the life and property of every Muslim as a sacred trust. Return the goods entrusted to you to their rightful owners. Hurt no one so that no one may hurt you. Remember that you will indeed meet your Lord, and that he will indeed reckon your deeds. God has forbidden you to

charge interest, therefore all interest obligations shall henceforth be waived. Your capital, however, is yours to keep. You
will neither inflict nor suffer inequity.

Every right arising out of homicide in the pre-Islamic days
is henceforth waived . . . O my people, it is true that you
have certain rights with regard to your women, but they also
have rights over you. If they abide by your right then to
them belongs the right to be fed and clothed in kindness. Do
treat your women well and be kind to them for they are
your partners and committed helpers . . .

O my people, listen to me in earnest, worship God, say
your daily prayers, fast during the month of Ramadan, and
give alms. Perform the Hajj if you can afford to.

All humankind is from Adam and Eve, an Arab has no
superiority over a non-Arab nor a non-Arab has any superiority over an Arab: also a white has no superiority over black
nor a black has any superiority over white except by piety
and good action. Learn that every Muslim is the brother of
another Muslim, and that Muslims constitute one brotherhood. Nothing shall be legitimate to a Muslim which
belongs to a fellow Muslim unless it was given freely and
willingly. Do not therefore, do injustice to yourselves.

Remember, one day you will appear before God and
answer for your deeds. So beware, do not stray from the
path of righteousness after I am gone.

O my people, no prophet or apostle will come after me
and no new faith will be born. Reason well, therefore, my
people, and understand my words which I convey to you. I
leave behind me two things, the Qur'an and my example, the
Sunnah, and if you follow these you will never go astray.

All those who listen to me shall pass on my words to
others and those to others again; and may the last ones

understand my words better than those who listen to me directly. Be my witness O God, that I have conveyed your message to your people.

With one voice the thousands of assembled Muslims replied. The hills and the valleys echoed to the great cry, 'Most assuredly he has.'

☾

Muhammad returned to Medina and spent the next months in his household there. One night in June he felt a sudden summons to go out and pray over the dead in the cemetery. The following morning he collapsed with a violent headache. By binding his head tightly with a cloth he managed to control the pain sufficiently to lead the prayers in the mosque and then afterwards to present a war banner to the young Usamah (the twenty-year-old son of Zayd) who was leading a military expedition back into Syria.

Afterwards Muhammad collapsed with a burning fever, which consumed him for the next ten days. Despite his insistence that he was a mere mortal, and the warning implicit in his farewell sermon, the news of the Prophet's illness tormented Arabia. There was no desire to hide the truth, nor any ability to do so. The Prophet's household was arranged around the courtyard of the mosque at Medina. Every believer who attended the daily prayers could see, hear and sense the situation for himself. Not for the Prophet of God the high walls, the silent, implacable bodyguard at the gate, the sober courtiers, the discreet ministers spinning a tale to the world.

Muhammad was now too ill to share himself equally among his women. They had met and agreed that it was better for his health, and perhaps for his heart, if he stayed solely in the room of his beloved Aisha. She was given the honour of nursing him, though they all conspired to bathe him in cold water and tempt him with various cures. He was lucid enough only to insist that, in his absence, Abu Bakr should lead the prayers.

At dawn on the tenth day of his fever, Muhammad dragged himself out of Aisha's room by an enormous effort of will to attend – though not to lead – the prayers. The news of this partial recovery spread like wildfire through Medina. He returned to Aisha's room immediately afterwards, laid his head on her breast and clasped her hand firmly in his own. He lay quite still as the heat intensified over the morning. Then Aisha felt his head grow heavy and heard him say 'Lord, grant me pardon.' The grip on her hand loosened. The Prophet had left this world.

EPILOGUE
The Successor

Abu Bakr had been greatly relieved to see the Prophet attend dawn prayers. He felt that his vigil was now over and left Muhammad's courtyard to visit his own family. By midday he knew something was wrong. The oasis was filled with the screams of men and the wailing of women. By the time Abu Bakr returned to the courtyard of the mosque the place was in uproar. Abu Bakr slipped through the hysterically grieving crowd and quietly entered his daughter's room. A thick cloak covered in the embroidery of the Yemen was draped over the still body of Muhammad. He raised the cloth to kiss the forehead of the dead Messenger of God: 'You are dearer to me than my father and mother. You have tasted death as God decreed,' he murmured. Outside again, he pushed his way through the crowd and tried to calm 'Umar who was ranting and raving. 'Umar was threatening the people with the direst punishments if he heard any more rumours about the death of the Prophet. He promised to cut off both the hands and feet of any man who dared whisper that Muhammad was dead. 'Umar tried to explain to the crowd that Muhammad had gone to God, but, like the prophet Moses, he would return to them in forty days. Nothing that Abu Bakr said could halt the passionate flow of 'Umar's rhetoric. He moved to another corner of the courtyard, where his calm, measured voice gradually attracted the people over to him.

'O people. To those who used to worship Muhammad, Muhammad is dead. But for those who used to worship God, God is alive and can never die.' He reminded the crowd of the Prophet's own Qur'anic recitation of his mortality: 'Muhammad is but a messenger, messengers the like of whom have passed away before him. Will it be that, when he dies or is slain, you will turn back on your heels?'

'Umar's passion dried up at the sound of Abu Bakr's words. According to his own recollection, 'directly I heard Abu Bakr . . . my feet were cut beneath me and I fell to the ground'. If this was the reaction of 'Umar, the most steadfast and iron-willed of believers, the panic that filled the hearts of the rest of the Muslims can be readily imagined. One contemporary account recalled the mood of that day as being 'like sheep on a rainy night'.

Ironically Abu Bakr, known as a highly sensitive man, not loud of voice and much given to weeping when he recited the Qur'an, now emerged as the strongest leader. Most of the prominent Muslims of Meccan origin gathered around him in the mosque, but it soon became noticeable that the Muslims of Medina were absent. They had been called together by one of their more ambitious hereditary chieftains, Sa'd of the Beni Sa'dah, who aspired to take over the leadership. 'Umar got wind of the meeting and with it the incipient threat of a schism. He had by now recovered his poise and insisted that he would escort Abu Bakr to the place where the Muslims of Medina were meeting. They arrived at a critical moment when the future leadership of the Muslim community was being debated. Abu Bakr's intervention proved decisive. In a measured, calm and tactful speech he repeated the Prophet's praise for the men of Medina, but insisted now that Islam was a faith across Arabia they would have to choose a candidate from the Quraysh if they wished to retain the respect of the great Bedouin tribes. Abu Bakr, who was by now quite old, proposed two candidates from which the assembly could choose. He made no mention of himself. A clamour of excited voices soon filled the hall as Abu Bakr's ideas were debated by the rival clans of Medina. It was broken by 'Umar who roared, 'Who will willingly take precedence over the man that the Prophet ordered to lead the prayer!' It was an unanswerable case. 'Umar made use of the silence to seize the hand of Abu Bakr and pledge public allegiance to him. One by one his example was followed.

The next day, after the dawn prayers, 'Umar repeated his oath to Abu Bakr before the packed ranks of the faithful in the mosque. He described Abu Bakr to the congregation as 'the best of you, the Companion of God's Messenger, the second of two when they were both in the cave' (fleeing from the persecution at Mecca). With one voice the congregation acclaimed Abu Bakr as 'Khalifat Rasul Allah', the successor to the Messenger of God. The title Khalifat can also be translated as 'vice-regent' and by long-established English usage is customarily rendered as 'caliph'.

Thus was the caliphate founded, by acclamation of the assembled faithful at the end of the morning prayer. Abu Bakr's reply to the congregation took the form of an oath in exchange for their pledge of allegiance, just as Muhammad had replied to that first midnight pledge of faith at Aqaba. It should be engraved in stone on the gates of every presidential palace and in the public reception hall of every Muslim monarch. It should be stamped on the front of every identity card and passport so that the police and security forces of the Muslim world are daily reminded of this great and noble contract between the governed and the governor:

I have been given the authority over you, and I am not the best of you. If I do well, help me; and if I do wrong, set me right. Sincere regard for truth is loyalty and disregard for truth is treachery. The weak amongst you shall be strong with me until I have secured his rights, if God will: and the strong amongst you shall be weak with me until I have wrested from him the rights of others, if God will. Obey me for so long as I obey God and His Messenger. But if I disobey God and His Messenger, you owe me no obedience. Arise from your prayer, God have mercy upon you!

During this time Ali had withdrawn to his house, where he must have recalled with a heavy heart the last whispered conversation that had taken place between the Prophet and his daughter Fatimah. She had been seen to weep and then to laugh. She now explained that she had wept when her father had warned her that he was about to die. 'Then he told me that I would be the first of the people of his house to follow him' and therefore I laughed. This was to be Ali's inheritance: the death of his beloved wife just a few months after the death of his adopted father, his cousin, his mentor, his father-in-law, Muhammad the Prophet of God.

It was Ali who took charge of the burial. The body of the Prophet was not stripped bare. Instead Muhammad was reverently washed in his woollen garments and wrapped in a rich cloak. There was some debate about the proper place of burial. The obvious spot was beside his three daughters and his infant son Ibrahim in the Baqi al-Gharqad cemetery. However, eventually it was decided to dig a grave within the chamber of Aisha, just beside the mat upon which he had died. It was a very odd decision and went against the practice the Prophet had established in his life, not to mention the ancient practice of the Arabs and all civilised nations of the Middle East, to keep a clear division between the living and the dead. There is a story that Abu Bakr quoted a saying of Muhammad's, that 'no Prophet dieth but is buried where he died'. It is a neat explanation but only half-convincing. The action, even at this great distance in time, has an air of panic about it. Perhaps it was simply that his family and close friends feared his body might be desecrated by the enemies of Islam, a vengeful pagan or a hired sorcerer. As a result, the tomb of the Prophet is to this day within the walls of Medina's great mosque.

Ali was clearly too preoccupied by the burial of the Prophet to take part in the discussions about the succession. He may have hoped to be nominated as successor to Muhammad; at the very least he expected to be consulted. He was certainly the most conspicuous of the Muslims to abstain from joining in the oath to the first caliph. His was a very noticeable absence. Ali explained his position in a meeting with Abu Bakr some months later: 'I know well your pre-eminence and what God hath bestowed upon you, and I am not jealous of any benefit that He hath caused to come unto you. But you did confront us with a thing accomplished, leaving us no say in the matter, and we felt that we had some claim as the nearest in kin-ship to the Messenger of God.' Abu Bakr immediately replied that he would rather get on badly with his own family than suffer any disagreement with the family of Muhammad. They then made a public show of accord at the end of the noon-day Friday prayers.

Islam owes a great deal to the modesty of Abu Bakr. He was determined to keep the caliphate clear of the pomp and ritual of kingship. He left no doubt that the age of prophecy had ended with the death of Muhammad. The caliph collectively held the political authority of the community but Abu Bakr was adamant that the office conferred no spiritual powers. Nothing should be allowed to stand between God and a believer.

☾

As the sun rises over each successive longitude of the globe, the dawn prayer ripples out from the throats of the faithful, so that the whole world is now encircled in a continuous wave of praise. Muhammad's greatest gift to the world is revealed every time a Muslim stands alone to pray directly to God. This revolution in spiritual attitude, the direct communion between believer and the divine, is Muhammad's triumphant achievement. He himself always possessed an extraordinarily close relationship with God, revealed in that haunting revelation that 'God is closer to you than your jugular vein'. This intimacy had its own personal price, for he was overwhelmed by the sense of the omnipotence of the divine and the insignificance of humankind, leading to a fear that the end of the world was but a breath away. This heavy sense of foreboding helps explain the decisiveness with which he acted in the last years of his life.

Muhammad was enormously proud to stand in a line of succession with the prophets of old. He was deeply touched by the ethical teachings of Jesus and the family and community centred religious life of the Jews. But Muhammad was the Prophet of the Arabs, and his faith also rested on the noble traditions of the Arabs. Muhammad's message took the loyalty and strong sense of community that had been hitherto focused on the clan and tribe, and extended it to embrace the whole society of believers. It extracted the virtues of the Bedouin: their exquisite sense of hospitality, their generosity and their reckless chivalry, but rejected their intemperance, casual cruelty and ignorance. It elevated the fine qualities of the successful caravan merchants (their *hilm* – self-control – and *aql* – rational judgement) but directed it away from personal ambition to the communal care of the weak and the poor. Islam suppressed the blood feud and replaced it with a community that collectively enforced public justice, defended itself and took responsibility for education and social welfare. It combined an intellectually elegant and conceptually sturdy monotheism with a passionate awareness of a Day of Judgement. The old traditions of tribal raiding were replaced by the *jihad*, the struggle against the unbelievers on the frontiers of Islam and in the hearts of the hypocrites.

A Muslim must believe that the Qur'an comes from God. Muhammad's role was to shape this divine inspiration into a language that could not only be understood but could inspire his fellow Arabs. This was his genius; to transform his own religious experience, which was by its very nature highly individual, and create from it something of relevance to a whole society and indeed to all succeeding generations. There is an unearthly, timeless magic about the Qur'an. There are verses in it that must have seemed mysterious and indecipherable for centuries, but which suddenly glow with an acute relevance in later ages whose outlook has been changed by scientific discoveries and an expanding understanding of the world. In the farewell sermon, the Prophet had declared to his people, 'I leave behind me two things, the Qur'an and my example, the Sunnah, and if you follow these you will never go astray.'

It has been a challenge that many societies have grappled with but very few have managed to meet. Within Islam all that is of merit in humankind is embodied by the Prophet Muhammad. As Rumi, the great mystic medieval poet, declared, 'He is the evidence of God's existence', while Muhammad said of himself, 'I, too, am a man like you.'

Peace be upon you, Prophet of God.

THE NINETY-NINE
NAMES OF ALLAH

The ninety-nine names of Allah are a foundation of Muslim identity. Most given names are formed from one of these, with the
addition of the vital prefix of 'Abd' – 'servant or slave of'. The
prefix 'Al' – 'the' – makes each immediately applicable only to
Allah.

They are a brilliant achievement for a monotheistic faith. One
of the essential dualities of all religious experience is the acknowl-
edgement of unity, but the need for diversity. All religions,
however dazzling their pantheon, however bewildering their
mythology, accept a single fundamental source. But in so doing, a
God is created of such vast power and mindless distance from the
bustling masses of humanity that intercessors – be they Catholic
saints, revered Sufi masters, Hindu Avatars, Shaman healers or
Judaic angels – must also be created. The beautiful Islamic names
of Allah encourage communication from the faithful and pro-
mote an intimacy in prayer, without deflecting from unity.

Ar-Rahman, the Beneficent

Ar-Rahim, the Merciful

Al-Malik, the Sovereign Lord

Al-Quddus, the Holy

As-Salam, the Source of Peace

Al-Mu'min, the Guardian of Faith

Al-Muhaymin, the Protector

Al-Aziz, the Mighty

Al-Jabbar, the Compeller

Al-Mutakabbir, the Majestic

Al-Khaliq, the Creator

Al-Bari, the Evolver

Al-Musawwir, the Fashioner

Al-Ghaffar, the Forgiver

Al-Qahhar, the Subduer

Al-Wahhab, the Bestower

Ar-Razzaq, the Provider

Al-Fattah, the Opener

Al-'Alim, the All-knowing

Al-Qabi, the Constrictor

Al-Basit, the Expander

Al-Khafid, the Abaser

Ar-Rafi, the Exalter

Al-Mu'izz, the Honourer

Al-Muzill, the Dishonourer

As-Sami, the All-hearing

Al-Basir, the All-seeing

Al-Hakam, the Judge

Al-'Adl, the Just

Al-Latif, the Subtle One

Al-Khabir, the Aware

Al-Halim, the Forbearing One

Al-Azim, the Great One

Al-Ghafur, the All Forgiving

Ash-Shakur, the Appreciative

Al-Ali, the Most High

Al-Kabir, the Most Great

Al-Hafiz, the Preserver

Al-Muqit, the Maintainer

Al-Hasib, the Reckoner

Al-Jalil, the Sublime One

Al-Karim, the Generous One

Ar-Raqib, the Watchful

Al-Mujib, the Responsive

Al-Wasi, the All-embracing

Al-Hakim, the Wise

Al-Wadud, the Loving

Al-Majid, the Most Glorious One

Al-Ba'ith, the Resurrector

Ash-Shahid, the Witness

Al-Haqq, the Truth

Al-Wakil, the Trustee

Al-Qawi, the Most Strong

Al-Matin, the Firm One

Al-Wali, the Protective Friend

Al-Hamid, the Praiseworthy

Al-Muhsi, the Reckoner

Al-Mubdi, the Originator

Al-Mu'id, the Restorer

Al-Muhyi, the Giver of Life

Al-Mumit, the Creator of Death

Al-Hayy, the Alive
Al-Qayyum, the Self-subsisting
Al-Wajid, the Finder
Al-Majid, the Noble
Al-Wahid, the Unique
Al-Ahad, the One
As-Samad, the Eternal
Al-Qadir, the Able
Al-Muqtadir, the Powerful
Al-Muqaddim, the Expediter
Al-Mu'akhkhir, the Delayer
Al-Awwal, the First
Al-Akhir, the Last
Az-Zahir, the Manifest
Al-Batin, the Hidden
Al-Wali, the Governor
Al-Muta'Ali, the Most Exalted
Al-Barr, the Source of all Goodness
At-Tawwab, the Acceptor of Repentance
Al-Muntaqim, the Avenger

Al-Afuw, the Pardoner
Ar-Ra'uf, the Compassionate
Malik-ul-Mulk, the Eternal Owner of Sovereignty
Dhul-Jalal-Wal-Ikram, Lord of Majesty and Bounty
Al-Muqsit, the Equitable
Al-Jame, the Gatherer
Al-Ghani, the Self-sufficient
Al-Mughni, the Enricher
Al-Mani, the Preventer
An-Nafi, the Propitious
Ad-Darr, the Distresser
An-Nur, the Light
Al-Hadi, the Guide
Al-Badi, the Incomparable
Al-Baqi, the Everlasting
Al-Warith, the Supreme Inheritor
Ar-Rashid, the Guide to the Right Path
As-Sabur, the Patient

A NOTE ON SOURCES

Soon after he succeeded to the caliphate in 644, 'Uthman started to create a definitive edition of the Qur'an. At first the work seems to have been solely for his private edification, but the project soon acquired enormous attention. 'Uthman called in all the earlier written drafts of verses from the garrison cities in the provinces and got Zayd to listen and record the three greatest reciters of the Qur'an. In addition he was able to make use of Hafsah's Qur'an, for it seems that 'Umar's daughter inherited various draft copies that had been made by one of the Prophet's scribes.

When the Qur'an was finally assembled in 650 it was found to contain 6,211 verses, which were divided into 114 surah (chapters). These were arranged by length, with no attempt to order the recitation by subject or by chronology. It is traditionally considered that four copies were made from 'Uthman's original – one for each point of the compass – and the fathers of all the tens of thousands of manuscript Qur'ans that would be written in the many centuries to come. It was a great and devout task, but inevitably there were murmurs of complaint. Many objected to the very idea of a written revelation, rather than the living sound of the recitation. The semi-professional reciters of the Qur'an who had become attached to the Muslim armies and the great mosques of the garrison cities were particularly scornful of the process. However, 'Uthman's editorial achievement becomes brilliantly clear when you compare the pristine state of the Qur'an to the tangled world of Hadith studies.

For the Hadith – the sayings and actions of the Prophet – were never edited into a single orthodox collection by any of his immediate successors. Instead as the decades passed a heterogeneous collection of folk wisdom, Bedouin traditions, epigrams and *wasiyya* – the treasured deathbed sayings of the Arabs – was slowly collected alongside the Prophet's actual words. It also became clear that some of the early politicians and tribal leaders had subtly altered the sayings of Muhammad to support their various cases, causes, schisms and grievances. By the eighth century this problem was at last being addressed by a determined group of scholars working in the Abbasid capital of Baghdad. Hadith studies attempted to grade the reliability of the Prophet's sayings by the character of the sources, the possible witnesses, multiple references and the chain of verbal succession that had preserved these sayings before they were first committed to paper. By the ninth century the work of dozens of scholars had been more or less completed. The rival editions of al-Bukhari, al-Qushayri, at-Tirmidhi, ibn Hanbal, an-Nasai, as-Sijisatni, ad-Darimi and ibn Majah would in time become accepted as the eight traditional texts. However, no canonical edition has ever been accepted. It is also clear that much has been lost, especially from the real intimates of the Prophet such as his wives, his daughters and Ali.

The first biography of the Prophet, written by Ibn Ishaq, who died in 767, was also produced in this same period. Ibn Ishaq was not a freeborn Arab of the desert, but of Persian descent. Indeed his grandfather had been made captive during the Muslim conquest of the Persian Empire. His work was quickly followed by the first histories

of the Arabs and their conquests, as well as the first textual commentary on the Qur'an by another Persian – Muqatil ibn Salaiman.
Arabic grammar soon developed into an intimate part of Islamic
faith as earnest (and largely non-Arabic) scholars sought to define the
exact meaning and nuance of the words used in the Qur'an. It also
became important to try to fix the timing and references for each of
the verses. Within a hundred and fifty years of Muhammad's death
Sibawayhi, the first great Arab grammarian but by birth an Afghan
from the Central Asian city of Balkh, would be hard at work.
Sibawayhi would send young scholars out into the Arabian desert to
make notes of the ordinary speech of the Arab Bedouin and to question them on abstruse points of grammar, as well as taking down
notes on their tribal history. The pre-Islamic poetry of the desert was
also carefully collected – for its own pleasure, but also as an indis-
putable aid to understanding the vocabulary of the Qur'an.

Much Western scholarship in the last twenty years has been
devoted to examining this gap between the life of the Prophet and
this first wave of Muslim scholarship in the eighth century. A close
examination of the political context in which these first historians
worked, their separation from the desert culture of the Arabs and the
prevailing theological debates against which they wrote has been
enormously illuminating. It is also fascinating to look at the few documents written by Jews and Christians that survive from this period.
This new criticism was formulated by John Wansbrough in the late
1970s and further developed by Patricia Crone and Michael Cook
in the 1980s. It has been a very useful corrective to generations of
uncritical scholarship. New focus has been given to the enlarged role
that the biographers probably created for Muhammad's uncle Abbas
(founder of the Abbasid dynasty), the possibly influential role of the
Jews in Arabia, while the natural tendency to give enhanced status to
Mecca in pre-Islamic Arabia has been corrected. It also seems clear
that, right at the start of Islam, the Hadith stood side by side with

the Qur'an as a prime source for lawmakers and theologians. Current work on metallurgy and the archaeology of the Red Sea and caravan trades in seventh-century Arabia will continue to broaden our understanding of the period. There may be room for some recalculation of dates and both within, and outside, the world of Islamic scholarship there is always much work to be done on the likely order of the Qur'anic verses and the veracity of Hadith traditions. However, the current tendency completely to dismiss the early sources, because of a gap of over a hundred years, seems reckless. Much greater gaps separate Arrian from his biography of Alexander the Great and Eusebius from the Early Church while a roughly comparable period may separate the Gospel of John from the life of Christ, and Bede from his Anglo-Saxon kings. In an earlier period of scholarship the corpus of pre-Islamic poetry was for a while dismissed as inventions of eighth-century Baghdad. They have since been retrieved from the academic rubbish bin and are now thoroughly back in favour.

☾

You can collect a small library of the biographies of the Prophet Muhammad in English. Each has its own perspective, mood and relevance to a period. Karen Armstrong, author of best-sellers like *Muhammad* and *A History of God*, is an inspiring guide to the Prophet's quest for God. Young English-speaking Muslim pilgrims looking for a contemporary voice even take her books with them to Mecca. For sober academic respectability you could read through Montgomery Watt's twin volumes, *Muhammad at Mecca* and *Muhammad at Medina*. Martin Lings' *Muhammad: his life based on the earliest sources* has gone even further down this road, though his scholarly but uncritical reading of the early sources may be considered a little too pious and dry by some. Sir John Glubb (Glubb Pasha) brought his unique knowledge of the landscape of

Arabia, the Bedouin way of life and the tactics of desert warfare to his biography, *The Life and Times of Muhammad*. A similar authorial tone can be heard in *The Messenger* by R. V. C. Bodley, another great British authority on desert life, albeit the Sahara. Other popular biographies from the early twentieth century include one by Ali Shah (father to Idries Shah – a great disseminator of Islamic mysticism to the West). Looking further back into Western perceptions, the nineteenth-century view of Muhammad was dominated by two great Scottish writers: Thomas Carlyle's passionate championship of the Prophet (as a great heroic Hegelian agent of change) and William Muir's careful four-volume biography. This was first published in 1858 but enjoyed a long life as it was later updated by his son-in-law. From the same period came Washington Irving's *Life of Mahomet*, which also enjoyed endless reprintings as a cheap Everyman edition.

From the early eighteenth century comes Simon Ockley's *The History of the Saracens* (published between 1708 and 1718) and George Sale's translation of the Qur'an in 1734. Although they are now considered to be culturally offensive, a careful reading can easily breach the astonishing statements of prejudice to locate a bedrock of sympathy. It is also interesting to remember that they were in their day attacked for being too pro-Islamic. Their work was being mirrored in France, where Henri, Comte de Boulainvillieas, arguably produced Christendom's first impartial biography. His *La Vie de Mahomet* was published in 1728 and a pirated English translation was on sale in the streets of London just three years later. Such a book would have been impossible to sell in the seventeenth century. Indeed, Henry Stubbe (the second keeper of the Bodleian Library in Oxford, who was born in 1631) kept his sympathetic study safely locked up in a drawer in manuscript form.

☽

For an English reading of the Qur'an I recommend that you do not stay loyal to one translation but look at the verses through different eyes. Only then will you begin to appreciate the complexity of the task of the translation. To begin with you could try N. J. Dawood's 1956 translation as published in the Penguin Classics series; J. M. Rodwell's 1909 translation as published by the Everyman Library; and that prepared in Biblical English by Muhammad Marmaduke Pickthall in 1930. These proffer the scholarship of an Iraqi Jew, an Anglican clergyman and an English convert to Islam. You should also have a look at A. J. Arberry's *The Koran Interpreted*, New York, 1955 and the modernised 1989 version of Abdullah Yusuf Ali's translation, first published in Lahore in 1934.

Muhammad Ibn Ishaq's eighth-century *The Life of Muhammad* (*Sirat al-Nabi*) survives with two different early commentaries: that of 'Abd al-Malik ibn Hisham and 'Abd ar-Rahman ibn 'Abd Allah as-Suhayli. The English translation is by A. Guillame, Karachi, 1955. There is also the edition of the nineteenth-century Hungarian linguist of Bombay, Edward Rehatsek from which the Folio Society produced an edited version in 1964. Ibn Ishaq was born around 699 and died in Baghdad in 767.

Ibn Sa'd Muhammad's *Kitab al-Tabaqat al-kabir* (*The Great Book of Classes,* written in the ninth-century C.E.) was edited by Eduard Sachau and others and published by Brill between 1904 and 1940.

Abu Muhammad Ahmad ibn A'tham al-Kufi's ninth-century *Kitab al-futuh (The Book of Conquests)* was edited by Muhammad Ali al-Abbasi and Sayyid Abd al-Wahhab Bukhari in eight volumes and published in Hyderabad between 1968 and 1975.

Muhammad ibn 'Umar al-Waqidi's *Kitab al-maghizi, The Campaigns of the Prophet*, has been translated into English by Marsden Jones in three volumes and was published by Oxford University Press in 1966.

Also worth a look is Muhammad ibn Abdallah al-Azraqi's *History of Mecca.*

Muhammad Abu Jafar ibn Jarir al-Tabari (839-923 C.E.) wrote *The History of the Messengers and the Kings;* it has as its most recent edition thirty-nine volumes from the Department for Near Eastern Studies, SUNY Albany, published between 1985 and 1999 by SUNY Press. His *Tafsir*, his Qur'anic commentary (nearly as many volumes) is in an English translation by E. Yarshater.

The Hadith (the traditional sayings of the Prophet) presents a much greater difficulty. At any time there are always a number of personal selections available. I have long treasured a little 126-page red notebook, *The Sayings of Muhammad*, collected by Allama Sir Abdullah Al-Mamun Al-Suhrawardy and first published by John Murray in 1941. The Shambala Press has also just produced another elegantly printed collection, *The Wisdom of the Prophet*, translated by Thomas Cleary. For a serious study rather than an inspirational browse, there is no scholarly collection in print at the moment. You will need to go to a library and dig out a copy of A. J. Wensinck's *Handbook of Early Muhammadan Tradition*, published by Brill in 1927. After that the road leads back to the first great editions made in the ninth century. Of the eight traditionalists, the collections put together by Muhammad ibn Ismail al-Bukhari and Ahmad ibn Muhammad ibn Hanbal receive most attention.

Another good source, scattered over hundreds of different entries is the *Encyclopaedia Islamica*, especially the new (1960–2001) edition, edited by H. A. R. Gibb and others, published by Brill.

☾

With so many variant texts being cited, it seemed important to give some order to the process. I have given clear references for all the longer quotations from the Qur'an, with the traditional Arabic name of the surah and the number of the surah and the verse or verses.

FURTHER READING

Ahmed, A. S., *Discovering Islam: Making Sense of Muslim History and Society*, Routledge, 1988.

Akbar S. Ahmed, *Islam Today: A Short Introduction to the Muslim World*, I. B. Tauris, 1999.

Ali, Tariq, *The Clash of Fundamentalisms: Crusades, Jihads and Modernity*, Verso, 2002.

Arberry, Arthur, *The Seven Odes*, George Allen & Unwin, 1957.

— *The Koran Interpreted*, Oxford University Press, 1983.

Armstrong, Karen, *Muhammad: A Biography of the Prophet*, Victor Gollancz, 1991.

— *Islam: A Short History*, Weidenfeld & Nicolson, 2000.

Atiyah, Edward, *The Arabs*, Penguin Books, 1955.

Bakhtiar, Laleh, *Sufi: Expressions of the Mystic Quest*, Thames & Hudson, 1976.

Ball, Warwick, *Rome in the East: The Transformation of an Empire*, Routledge, 2000.

Barlas, Asma, *Believing Women in Islam: Unreading Patriarchial Interpretations of the Qur'an*, University of Texas Press, 2002.

Bell, R., *The Origins of Islam in its Christian Environment*, London, 1968.

Brockelmann, Carl, *History of the Islamic Peoples* (1939 German edition translated by Joel Carmichael and Moshe Perlmann), Capricorn Books, 1960.

Brooks, Geraldine, *Nine Parts of Desire: The Hidden World of Islamic Women*, Anchor Books, 1994.

Bulliet, R., *The Camel and the Wheel*, Harvard University Press, 1975.

Cameron, Averil, *The Mediterranean World in Late Antiquity AD 395–600*, Routledge, 1993.

Chadwick, Henry, *The Early Church*, Penguin, 1967.

Clarke, Peter (ed.), *Islam: The World's Religions*, Routledge, 1988.

Cook, Michael, *Muhammad*, Oxford University Press, 1985.

Creswell, K. A. C., *Early Muslim Architecture*, Oxford University Press, 1932.

Crone, Patricia and Cook, M., *Hagarism: The Making of the Islamic World*, Cambridge University Press, 1977.

Epstein, (Rabbi Dr) Isidore, *Judaism*, Pelican Books, 1959.

Esin, Emel, *Mecca the Blessed, Madinah the Radiant*, Paul Elek Books, 1963.

Frye, Richard, *The Golden Age of Persia*, Weidenfeld & Nicolson, 1993.

Glubb, John Bagot (Glubb Pasha), *The Life and Times of Muhammad*, Hodder & Stoughton, 1970.

— *Empire of the Arabs*, Hodder & Stoughton, 1963.

— *A Short History of the Arab Peoples*, Quartet Books, 1978.

— *Great Arab Conquests*, Quartet Books, 1980.

Glueck, Nelson, *Deities and Dolphins: The Story of the Nabateans*, Farrar, Straus & Giroux, 1965.

Grant, Michael, *The Jews in the Roman World*, Weidenfeld & Nicolson, 1973.

Groom, Nigel, *Frankincense and Myrrh: A Study of the Arabian Incense Trade*, Longman, 1981.

Grunebaum, G. E. von., *Muhammadan Festivals*, Curzon, 1976.

Guillame, Alfred, *The Traditions of Islam*, Oxford University Press, 1924.

— *Islam*, Penguin Books, 1954.

— *Life of Muhammad* (trans of Ibn Ishaq), Oxford University Press, 1955.

Haag, Michael, *Syria and Lebanon*, Cadogan, 1995.

Henze, Paul, *Layers of Time: a History of Ethiopia*, C. Hurst, 2000.

Hitti, Philip K., *History of the Arabs*, Palgrave, 1951.

— *Makers of Arab History*, Macmillan, 1968.

Hourani, G. F., *Arab Seafaring*, Princeton University Press, 1995.

Hoyland, Robert G., *Arabia and the Arabs: From the Bronze Age to the Coming of Islam*, Routledge, 2001.

Insoll, Timothy, *The Archaeology of Islam*, Blackwell, 1999.

Irving, Washington, *Life of Mahomet*, Everyman, 1911.

Irwin, Robert, *Night & Horses & The Desert: An Anthology of Classical Arabic Literature*, Allen Lane, 1999.

Isaac, Benjamin, *The Limits of Empire: The Roman Army in the East*, Oxford University Press, 1990.

Kabbani, Rana, *Europe's Myths of Orient*, Macmillan, 1986.

Kaegi, Walter, *Byzantium and the Early Islamic Conquests*, Cambridge University Press, 1992.

Kennedy, Hugh, *The Prophet and the Age of the Caliphates*, Longman, 1986.

— *The Armies of the Caliphs*, Routledge, 2001.

Kepel, Gilles, *Jihad: The Trail of Political Islam*, I. B.Tauris, 2002.

Khan, Muhammad Zafrulla, *Islam: Its Meaning for Modern Man*, Routledge, 1962.

Lane-Poole, Stanley, *The Speeches and Table Talk of the Prophet Muhammad*, Ashraf, Lahore, 1979.

Lapidus, Ira, *A History of Islamic Societies*, Cambridge University Press, 1988.

Lewis, Bernard, *The Arabs in History*, Oxford Paperbacks, 2002.

— *The Muslim Discovery of Europe*, Weidenfeld and Nicolson, 1982.

Lieu, Judith, North, John and Rajak, Tessa (eds), *The Jews Among Pagans and Christians in the Roman Empire*, Routledge, 1992.

Lings, Martin, *Muhammad, his life based on the earliest sources*, Islamic Texts Society, 1991.

Makiya, Kanan, *The Rock: A Tale of Seventh-Century Jerusalem*, Constable Robinson, 2002.

Miller, J. Innes, *The Spice Trade of the Roman Empire, 29 BC to AD 641*, Oxford University Press, 1969.

Mokhtar, G. (ed.), *Ancient Civilizations of Africa*, University of California Press, 1981.

Muir, William, *The Life of Mahomet: From Original Sources*, Edinburgh, 1861 (4 vols), Fourth Edition revised and edited by T.H. Weir, published as *The Life of Mohammad: From Original Sources,* John Grant, Edinburgh, 1912.

Muzafferedin, Shaikh Shemseddin Halveti al-Jerrahi, *Ninety-Nine Names of Allah*, Sultan & Co., Karachi.

Nasr, Seyyed Hossein, *Islamic Art & Spirituality*, Golgonooza Press, 1987.

Nicholson, Reynold, *Translations of Eastern Poetry and Prose*, Cambridge University Press, 1922.

— *A Literary History of the Arabs*, Cambridge University Press, 1930.

Nigosian, Solomon, *Islam*, Crucible, 1987.

Norris, Harry Thirlwall, *The Adventures of Antar*, Aris & Phillips, 1980.

Norwich, John Julius, *Byzantium: The Early Centuries*, Viking, 1988.

Pankhurst, Richard, *The Ethiopians*, Blackwell, 1998.

Pawick, Constance, *Muslim Devotions: A Study of Prayer-manuals in Common Use*, SPCK, 1961.

Peters, F. E., *Children of Abraham: Judaism, Christianity, and Islam*, Princeton University Press, 1982.

— *The Hajj: The Muslim Pilgrimage to Mecca and the Holy Places*, Princeton University Press, 1994.

— *A Reader on Classical Islam*, Princeton University Press, 1994.

— *Muhammad and the Origins of Islam.* SUNY Press, 1994.

Pitts, Joseph, *A Faithful Account of the Religion and Manners of the Mahometans*, 1731.

Reeves, Minou, *Muhammad in Europe: A Thousand Years of Western Myth-Making*, Garnet, 2000.

Rodinson, Maxime, *Muhammad: Prophet of Islam*, Allen Lane, Penguin Press, London, 1971.

Ruthven, Malise, *Islam in the World*, Penguin, 2000.

— *A Fury for God: the Islamist Attack on America*, Granta Books, 2002.

— *A Satanic Affair: Salman Rushdie and the Rage of Islam*, Hogarth Press, 1991.

Sardar, Ziauddin and Zafar Abbas Malik, *Muhammad for Beginners,* Icon Books, 1994.

Sells, Michael, *Desert Tracings*, Wesleyan University Press, 1989.

Shadid, Irfan, *Byzantium and the Arabs in the Fifth Century,* Washington, Dumbarton Oaks, 1989.

— *Byzantium and the Semitic Orient before the Rise of the Rise of Islam,* London, Variorum, 1988.

— *Rome and the Arabs,* Washington, Dumbarton Oaks, 1984.

Shah Ikbal Ali, *Muhammad: The Prophet*, Wright & Brown, London, 1932.

Stoneman, Richard, *Palmyra and its Empire*, University of Michigan Press, 1992.

Thomas, Bertram, *The Arabs: the Life-Story of a People Who Have Left Their Deep Impress on the World*, Simon Publications, 1937.

Tisdall, W. St Clair, *The Original Sources of the Qoran*.

Trimingham, John Spencer, *Islam in Ethiopia*, Oxford University Press, 1952.

— *Christianity Among the Arabs in Pre-Islamic Times*, Longman, 1979.

Uzunoglu, Nurettin, *History of the Prophets*, Istanbul, 1995.

Wansbrough, John, *Quranic Studies: Sources and Methods of Scriptural Interpretation*, Oxford University Press, 1977.

— *The Sectarian Milieu: Content and Composition of Islamic Salvation History*, Oxford University Press, 1978.

Waines, David, *Introduction to Islam*, Cambridge University Press, 1995.

Watt, Montgomery W., *Muhammad at Medina*, Oxford University Press, 1956.

— *Muhammad at Mecca*, Oxford University Press, 1956.

Westermarck, E., *Pagan Survivals in Mohammedan Civilisation*, Macmillan, 1933.

ACKNOWLEDGEMENTS

My first debt of gratitude is to those who have laboured in translating the Qur'an, the Hadith and the first histories of the Arabs into English. Although I have now travelled for more than twenty years through the lands of Islam, I remain at the level of a three-year-old in my grasp of language and Arabic letters. This also means that I have always been dependent on local guides to show me the treasures of their nations as well as acting as translators. Long embarrassed by my lack of felicity with language, I would not have it otherwise now, for many of these guides have grown into friends and interpreters not just of a language but of a living culture.

A short draft of this book first appeared in 1998 as a one of the seven-thousand-word essays published in Charlie Boxer's innovative narrative history series, the Orange Blossom Specials. Marketed at sixteen-year-olds they were in fact avidly read by all ages of subscribers. Number 33, *The Life of the Prophet Muhammad* by Barnaby Rogerson, very nearly exceeded the wildest hopes of both its publisher and author. For one heady moment it was keenly championed by one of the members of the Prince of Wales's inter-faith committee, who planned to print sufficient copies to give each school child in Britain a free copy.

Three years later my agent, Michael Alcock, was given a copy for his children, but read it on the train home. A week later I met Alan Samson of Little, Brown and, perching amongst tottering piles of manuscripts, we talked about the books and films that we both liked. It proved a gentle and effective way in which to commission a book.

My first draft was patiently and carefully edited by both Catherine Hill, desk editor at Little, Brown publishers and Rose Baring, a freelance book doctor, mother and managing editor of Sickle Moon & Eland Books. The maps were drawn by John Gilkes; Richard Collins was the attentive copy editor and David Atkinson compiled the index. It only remains for me to thank Professor Hugh Kennedy of St Andrews, Professor M. A. Zaki Badawi of the London-based Muslim College and Bruce Wannell for their critical readings and kind words of support.

INDEX

Index

فَادْعُوهُمْ فَلْ ... صَادِقِينَ

أَرْجُلٌ يَمْشُونَ بِهَا أَمْ لَهُمْ أَيْدٍ يَبْطِشُونَ بِهَا أَمْ

لَهُمْ أَعْيُنٌ يُبْصِرُونَ بِهَا أَمْ لَهُمْ آذَانٌ يَسْمَعُونَ

بِهَا قُلِ ادْعُوا شُرَكَاءَكُمْ ثُمَّ كِيدُونِ فَلَا تُنْظِرُونِ

إِنَّ وَلِيِّيَ اللَّهُ الَّذِي نَزَّلَ الْكِتَابَ وَهُوَ يَتَوَلَّى الصَّالِحِينَ

وَالَّذِينَ تَدْعُونَ مِنْ دُونِهِ لَا يَسْتَطِيعُونَ نَصْرَكُمْ

وَلَا أَنْفُسَهُمْ ... وَإِنْ تَدْعُوهُمْ إِلَى

الْهُدَى ... لَيْكَ وَ

... وَأَعْرِضْ

... عَنِ ...طَانِ

... الَّذِينَ

إِذَا مَسَّهُمْ طَائِفٌ مِنَ الشَّيْطَانِ تَذَكَّرُوا